OLD TESTAMENT

BIG PICTURE
of the
BIBLE

OLD TESTAMENT

BIG PICTURE
of the
BIBLE

LORNA DANIELS NICHOLS

WINEPRESS WP PUBLISHING

WinePress Publishing (PO Box 428, Enumclaw, WA 98022) functions only as book publisher. As such, the ultimate design, content, editorial accuracy, and views expressed or implied in this work are those of the author.

Unless otherwise noted, all Scriptures are taken from the Holy Bible, *New Living Translation,* copyright © 1996, 2004 by Tyndale Charitable Trust. Used by permission of Tyndale House Publishers, Wheaton, Illinois 60189. All rights reserved.

Scripture references marked AMP are taken from *The Amplified Bible,* Old Testament, © 1965 and 1987 by The Zondervan Corporation, and from The Amplified New Testament, © 1954, 1958, 1987 by The Lockman Foundation. Used by permission.

Scripture references marked CEV are taken from *The Contemporary English Version:* Thomas Nelson, 1997, c1995 by the American Bible Society. Used by permission. All rights reserved.

Scripture references marked KJV are taken from the *King James Version of the Bible.*

Scripture references marked KJ21 are taken from The Holy Bible, *21st Century King James Version* (KJ21®), Copyright © 1994, Deuel Enterprises, Inc., Gary, SD 57237, and used by permission.

Scripture references marked MSG are taken from *The Message Bible* © 1993 by Eugene N. Peterson, NavPress, PO Box 35001, Colorado Springs, CO 80935, 4th printing in USA 1994. Published in association with the literary agency—Alive Comm. PO Box 49068, Colorado Springs, CO 80949. Used by permission.

Scripture references marked NASB are taken from the *New American Standard Bible,* © 1960, 1963, 1968, 1971, 1972, 1973, 1975, 1977 by The Lockman Foundation. Used by permission.

Scripture references marked NCV are taken from the *New Century Version.* Copyright © 1987, 1988, 1991 by Thomas Nelson, Inc. Used by permission. All rights reserved.

Scripture references marked NIV are taken from the Holy Bible, *New International Version®, NIV®.* Copyright © 1973, 1978, 1984 by the International Bible Society. Used by permission of Zondervan. All rights reserved.

Scripture references marked NKJV are taken from the *New King James Version,* © 1979, 1980, 1982 by Thomas Nelson, Inc., Publishers. Used by permission.

Scripture references marked TNIV are taken from the Holy Bible, *Today's New International® Version TNIV©.* Copyright 2001, 2005 by International Bible Society®. Used by permission of International Bible Society®. All rights reserved worldwide.

Scripture references marked ESV are taken from The Holy Bible: *English Standard Version,* copyright © 2001, Wheaton: Good News Publishers. Used by permission. All rights reserved.

ISBN 13: 978-1-57921-929-1
ISBN 10: 1-57921-929-2
Library of Congress Catalog Card Number: 2007935556

Printed in China.
APC-FT5406

DEDICATION

This book is dedicated to my mother, Ruth Mae Meadows Daniels, who is now with the Lord. Thank you so very much for your prayers, love, and guidance. You encouraged each of your seven children to read the Bible and "let God speak to us through Scripture." You so wisely set an example and then created an environment that allowed each of us to discover Truth and the reality of Jesus Christ for ourselves.

TABLE *of* CONTENTS

ILLUSTRATIONS

MAPS OF KEY LOCATIONS

PICTURES

PREFACE

God. Who exactly is God? How can I be certain He exists? What should I know about Him?

Perhaps you're like me, and you've reached a point in life where you've started asking these questions. When I started asking these questions, my mother very wisely advised me to explore the Bible for the answers I sought about God. She told me to read the Bible and "let God speak to me." I was a teenager when I started that journey, and didn't yet have the maturity and wisdom to understand what she meant, but nevertheless I decided to take her advice.

The first time I tried to read the Bible and encountered Jesus on its pages, I had even more questions: Who is Jesus? Can I believe His promise of eternal life? Should I put my faith in Him as my Savior? Since I wanted God to answer my questions, I decided to read the Bible from cover to cover and "let God speak to me" as my mother had suggested.

Despite my ambitious intentions, I didn't quite make it all the way through the Bible, yet God still spoke to my heart and planted a strong desire in me to get to know Him better through the Bible–His Word.

Bible reading became a regular part of my life, but I still didn't understand much of what I was reading. What was it saying? All the different books and stories about so many people and their relationships with God–they just didn't seem to be connected.

I reached a crossroads in my Bible-reading journey: I could continue "just reading" or really make a determined effort to better understand God's Word. After investing in several study aids to guide me on my journey, I turned serious about my Bible study. Not so amazingly, the more I studied, the more I understood and saw that stories and people are connected. They are sequels of the same story and communicate the same message of God's Plan of Redemption and Salvation for all mankind. This is the message that resonates throughout the pages of both the Old and New Testaments and is the *Big Picture of the Bible*.

The overall message of the Bible became clear to me after countless hours of reading and study. It is God's Plan of Redemption and Salvation. The books of the Bible fit together like pieces of a puzzle to complete that picture. How wonderful it would be, I thought, if I could share the rewards of my study of the Bible with others, to help them see the *Big Picture of the Bible*. This study is the result of that effort.

Please use this as a tool to assist you in your Bible reading–not as a substitute. It's designed to help you better understand the Bible's message. Emphasis is on scriptures that refer to God's Plan of Redemption and Salvation and show how Jesus Christ fulfilled that plan.

My prayer for you is that God will plant in you a strong desire to read His Word more often and more consistently. God wants to speak to you. Allow Him to speak to you through the pages of the Bible.

Lorna Daniels Nichols

ACKNOWLEDGMENTS

First and foremost, my sincere thanks to God for Your inspiration and guidance. I especially thank You for sending the right people at the right time, and with the right talents to assist me with this book. My gratitude and affection for each of them is without measure. My personal thanks to:

My husband, best friend and wonderful partner, John W. Nichols III, for your love, patience, support, and encouragement throughout the long hours of study and writing for this project.

My father, George Earl Daniels Jr., for your awesome leadership as family patriarch. Your love, hard work, and values capture the essence of what fatherhood is all about.

Mary Ruth Crawford for editing and proofing the manuscript numerous times. Your command of English grammar and writing skills were exactly what I needed for this project. You have been a blessing and a true friend.

My sister, Rhonda L. Daniels, for your artwork. Your talent brings to life the personalities of the Old Testament. Your persistence and enthusiasm are contagious.

Gino Santa Maria for designing the maps and icons, identifying key locations and concepts. God has given you an incredible gift and we are blessed that you continue to use it to glorify His name.

My many friends and relatives who have read and given me their invaluable input on this project—Sheryl Smith Belson, Claudia Inman Brown, Dianne Dawson Daniels, Rita L. Daniels, William Dwayne Daniels, Derrick Dawson, Kathy Lauria Dismore, Mark and Janet Furlong, Madeline Norris Legler, Howie Meloch, Bonita McClellan Sams, and Cynthia Walker Watson.

A special thanks to Grace Church–Saint Louis and Pastor Ron Tucker for the opportunity to teach and further develop material for *Big Picture of the Bible*.

May God bless and keep each of you in His care always!

INTRODUCTION

What is the Bible?

The Bible is a compilation of writings written by men inspired by God. Although men wrote the Bible, its words are not those of mere men, but of God. The authors of the Bible were divinely chosen by God to write His words and deliver His message. The Apostle Peter makes this point clear in Scripture when he writes, *"Above all, you must realize that no prophecy in Scripture ever came from the prophet's own understanding, or from human initiative. No, those prophets were moved by the Holy Spirit, and they spoke from God"* (2 Peter 1:20–21).

Writings included in our Bible were authored by at least forty men over a period of about 1600 years. These writings were collected, organized, and published as the sixty-six books of our Bible. These books, when combined, tell the story of God's love and desire for a close personal relationship with each of us.

The Bible is sectioned into two main divisions: the *Old Testament* and the *New Testament*. The word *testament* could easily have been translated *covenant*. Both terms are used to describe the various promises and agreements God entered into with mankind.

What is the Old Testament?

There are thirty-nine Old Testament books, written from about 1445 B.C. to 430 B.C. Most of the Old Testament was written in Hebrew, a Semitic language similar to Arabic. A small portion was written in Aramaic, a language spoken in Palestine during Jesus' day. The Old Testament provides a record of God's relationship with mankind, covering history from the beginning of the world to about 400 years before the birth of Jesus Christ. It includes the covenants God entered into with mankind during this period. The primary focus of the Old Testament is on how God taught the world about the One True God through His relationship and interactions with the nation of Israel. Throughout the pages of the Old Testament is God's promise of a Messiah, the Anointed One, who would provide a way for all mankind to enjoy a close personal relationship with the One True God.

What is the New Testament?

There are twenty-seven New Testament books, written in Greek between 45 A.D. and 100 A.D. The New Testament includes writings, covering the historical period from just prior to Jesus' birth to about one hundred years after His death and resurrection. It provides the gospel (good news) of the new covenant God entered into with humanity after Jesus completed His mission on earth. The New Testament's primary focus is on how God fulfilled His promise of a Messiah through Jesus Christ, providing a way for all mankind—Jews and non-Jews alike—to commune with Him in an intimate and personal way.

 Note: See Appendix 1 for information about how we got the Old Testament; Appendix 2 for the organization of the Old Testament; and Appendix 3 for a timeline of the Old Testament books.

Why Read the Bible?

The Bible is the Word of God. It is God's message to mankind. It tells us what God (the Creator) wants us (His creation) to know about fellowshipping with Him and living a life that is full of successes and not failures. When we read the Bible, we gain a better understanding of who God is and why we need Him in our lives. God loves us and wants each of us to enjoy a good life, full of promise and direction. This can only happen if we allow God to guide us instead of living life apart from Him, doing things our own way.

The Bible provides all the power, wisdom, and knowledge needed to help us develop a close personal relationship with God, who is ready, willing, and able to help us navigate through life's challenges. God speaks to us as we read the Bible, guiding and equipping us for success. The Apostle Paul said, *"All Scripture is God-breathed and is useful for teaching, rebuking, correcting and training in righteousness, so that the man of God may be thoroughly equipped for every good work"* (2 Timothy 3:16–17 NIV).

 Note: See Appendix 4 for information on selecting a Bible, and Appendix 5 for a comparison of various Bible translations.

Who Is God?

God is the Creator of the universe and everything in it. God is not limited by time or space and has no beginning or end. God is all-knowing, all-powerful, and He is in all places at all times.

God is a Being with a personality. He has emotions just as we do. God feels, thinks, acts, sympathizes, hopes, desires, and enters into relationships. God is merciful, righteous, and just. However, one of the most important characteristics of God's nature is that of love. Scripture tells us that God is love (1 John 4:8, 16).

Who Is Jesus?

Jesus is God made human (John 1:1–3, 14; Colossians 2:9). Jesus came to earth and is the exact representation of God (Hebrews 1:3). The Bible explains that God revealed Himself to us through Jesus Christ. God is love and so is Jesus. God is merciful, righteous, and just. So is Jesus. By sending Jesus, God was saying to mankind, "Here I am. This is Who I am. Come fellowship with Me and let Me guide you through life's journey." It is possible to develop a close personal relationship with God and commune with Him now and throughout eternity when we accept Jesus Christ as our Lord and Savior.

Who Is the Holy Spirit?

The Holy Spirit is God. He is the Spirit of God. After Jesus delivered God's message and completed God's mission on earth, He sent the Holy Spirit to live inside everyone who believes in God's Word. The Holy Spirit helps us recognize sin and points us towards the righteousness of God (John 14:16–17; 16:7–8). By sending the Holy Spirit to live inside us, Jesus is saying, "I am with you always, living inside you through the Holy Spirit. I am here to help you develop a close personal relationship with God. I will encourage you, strengthen you, and guide you to the Truth of God." The Holy Spirit helps us grow in righteousness so that we become more like Jesus, displaying God's character and reflecting God's glory.

What Is the Trinity?

Our one God is three distinct beings: God the Father; Jesus the Son; and the Holy Spirit. These three beings are collectively referred to as the Trinity. All three are fully God, and yet these three beings are one God, and not three Gods.

The Trinity, although not a biblical term, is commonly used to describe our (one) God in (three) beings. It is a profound mystery and difficult to understand because humans are not created in this way. We must remember that this existence is unique to God.

 Note: The Trinity is God the Father, Jesus the Son, and the Holy Spirit united as One God. We can gain a little insight into this concept through analogies. Think about the three dimensions of a cube. Its dimensions are length, width, and height. Each dimension can be used individually to describe a given cube, yet all three can be used in combination to describe one and the same cube. Similarly, there are three distinct beings of the Trinity, each of whom is one and the same God. Another analogy is that of water which can be manifested as a liquid (water), a solid (ice), or a gas (steam). Three forms of one and the same water. Just as water manifests itself in three distinct forms, so our God manifests Himself as three distinct beings.

What is God's Plan of Redemption and Salvation?

God's Plan of Redemption and Salvation is the series of events God so lovingly orchestrated to provide a way for mankind to live in fellowship with Him on earth and throughout eternity. Mankind was originally created to live in fellowship with God. However, fellowship with our Creator was severed when the first man and woman rebelled against God and chose to follow their own selfish desires. As a result of the first man and woman's rebellion, every man and woman is born with this same rebellious attitude, doing things his or her own way apart from God, rather than allowing God to guide their lives. Rebellion against God is called sin. All of us are born spiritually separated or out of fellowship with God because of sin (Romans 3:10–12; 23).

God lovingly developed a plan to free mankind from sin (the spirit of rebellion) so that we can live in fellowship with Him. God's plan called for our redemption (deliverance by payment of a price) and salvation (freedom from the power of sin). God's plan required payment for our deliverance, but what would be the price and who would be willing and able to pay it? The Old Testament answers these questions for us. God promised to send a Messiah, who would die for our iniquities and cleanse us from our sins (Isaiah 53; Zechariah 3:8–9; 13:1). Throughout Scripture, it becomes clear that Jesus Christ is the promised Messiah and that He paid the price of redemption with His blood (Hebrews 9:11–12).

God became a man, in the person of Jesus, and lived with mankind on earth. Jesus suffered death by crucifixion, paying the price for humanity's deliverance with the shedding of His blood. After three days in the grave, Jesus rose from the dead, conquering death and freeing humanity from the power of sin. Jesus' death and resurrection fulfilled God's Plan of Redemption and Salvation and provided a way for all mankind to live in fellowship with God now and throughout eternity (1 Corinthians 15:3–8; Romans 6:3–5).

Accepting God's Offer of Redemption and Salvation

God offers redemption and salvation to all mankind as a free gift. God says, "I love you and want a close personal relationship with you. I knew you could neither redeem nor save yourself, so I sent My Son, Jesus Christ, to do it for you." Jesus paid the price for our redemption with His blood and provided for our salvation by conquering death and the power of sin.

Although God's Plan of Redemption and Salvation is a free gift from God, most people think it is something that must be achieved or earned. Many try to earn salvation by doing good deeds, such as giving to the poor, attending church, or giving up the things they know are morally wrong. However, our good deeds cannot save us. The only way we can be saved is by accepting God's offer of redemption and salvation. God's offer is a free gift and cannot be earned.

Accepting God's offer of redemption and salvation is simple. Jesus has done everything for us. All we have to do is have faith in (believe and trust in) Jesus Christ as our Lord and Savior (John 3:16; Romans 10:9–10). We are saved by God's grace (unmerited favor) when we believe in Jesus as our Lord and Savior (Romans 3:21–26; Ephesians 2:4–10). Jesus Christ invites you to believe and trust in Him. Jesus is saying, *"Here I am! I stand at the door and knock. If anyone hears my voice and opens the door, I will come in and eat with him, and he with me"* (Revelation 3:20 NIV).

There are numerous references to the Messiah and God's Plan of Redemption and Salvation in the Old Testament. As you read through this study, you will find these references highlighted with explanations of how Jesus Christ fulfilled God's plan. If you have accepted Jesus as your Lord and Savior, my prayer is that this study will strengthen your relationship with God. If you have not accepted Jesus, I pray that it will help you see how Jesus Christ fulfilled God's plan and that you will accept God's offer. All you have to do is believe in Jesus Christ as the One who has provided for your redemption and salvation.

USING THIS STUDY

Big Picture of the Bible provides a summary of Bible stories and events in an easy-to-read bulleted format. It organizes events in historical sequence so readers can see the continuity and overall message of the Bible.

This study has been designed to be used as either an individual or group study. It is not a replacement for reading the Bible, but should supplement it. When using this study, it is recommended that you follow a lesson plan similar to this:

✓ Find a good Bible translation you can read and understand. *Big Picture of the Bible* is not a translation, but a tool to help you with your study.

✓ Each chapter begins with an opening prayer and summary. The chapters are divided into five sections so you can easily read a section each day and read through a chapter each week. However, you can read at your own pace. Read each chapter according to whatever schedule you've chosen for yourself.

✓ Read the recommended Bible reading listed at the end of each section to experience God's Word speaking to you.

✓ You might decide to follow along in your Bible and read all scriptures or scriptures other than those selected as recommended reading. If so, you will find the corresponding Bible scriptures for *Big Picture of the Bible* summaries included in the sub-heading lines.

✓ Go to the Bible review section of this study and answer the questions before proceeding to the next chapter. This will help you verify your understanding and reinforce the material covered in each chapter.

✓ After completing this study, make the Bible a part of your daily activity.

Icons Used in this Study

As you read through *Big Picture of the Bible*, you will see the following icons. They are there to guide you in thought, prayer, or to provide supplemental information to enhance your knowledge of the section you're reading.

 Prayer for beginning and ending each chapter. The prayers at the end of the chapter are prefaced with scripture, on which you may wish to meditate.

 Indicates God's Plan of Redemption and Salvation or a Foreshadowing of the Messiah, Jesus Christ.

 Supplemental information provided by the author to enhance the reader's knowledge of the section.

 Recommended Bible Reading. References include passages from both the Old and New Testaments and complement one another.

 Review Questions. A set of questions is provided at the end of each chapter, along with space to answer them. Answers are found in the back of the book.

Personal Reflections. Questions designed for prayerful thought as you discover how God is speaking to you through this study.

Bible Versions Used in This Study

AMP–Amplified Bible

CEV–Contemporary English Version

ESV–English Standard Version

KJV–King James Version

KJ21–21st Century King James

MSG–The Message

NASB–New American Standard Bible

NCV–New Century Version

NIV–New International Version

NKJV–New King James Version

NLT–New Living Translation (2nd Edition)

TNIV–Today's New International Version

 Note: See Appendices 4 and 5 for more information about Bible Versions and Translations.

CHAPTER 1

THE BEGINNING OF MANKIND

OPENING PRAYER

Heavenly Father,

Prepare my mind and heart to receive fresh new insights into Your Word. Speak to my heart and teach me about creation and the beginning of mankind. Reveal Yourself to me as the just and merciful God that You are. I praise Your Holy Name, for You are the Creator of the universe, the Giver and Sustainer of life.

Amen

CHAPTER SUMMARY

THE BEGINNING OF MANKIND

(Genesis 1–16)

Genesis is the book of beginnings. It opens with the formation of the universe and tells us that God created the world and everything in it. The culmination of God's handiwork was the creation of human life, a man and woman named Adam and Eve. In the beginning, the first man and woman enjoyed an intimate, personal relationship with God. However, this relationship was forever changed when they disobeyed the rules God established for their lives. Their rejection of God's rules, commonly referred to as the Fall, marked the beginning of sin and unrighteousness in the world.

Our righteous and holy God could not coexist with sin and unrighteousness, so a barrier was created spiritually separating Adam and Eve from God. Their rebellion against God severed their relationship with Him. The first man and woman would not be the only ones affected. As a result of their disobedience, every member of the human race would be born spiritually separated from God, repeating Adam and Eve's act of rebellion in their own way each and every day.

Our Creator still loved mankind and wanted the relationship restored. Immediately after the Fall, God initiated a plan to remove the barrier that spiritually separated mankind from Himself. God's plan is called *Redemption and Salvation through Jesus Christ* and we see it unfolding throughout the pages of the Old Testament. God's plan would actually happen through Jesus Christ in accordance with God's timing thousands of years later.

Genesis goes on to tell the story of God's relationship with mankind after the Fall. Early mankind soon became so unrighteous and immoral that God regretted having made man. God caused a great flood to cover the entire earth, destroying all life except that of a righteous man named Noah, his family, and two of every kind of animal. After the Flood, the world was repopulated through Noah's descendants.

God later chose another righteous man named Abram (Abraham), a descendant of Shem, one of Noah's sons, and entered into a covenant with him. God promised to make Abraham's descendants a great nation and to bless the entire world through his offspring. Jesus Christ, a descendant of Abraham, is the manifestation of that promise.

	Approximate Timeline	**Location**	**Biblical Scriptures**	**Author**
The Creation	In the Beginning	The Universe	Genesis 1–2	Moses
The Fall	After the Creation	Garden of Eden	Genesis 3–5	Moses
The Flood	After the Fall	Mountains of Ararat	Genesis 6–9	Moses
The Tower	After the Flood	Babylonia	Genesis 10–11:9	Moses
A Man Named Abram	2166 B.C.–2080 B.C.	Canaan (Israel)	Genesis 11:10–16:16	Moses

MAP OF KEY LOCATIONS

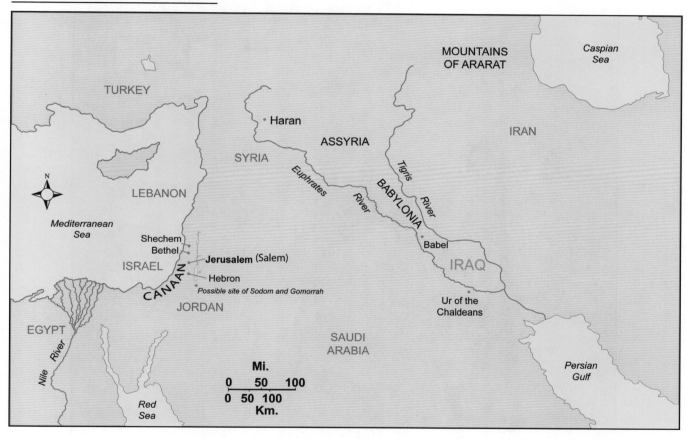

ABRAHAM

"Now [in Haran] the Lord said to Abram, Go for yourself [for your own advantage] away from your country, from your relatives and your father's house, to the land that I will show you. And I will make of you a great nation, and I will bless you [with abundant increase of favors] and make your name famous and distinguished, and you will be a blessing [dispensing good to others]." (Genesis 12:1–2 AMP)

SECTION 1: THE CREATION

The Creation of the World: (Genesis 1:1–2:3)

- Genesis describes the beginning of the universe, not the beginning of God. God has always existed and always will.

- In the beginning, God created our world from nothing. Before time began, the earth had no shape or form and was totally dark.

- The Holy Spirit was present and *"hovering over the waters"* (Genesis 1:2 NIV).

- God spoke and by His Word the world came into being. God's Word caused the action that created the world and everything in it.

 The Apostle John tells us that Jesus is the Word of God.

"In the beginning the Word already existed. The Word was with God, and the Word was God. He existed in the beginning with God. God created everything through him, and nothing was created except through him. . . . So the Word became human and made his home among us. He was full of unfailing love and faithfulness. And we have seen his glory, the glory of the Father's one and only Son" (John 1:1–3, 14).

- The world was created in seven days. On the first day, God created the light of day and dark of night. On the second day, the sky and atmosphere were created.

- On the third day, God created the earth, seas, and vegetation. On the fourth day, the sun, moon, and stars were created. Sea life and birds came into being on the fifth day.

- On the sixth day, God created land animals. *"Then God said, 'Let us make man in our image, in our likeness . . .'"* (Genesis 1:26 NIV).

- God created man to display His righteous character and reflect His glory.

Note: All three beings of the Trinity (God, Jesus, and the Holy Spirit) were present during creation. This truth is supported in Scripture as follows: 1.) Genesis 1:2 tells us that the Holy Spirit was present and hovering over the waters; 2.) God spoke in Genesis 1:26, saying "Let us make man in our image." God's use of plural pronouns "us" and "our" indicates He was not alone; 3.) *Elohim* is the primary Hebrew name used in the Old Testament for references to God as Creator. *Elohim* is the plural form of the Hebrew word *El* meaning "mighty" or "strong." Although *Elohim* is translated "God" in Scripture, it is a plural word, meaning "Gods" as in God the Father, God the Son, and God the Holy Spirit–The Trinity. For more information about the Trinity, see "What is the Trinity?" in the Introduction.

- After creating man, God declared that all His creations were very good. On the seventh day, God's creative work was done, so He rested. God blessed the seventh day and declared it a holy day.

The Seven Days of Creation

Day 1	Light of Day and Dark of Night
Day 2	The Sky and Atmosphere
Day 3	The Earth, Seas and Vegetation
Day 4	The Sun, Moon and Stars
Day 5	Sea Life and Birds
Day 6	Land Animals and Man
Day 7	Finished, Rested and Blessed the Day

The Creation of Man and Woman: (Genesis 1:26–2:25)

- God formed man (Adam) from the dust of the ground, breathed life into him, and placed him in the Garden of Eden.

- The Lord planted all kinds of fruit-bearing trees in the Garden of Eden. The Tree of Life and the Tree of the Knowledge of Good and Evil were planted in the middle of the garden.

- God told the man that he could eat fruit from any tree in the garden except from the Tree of Knowledge of Good and Evil. The Lord specifically warned the man saying, *"If you eat its fruit, you are sure to die"* (Genesis 2:17b).

Note: Although the exact location of the Garden of Eden is unknown, Genesis tells us that branches of the Tigris and Euphrates Rivers flowed from the river that watered Eden (Genesis 2:10–14). This suggests a location in the ancient Near East. Many scholars believe it was located in what is present day Iraq.

- God later said, *"It is not good for the man to be alone"* (Genesis 2:18a).

- God brought every kind of land animal and bird to Adam. As Adam looked at each kind of animal, he gave it a name. After choosing names for the land animals and birds, Adam still needed a companion for himself.

- God caused Adam to fall into a deep sleep and created a woman using a rib taken from Adam's side. The man and woman were naked, but did not realize it and felt no shame.

- God made the woman to be man's companion. The man and woman were to live together and be united as one.

Note: The Hebrew word *ehad* means "one" and is the word used in Scripture when God told the first man and woman that they were to become united as one (Genesis 2:24). It is interesting to note that this same Hebrew word was used in Scripture when God said, "Hear, O Israel! The LORD is our God, the LORD is one!" (Deuteronomy 6:4 NASB). When a man and woman are married, they are to become one just as God the Father, Jesus the Son, and the Holy Spirit are One.

- God gave the man and woman rules to live by and instructed them to:

  ✓ Populate and inhabit the earth.

  ✓ Take care of the Garden of Eden.

✓ Rule over and care for the animals, birds and fish.

✓ Eat seed-bearing plants and fruit from every tree in the garden except fruit from the Tree of Knowledge of Good and Evil.

RECOMMENDED BIBLE READING

Genesis 1:1–2:25 **The Creation of the World and Mankind**

John 1:1–14 **Jesus, The Word of God**

SECTION 2: THE FALL

The Fall of Mankind: (Genesis 3)

- All was indeed very good until Satan, through a serpent, tempted the woman:

    ✓ The serpent questioned God's Word: *"He said to the woman, 'Did God really say, "You must not eat from any tree in the garden"?' The woman said to the serpent, 'We may eat fruit from the trees in the garden,' but God did say, 'You must not eat fruit from the tree that is in the middle of the garden, and you must not touch it, or you will die'"* (Genesis 3:1b–2 NIV).

    ✓ He distorted and denounced God's Word: *"'You will not surely die,' the serpent said to the woman"* (Genesis 3:4 NIV).

    ✓ He appealed to man's ego, appetite, and desire for power and control: *"'For God knows that when you eat of it your eyes will be opened, and you will be like God, knowing good and evil.' When the woman saw that the fruit of the tree was good for food and pleasing to the eye, and also desirable for gaining wisdom, she took some and ate it"* (Genesis 3:5–6 NIV).

- The woman gave in to temptation and ate fruit from the forbidden Tree of Knowledge of Good and Evil. She gave some to her husband and he too ate the fruit.

- Immediately after eating the fruit, the man and woman realized for the first time that they were naked and covered themselves with fig leaves.

- When God confronted Adam, he said it was the woman's fault and she, in turn, passed blame to the serpent. God cursed the serpent and judged Satan.

 God said to the serpent, *"And I will put enmity between you and the woman, and between your offspring and hers; he will crush your head, and you will strike his heel"* (Genesis 3:15 NIV).

Many Bible scholars believe this passage is a foreshadowing of Jesus Christ as the offspring of the woman. Satan would strike at Jesus' heel, but Jesus would crush Satan's head and prevail.

Note: What is a "Foreshadowing of Jesus Christ" or "A Picture of Redemption?" It is when Scripture gives a preview of how God would send Jesus Christ to save mankind and restore our relationship with Him. It is also any Scripture that illustrates an aspect of Jesus' character or ministry, or one that provides a symbolic representation of Jesus as Redeemer and Savior.

- The consequences of the first man and woman's disobedience affected all mankind:

    ✓ The woman would experience great pain during childbirth.

    ✓ The woman's relationship with her husband would not be as she desired.

    ✓ The ground would bring forth weeds.

    ✓ Only through great toil would man be able to grow crops for food.

    ✓ Both the man and woman died spiritually.

    ✓ Both would also experience physical death.

- Adam named his wife Eve because she would be the mother of all humanity. God clothed Adam and Eve with animal skins and then banished them from the Garden of Eden.

> God responded to Adam and Eve's disobedience with justice and mercy. Banishing Adam and Eve from the Garden was a demonstration of God's justice. God held them accountable for their actions. There were consequences for their disobedience.
>
> Clothing Adam and Eve with animal skins demonstrated God's mercy. God loved them and wanted a relationship with them, so He allowed them to live outside of the Garden of Eden.
>
> An animal had to be sacrificed and its blood shed to clothe Adam and Eve, which foreshadowed the significance of blood in atoning (reconciling or making amends) for sin. Jesus' blood was shed to atone for our sins, an act which demonstrated God's justice and mercy.

Note: At this point, God's Plan of Redemption and Salvation begins to unfold throughout the remaining pages of the Bible. In fact, the rest of the Bible is all about God's plan to restore man's relationship with Himself.

Adam and Eve's Sons (Cain, Abel, and Seth): (Genesis 4–5)

- After Adam and Eve left Eden, they began having children. Their firstborn child was Cain; Abel was their second.

- When Adam and Eve's sons grew up, Abel became a shepherd and Cain farmed the land, growing crops for food.

- Both brothers offered sacrifices to the Lord. Cain brought the Lord crops from his garden as a gift, while Abel gave the very best from his flock.

- God accepted Abel's offering, but was displeased with the spirit in which Cain made his offering.

Note: The author of Hebrews later explained, *"It was by faith that Abel brought a more acceptable offering to God than Cain did. Abel's offering gave evidence that he was a righteous man, and God showed his approval of his gifts"* (Hebrews 11:4).

- Filled with envy and hatred, Cain killed his brother, Abel. Cain's children followed in his footsteps, perpetuating an ungodly line of descendants.

- In time, Adam and Eve had another son named Seth, who became the father of a godly line of descendants.

- Included in Seth's lineage were: Enoch, who followed the Lord and never saw death (Hebrews 11:5); Methuselah, who lived to be 969 years old, older than any other person recorded in the Bible; and Noah, a righteous man who found grace in God's sight.

> Jesus Christ was a descendant of Seth, the son born to Adam and Eve after Cain killed Abel.

RECOMMENDED BIBLE READING

Genesis 3:1–24 **The Fall of Mankind**

Romans 5:12–21 **Death through Adam, Life through Christ**

SECTION 3: THE FLOOD

Noah and the Flood: (Genesis 6–9)

- In time, everyone except Noah was living a life filled with sin and unrighteousness. In fact, evil was so prevalent that the world had become an abomination to God.

- God decided to wipe out mankind and repopulate the world through Noah.

- The Lord spoke to Noah and told him it was going to rain. God said the downpour would be so heavy that it would flood the entire earth and choke out all living beings except those God chose to spare.

- God instructed Noah to build an ark (boat) and told him that he, along with his wife, his sons (Shem, Ham, and Japheth), and their wives, would be safe inside it.

- God then commanded Noah to round up a male and female of every kind of animal and put them inside the ark. God also told Noah to gather plenty of food and store it inside the ark.

- Noah faithfully obeyed and did everything God commanded him to do. After the ark was built, God shut Noah, his family, and the animals inside.

- In the course of time, it began to rain. It rained for forty days and forty nights until the waters covered the earth, killing every living thing except those God had shut up in the ark.

- The waters subsided and the ark came to rest on the mountains of Ararat.

 God used the ark as a savior. Just as the ark saved Noah and his family, Jesus Christ is our Savior with the power to save us from God's righteous judgment.

- When Noah finally set foot on dry ground, he offered a sacrifice of praise and thanksgiving to God.

- God blessed Noah and his family and gave them these commandments:

  ✓ Repopulate the earth.

  ✓ Rule over the animal kingdom.

  ✓ Eat both plants and animals for food.

  ✓ Do not eat meat that still has its lifeblood in it.

  ✓ Do not shed another man's blood, for life is sacred.

- God established a covenant with Noah, declaring that He would never destroy the earth with floodwaters again. The rainbow is God's permanent reminder of that covenant.

Note: What is a covenant? Covenant is the term used to describe the various promises and agreements God entered into with mankind, and man entered into with his fellowman. When God enters into a covenant, He commits Himself and declares to bring promised blessings to pass some time in the future.

RECOMMENDED BIBLE READING

Genesis 6:5–8:22 **Noah and the Flood**

Hebrews 11:1–7 **Noah's Faith**

Section 4: The Tower

The Tower of Babel: (Genesis 10–11:9)

- After the Flood, Noah's sons, Shem, Ham, and Japheth, began having children and the earth was gradually repopulated through their descendants.

- One of Ham's descendants was a man named Nimrod, a mighty hunter and leader, who established several great cities in the plains of Shinar (Babylonia) and in Assyria.

- At that time, the entire world spoke one language. The people, who had migrated eastward to Babylonia, wanted a great city, so they decided to build a tower that would reach up into the skies.

- Thinking that a skyscraper would make them famous, the people began constructing the tower.

Note: The tower was the result of a prideful people's desire for power and control. God told the people to multiply and populate the earth (Genesis 9:1). They disobeyed God, choosing to stay together in one place instead of populating the earth.

- The Lord saw what was happening and stopped construction of the tower by causing the people to speak different languages.

- The people were no longer able to work together because they spoke different languages and could not understand each other. They gave up and moved on.

- The word *babel* means "confusion." The tower the people were building is called the *Tower of Babel* because it was there that the Lord changed the people's language, causing great confusion.

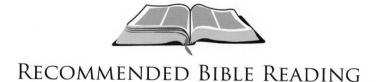

Recommended Bible Reading

Genesis 9:1–17 **God's Covenant with Noah**

Genesis 11:1–9 **The Tower of Babel**

James 4:1–10 **God Opposes the Proud**

Section 5: A Man Named Abram

Abram Chosen by God: (Genesis 11:10–12:9)

- A man named Abram was a descendant of Shem, one of Noah's three sons. One day God spoke to Abram and instructed him to leave his father's house in Haran and go to a land the Lord would show him.

 Note: Abraham was called Abram in Scripture until God changed his name to Abraham in Genesis 17:5.

- God promised to bless Abram, saying *"I will make you into a great nation. I will bless you and make you famous, and you will be a blessing to others. I will bless those who bless you and curse those who treat you with contempt. All the families on earth will be blessed through you"* (Genesis 12:2–3).

 God promised Abram that all peoples on earth would be blessed through him, which did happen. All peoples on earth were blessed through Jesus Christ, who was a descendant of Abram (Abraham).

- Abram obeyed the Lord and was seventy-five years old when he left his father's house and began traveling with his household and his nephew, Lot.

- When they reached Canaan, God appeared to Abram and told him that He was giving him this land.

Abram's Deception in Egypt: (Genesis 12:10–20)

- When a famine occurred in Canaan, Abram went to Egypt for a period of time.

- Abram's wife, Sarai, was a very beautiful woman. Because of this Abram was afraid the Egyptians would kill him and take her away.

- Abram decided to tell the Egyptians that Sarai was his sister—not his wife—so they would be good to him and spare his life.

- Sure enough, the Egyptians did find Sarai to be very beautiful. Pharaoh (the Egyptian king) added Sarai to his harem and allowed Abram to live because he thought Sarai was Abram's sister and not his wife.

- God became angry with Pharaoh and sent a plague to his household. When Pharaoh realized the plague was because of Sarai, he gave her back to Abram and sent them away.

 Note: Abram acted out of fear, asking Sarai to tell a half-truth instead of trusting God for protection. Sarai was Abram's half-sister (Genesis 20:12), but more importantly, she was his wife. Abram knew that as Sarai's brother, his life would be spared. As Sarai's husband, the Egyptians would try to kill him so that Sarai could be added to Pharaoh's harem.

Abram and Lot's Separation: (Genesis 13)

- After leaving Egypt, Abram traveled back to Canaan. God blessed Abram with great wealth.

- Abram and his nephew, Lot, became successful herdsmen with large numbers of sheep and cattle. Eventually, it became difficult to keep their livestock in close proximity because the same pasturelands could not support both herds.

- Since there was plenty of land, Abram suggested they choose different areas and separate. Abram gave Lot first choice.

- Lot chose the best land for himself, a well-watered section near the Jordan River, which was also the section nearest to the wicked cities of Sodom and Gomorrah.

Abram Rescues Lot and Gives Tithes to Melchizedek: (Genesis 14)

- Several kings started fighting among themselves near the area where Lot lived. The kings eventually captured Lot. Abram came to Lot's rescue by defeating the kings.

- On the return trip home, Abram met Melchizedek, King of Salem and Priest of God.

 Salem means "peace" and is another name for Jerusalem. Just as Melchizedek was King of Salem and High Priest, Jesus is Prince of Peace and our High Priest.

- Melchizedek brought bread and wine. As he and Abram prepared to eat together, Melchizedek called upon *El Elyon,* which means "God Most High," to bless Abram (Genesis 14:19).

 Note: *El Elyon* is the Hebrew name of God as Supreme and Sovereign Ruler of the universe.

- As an expression of thanks to God for the victory, Abram gave Melchizedek a tithe, one tenth of his plunder won in battle.

 Abram's encounter with Melchizedek foreshadowed what would later be called the Lord's Supper and is the first time tithing is mentioned in the Bible.

God's Covenant with Abram: (Genesis 15)

- Abram and his wife, Sarai, were old and childless. As time passed, Abram became discouraged and cried out to *Adonai,* which means "Lord" (Genesis 15:2).

 Note: Scripture translates the Hebrew name *Adonai* as "Lord," denoting authority. The term is a plural reference to God as Master and could also have been translated "Lords," thereby giving further credibility to the Trinity.

- Abram wondered how the Lord would bless him to become a great nation since he still had no sons.

- The Lord later came to Abram in a prophetic dream and told him that he would have descendants who would be enslaved in a foreign country for 400 years, but they would come back to the land of Canaan.

- God confirmed His covenant with Abram and outlined the boundaries of the land his descendants would one day occupy.

Ishmael, the Son of Abram and Hagar: (Genesis 16)

- After Abram and Sarai had been in Canaan for ten years with no children, Sarai suggested Abram have a child with Hagar, her handmaiden. Abram agreed.

- When Hagar became pregnant, she became haughty and disrespectful towards Sarai. Hagar's irreverent attitude became so offensive that Sarai went to Abram and asked him to send Hagar away.

- Abram gave Sarai permission to deal with Hagar any way she wished. Sarai began treating Hagar harshly, so she (Hagar) ran away.

- An angel of the Lord came to Hagar and said, *"Return to your mistress, and submit to her authority"* (Genesis 16:9).

- The angel told Hagar that she would give birth to a son who would be named Ishmael, and she would be blessed with numerous descendants. The angel also said Hagar's son would be wild, living at odds against everyone.

- After Hagar's encounter with the angel, she began calling God, *El Roi*, which means "The God Who Sees" (Genesis 16:13).

 Note: *El Roi* is the Hebrew name Hagar gave God. It refers to God's omnipresence. *El Roi* is always present and sees everything.

- Hagar returned and gave birth to Abram's son, who was named Ishmael, meaning "God hears." Abram was eighty-six years old when Ishmael was born.

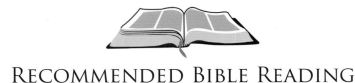

RECOMMENDED BIBLE READING

Genesis 12:1–7 **The Call of Abram**

Genesis 15:1–6 **God's Promise to Abram**

Genesis 16:1–16 **The Birth of Ishmael**

Hebrews 5:1–10 **Jesus Is Like Melchizedek**

MEDITATION & PRAYER

A Psalm of praise to the Lord God of all creation:

"Praise the LORD! Praise the LORD from the heavens!
Praise him from the skies!

Praise him, all his angels!
Praise him, all the armies of heaven!

Praise him, sun and moon!
Praise him, all you twinkling stars!

Praise him, skies above!
Praise him, vapors high above the clouds!

Let every created thing give praise to the LORD,
for he issued his command, and they came into being."

(Psalm 148:1–5)

Dear Lord God,

I praise Your Holy Name! You are Elohim, Creator of the universe. You spoke and all life came into existence as an expression of Your awesome power and love. I acknowledge my dependence on You as the Giver and Sustainer of life. I, along with all creation, praise Your Holy Name!

Amen

REVIEW QUESTIONS

1. Which members of the Trinity were present during creation? What Scriptures would you use to support your position?

_____

_____

_____

_____

_____

_____

2. What strategies did Satan use to tempt Eve?

_____

_____

_____

_____

_____

_____

3. How did the Fall change man's relationship with God?

_____

_____

_____

_____

_____

_____

4. After Adam and Eve's disobedience, what did God do that demonstrated *justice*? What did God do that demonstrated *mercy*?

_____

_____

_____

_____

_____

_____

5. What is meant when we say that a particular scripture points to a picture of *God's Plan of Redemption and Salvation* or is a *Foreshadowing of Jesus*?

_____

_____

_____

_____

_____

_____

6. In what way does the story of Noah and the Flood provide a picture of *God's Plan of Redemption and Salvation*?

_____

_____

_____

_____

_____

7. How did Noah demonstrate his faith? How did God reward his faith?

_____

_____

_____

_____

_____

_____

8. What is a *covenant*? What was God's covenant with Abram (Abraham)? How was this covenant fulfilled?

_____

_____

_____

_____

_____

_____

Personal Reflections

9. What does creation reveal to you about God? How does God manifest Himself to you through nature (i.e., waterfalls, mountains, forests, etc.)?

_____

_____

_____

_____

_____

_____

10. What strategies does Satan use to tempt us today?

_____

_____

_____

_____

_____

_____

11. In what areas of your life are you vulnerable to temptation? List steps you can take to help you resist temptation in these areas.

_____

_____

_____

_____

_____

_____

12. As you read this chapter, what did God reveal to you about His justice and mercy?

_____

_____

_____

_____

_____

_____

13. What did God reveal to you about His character through His Hebrew names: *Elohim, El Elyon, Adonai,* and *El Roi?*

_____

_____

_____

_____

_____

_____

_____

CLOSING PRAYER

The author of Hebrews defines faith:

"Faith makes us sure of what we hope for and gives us proof of what we cannot see. It was their faith that made our ancestors pleasing to God.

Because of our faith, we know that the world was made at God's command. We also know that what can be seen was made out of what cannot be seen."

(Hebrews 11:1–3 CEV)

Dear God Most High,

You are El Elyon, the Supreme and Sovereign Ruler of the universe. By faith I understand that the entire world was made at Your command. By faith I know that You are the source of all life. Renew me with Your life-giving Spirit. Keep me spiritually connected to You. I will walk by faith and not by sight, for faith is what makes us pleasing to You!

Amen

CHAPTER 2

GOD'S RELATIONSHIP WITH THE PATRIARCHS

OPENING PRAYER

Dear God,

Speak to my heart through the Holy Spirit as I read about the patriarchs of old.
Help me to see that the patriarchs were just ordinary men with extraordinary faith.
Increase my faith, for I want to be ready when you call my name. Guide my steps
to a more personal and intimate relationship with You.

Amen

CHAPTER SUMMARY

GOD'S RELATIONSHIP WITH THE PATRIARCHS

(Genesis 17–50; Job 1–42)

Genesis 17 thru 50 tells of God's relationship with the Hebrew patriarchs Abraham, Isaac, Jacob and Joseph. God reached out to these men, taught them His ways, and used them to make Himself known to the world.

God established a relationship with Abram, a righteous man who served the One True God. God later entered into a covenant of circumcision with Abram and changed his name to Abraham, which means "father of many nations." In this covenant, God promised to make Abraham's descendants a nation of kings; to bless all the nations of the earth through Abraham's offspring; and to give Abraham and his descendants the land of Canaan. In return, Abraham and his descendants were to live righteous lives and always serve the One True God.

Abraham did not live to see the fulfillment of all God's promises. However, God's covenant was passed on to his son, Isaac, and then to Isaac's son, Jacob, whose name was changed to Israel. It was Jacob's twelve sons who became the twelve tribes of Israel. Their offspring would become the nation of Israel.

Jacob's eleventh son, Joseph, became a great and powerful man in Egypt. Genesis gives us the details of Joseph's life and how he saved his family (Jacob's entire household) from famine by arranging for their migration to Egypt. Genesis closes with God's Plan of Redemption and Salvation unfolding in Egypt through Jacob's descendants, the nation of Israel.

The story of Job occurred around the same time period as that of the Hebrew patriarchs (Abraham, Isaac and Jacob) and is included in this chapter. Job was a righteous man who served the Lord. Job's faith was tested when God allowed Satan to afflict him with adversity. Job suffered personal and financial loss, as well as sickness and great physical pain at the hands of Satan. Although Job did not understand the reason for his suffering, he continued to trust in the Lord. Job passed the test and was rewarded for his faith. God restored Job's health and wealth. Job was not a descendant of Abraham, but his story shows that some Gentiles (non-Jews) of this period knew God and had personal relationships with Him.

	Approximate Timeline	Location	Biblical Scriptures	Author
Abram to Abraham	2067 B.C.–1991 B.C.	Canaan	Genesis 17–20	Moses
Isaac	2066 B.C.–1886 B.C.	Canaan	Genesis 21–26	Moses
Jacob	2006 B.C.–1859 B.C.	Canaan	Genesis 27–36	Moses
Joseph	1915 B.C.–1805 B.C.	Egypt	Genesis 37–50	Moses
Job	Sometime between 2000 B.C.–1800 B.C.	Uz	Job 1–42	Unknown

MAP OF KEY LOCATIONS

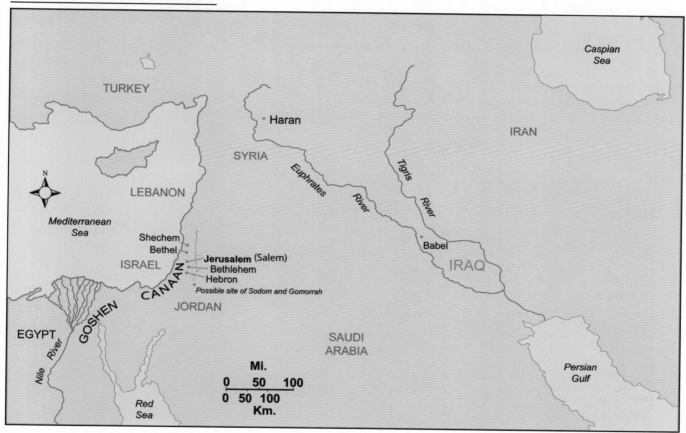

JOSEPH

"Joseph, being seventeen years old, was feeding the flock with his brethren. . . . Now Israel (Jacob) loved Joseph more than all his children, because he was the son of his old age: and he made him a coat of many colours." (Genesis 37:2b–3 KJV)

SECTION 1: ABRAM TO ABRAHAM

Abram's Name Changed (Genesis 17:1–8)

- When Abram was ninety-nine years old, God appeared to him, saying "I am *El Shaddai*," which means "God Almighty" (Genesis 17:1). The Lord, God Almighty, exhorted Abram to faithfully serve Him and to live a righteous life.

 Note: *El Shaddai* is the Hebrew name of God, the All-Powerful and All-Sufficient One.

- God changed Abram's name to Abraham, which means "father of many nations," and entered into a covenant with him saying:

> "I will make you extremely fruitful. Your descendants will become many nations, and kings will be among them! I will confirm my covenant with you and your descendants after you, from generation to generation. This is the everlasting covenant: I will always be your God and the God of your descendants after you. And I will give the entire land of Canaan, where you now live as a foreigner, to you and your descendants. It will be their possession forever, and I will be their God."
>
> (Genesis 17:6–8)

Circumcision Established as a Sign of the Covenant (Genesis 17:9–27)

- God told Abraham that his part in keeping the agreement was to have himself and all males in his household circumcised. God also said that circumcision would forever serve as a constant reminder of this covenant. Abraham obeyed God.

 Note: Circumcision is the removal of the male's genital foreskin. God initiated this rite as a sign of His covenant with Abraham saying, *"I will always be your God and the God of your descendants after you"* (Genesis 17:7). Abraham's willing submission to God's covenant of circumcision demonstrated his faith in God's Word. Circumcision has been performed from generation to generation among Abraham's Jewish descendants, identifying them as part of God's covenant.

- Sarai was ninety years old and still childless when God changed her name to Sarah, meaning "princess," for she would become the mother of nations.

- God told Abraham that His covenant would not be established with Ishmael, the son he had with Hagar, but with a son he would have with Sarah, his wife.

- The Lord blessed Ishmael and said his offspring would become a great nation, but Ishmael would not be the son of God's covenant promise.

 Note: Ishmael became the forefather of the present day Arab nations.

Abraham Intercedes for the People of Sodom: (Genesis 18)

- The Lord appeared to Abraham. When Abraham looked up, he saw three men standing nearby. One of the men told Abraham that Sarah would give birth to a son the next year.

- Overhearing their conversation, Sarah laughed to herself because she was very old and well past childbearing age.

- The men were on their way to Sodom when the Lord spoke to Abraham and told him about the wickedness of the people in Sodom.

- Abraham's nephew, Lot, was living in Sodom, so Abraham begged the Lord to spare the city for the sake of the righteous people living there.

- Abraham continued pleading until God said He would not destroy Sodom if He found as few as ten righteous people in the city.

The Destruction of Sodom and Gomorrah: (Genesis 19)

- When the Lord's angels arrived in Sodom, Lot greeted them at the city's entrance and took them to his house for a meal.

- Later that night, the men of Sodom surrounded Lot's house demanding that he hand over his guests so they could have sex with them.

- Lot begged the men of Sodom to stop, but they would not listen. The angels then told Lot to leave the city at once with his family.

- Lot hesitated, so the angels grabbed him, his wife, and his daughters and escorted them outside the city to safety.

- The angels told Lot and his family to run for their lives and not look back.

- The next morning, fire and burning sulfur rained down from heaven, completely destroying the wicked cities of Sodom and Gomorrah.

- As Lot and his family escaped, Lot's wife, in disobedience, looked back toward the city and turned into a pillar of salt.

- Only Lot and his two daughters were spared. The Lord had been merciful to Lot because of Abraham's petitions.

- Since Lot had no sons, his two daughters—in a scheme to preserve their family name—got their father drunk and slept with him so they could have children.

- Each of Lot's daughters had a son as a result of incestuous relations with their father. Their sons were the forefathers of the Moabites and the Ammonites, nations which would later become enemies of Abraham's descendants.

Abraham Deceives Again: (Genesis 20)

- Abraham moved to another part of Canaan and once again told the people that Sarah was his sister. Abraham feared he would be killed if the local people knew he was Sarah's husband.

- When the local king learned that Sarah was Abraham's sister, he sent for Sarah and spared Abraham's life.

- Even though Sarah was Abraham's half-sister, God was not pleased with this deception. The Lord intervened and made the king release Sarah unharmed.

RECOMMENDED BIBLE READING

Genesis 17:1–18:15 **God's Covenant with Abraham**

Romans 4:1–15 **Abraham's Faith Credited as Righteousness**

SECTION 2: ISAAC

Isaac, Son of Abraham and Sarah: (Genesis 21)

- Just as God had promised, Abraham and Sarah had a son whom they named Isaac, which means "laughter."

- Abraham was one hundred years old and Sarah was about ninety-one years old when Isaac was born. God gave them something to laugh about in their old age.

- Over the years, the relationship between Sarah and Hagar had been full of envy and strife. When Isaac was born, more problems developed, which created even more animosity between the two women.

- The situation became so unbearable that Sarah told Abraham to send Hagar and Ishmael away. This troubled Abraham because Ishmael was his son.

- The Lord reassured Abraham that he should do as Sarah had demanded, so Abraham sent Hagar and Ishmael away.

Abraham's Test of Faith: (Genesis 22)

- The Lord later instructed Abraham to sacrifice his son, Isaac, as a demonstration of his faith in God.

- Abraham obeyed the Lord and was about to sacrifice Isaac when an angel of the Lord stopped him. According to Hebrews 11:19, *"Abraham reasoned that God could raise the dead . . ."*

- When Abraham looked up, he saw a ram caught in a bush. Abraham built an altar and sacrificed the ram instead of his son to the Lord.

 Abraham's willingness to offer his son, Isaac, as a sacrifice foreshadowed events that would occur some 2,000 years later when God would offer His Son, Jesus Christ, as an atoning sacrifice. God provided a ram as a substitute for Isaac. He would later send His Son, Jesus, as a substitute for you and me. Jesus stood in our place as a substitute and was sacrificed to pay for our sins.

- Abraham named this place *Jehovah Jireh*, meaning "The LORD Will Provide" (Genesis 22:14). Once again God confirmed His covenant with Abraham.

 Note: *Jehovah-Jireh* is the Hebrew name of God as our Provider. *Jehovah Jireh* takes care of our every need.

Isaac Marries Rebekah: (Genesis 23:1–25:11)

- Sarah was 127 years old when she died. Abraham buried her in a cave located in Canaan.

- Abraham later decided it was time for Isaac to marry. He did not want Isaac to marry a Canaanite woman, so he sent one of his servants back to his relatives' country to find a wife for Isaac.

 Note: Abraham did not want Isaac to intermarry with the Canaanites because of their ungodliness. He feared they would lead his descendants into idolatry and away from God.

- The Lord led Abraham's servant to Rebekah, a young girl who happened to be Abraham's niece.

- Abraham's servant arranged for Rebekah to return to Canaan with him to marry Isaac.

- Isaac married Rebekah and they lived in Canaan near Abraham.

- Abraham was 175 years old when he died. Isaac and Ishmael buried him in the same cave in which Sarah was buried.

Jacob and Esau, Sons of Isaac and Rebekah: (Genesis 25:19–34)

- Isaac was forty years old when he married Rebekah. They were childless for twenty years.

- When Isaac was sixty years old, Rebekah became pregnant and gave birth to twin boys, Esau and Jacob.

- Before the twins were born, God told Rebekah the older child would serve the younger.

- Esau, the first born, was a skillful hunter and outdoorsman while Jacob, the second born, was quiet and preferred staying close to home.

- One day after hunting in the fields, Esau came home exhausted and was hungry. His brother, Jacob, offered him food in exchange for his birthright.

 Note: In ancient times, the birthright was an honor given to the oldest son. It included the privilege of becoming the family's leader and receiving a double portion of the family's wealth and possessions upon his father's death.

- Esau, famished and weak, had no use for his birthright at that moment, so he agreed to give it to Jacob for some bread and stew.

God's Covenant with Isaac: (Genesis 26:1–5)

- A severe famine later occurred in the land where Isaac lived. The Lord appeared to Isaac and told him to stay and not go to Egypt to avoid the famine.

- God confirmed His covenant with Isaac. It was the same covenant God had previously made with Isaac's father, Abraham.

Isaac's Deception: (Genesis 26:6–34)

- Isaac obeyed and stayed; however, when one of the kings in that region asked about his wife, Isaac responded in the same way his father had years earlier—by lying.

- Out of fear, Isaac told the king that Rebekah was his sister. Nevertheless, God blessed Isaac and worked everything out in his favor. Isaac became wealthy with large herds and flocks.

- When Esau was forty years old, he married two women from among the Hittites in Canaan. This greatly displeased his parents.

RECOMMENDED BIBLE READING

Genesis 21:1–21   **Isaac, Son of Abraham and Sarah**

Genesis 22:1–19   **Abraham's Test of Faith**

Galatians 3:6–9   **Righteous Because of Faith**

Hebrews 6:13–20   **The Assurance of God's Promises**

SECTION 3: JACOB

Jacob Deceives Isaac for Blessings: (Genesis 27)

- Jacob, encouraged by his mother, Rebekah, deceived his father and stole his brother's blessings.

 Note: Blessings were different from the birthright. Blessings bestowed God's special favor, while the birthright passed on the parent's wealth.

- Jacob and Rebekah tricked the aging and slightly blind Isaac into thinking he was blessing his oldest son, Esau, when he was really blessing Jacob, his second-born son.

- Having lost both his birthright and his blessing, Esau was enraged and vowed to kill Jacob.

- Rebekah heard about Esau's vow and did not want to see either of her sons harmed. She wanted Jacob to leave home and move far away so that he would be safe from Esau.

- Rebekah came up with a plan. She went to her husband, Isaac, and told him that it was time for Jacob to marry.

- Rebekah then convinced Isaac to send Jacob to Haran so that he could marry a woman from among her people. Rebekah knew that Jacob would be safe from Esau in Haran.

Jacob's Dream and God's Covenant with Jacob: (Genesis 28)

- Isaac blessed Jacob and sent him to Rebekah's brother, Laban, in Haran where he could find a wife.

- While on the way to Haran, Jacob stopped to rest and had a dream about a ladder on earth that extended up into the heavens with angels going up and down it.

- The Lord stood above the ladder and confirmed the covenant He had previously made with Jacob's grandfather, Abraham, and his father, Isaac, saying: *"I will give to you and your family the land on which you are now sleeping. Your descendants will spread over the earth in all directions and will become as numerous as the specks of dust. Your family will be a blessing to all people"* (Genesis 28:13b–14 CEV).

 Jacob's dream gives us a picture of Jesus. Just as the ladder reached upward providing a way up to God, Jesus provides a way for us to stand in God's presence.

Jacob Marries Both Leah and Rachel: (Genesis 29–30)

- When Jacob finally reached Haran, he found Laban, his mother's brother, and went to work for him tending sheep.

- Laban had two daughters. Jacob fell in love with Rachel, the younger daughter.

- Jacob made a deal with Laban, promising to work for him for the next seven years in exchange for Rachel's hand in marriage.

- Laban agreed. However, when seven years had passed, he gave Jacob his oldest daughter, Leah, instead of Rachel.

- Jacob was very angry with Laban when he realized what had happened. He confronted his uncle about the deception.

- Laban explained that it was customary for the older daughter to marry before the younger.

- Laban then offered to give Jacob both of his daughters in exchange for another seven years of work.

- Since Jacob loved Rachel and wanted to marry her, he agreed and became husband to both sisters.

- Jacob loved Rachel more than Leah, but Leah was the wife who was initially bearing children. Rachel remained childless for a long time.

- The two sisters argued and vied for their husband's affection.

- Over the next several years, Leah and Rachel, along with their handmaidens (Bilhah and Zilpah), gave birth to Jacob's twelve sons. Jacob also had one daughter, Dinah, born to him by Leah.

Jacob's Twelve Sons

Birth Order	Son's Name	Mother's Name
1st	Reuben	Leah
2nd	Simeon	Leah
3rd	Levi	Leah
4th	Judah	Leah
5th	Dan	Bilhah (Rachel's handmaiden)
6th	Naphtali	Bilhah
7th	Gad	Zilpah (Leah's handmaiden)
8th	Asher	Zilpah
9th	Isaachar	Leah
10th	Zebulun	Leah
11th	Joseph	Rachel
12th	Benjamin	Rachel

- When the eleventh son (Joseph) was born, Jacob decided it was time to return home, but Laban wanted him to stay.

- The two men reached an agreement. Laban agreed to give Jacob some of his sheep as wages, and Jacob agreed to stay and care for Laban's flock.

- Jacob devised a plan to increase his flock and God blessed him. Before long, Jacob became wealthy with a large number of sheep of his own.

Jacob Travels Back to Canaan: (Genesis 31)

- As Jacob prospered, Laban's sons became angry because they believed Jacob was stealing their father's sheep.

- The Lord spoke to Jacob and told him to return to his home in Canaan. After living in Haran for twenty years, Jacob packed up his family and his belongings and began the journey back to Canaan.

- Laban and his sons were not willing to let Jacob leave peacefully, so they went after him.

- Before Laban and his sons caught up with Jacob, the Lord appeared to Laban in a dream and cautioned him about saying anything against Jacob.

- Laban finally reached Jacob's campsite. Laban and Jacob exchanged hostile words, but ultimately agreed to never cross each other's path to do harm.

- Laban said farewell to his daughters and grandchildren and went back home.

Jacob's Name Changed to Israel: (Genesis 32)

- As Jacob and his household traveled on towards Canaan, he became afraid that his brother, Esau, might find out that he was returning and try to kill him.

- Jacob prayed that night. Suddenly, a man appeared and wrestled with Jacob until daybreak.

- Jacob's hip was pulled out of its socket, crippling him, but he continued holding on. Jacob finally asked the man for a blessing.

- After wrestling all night, the man spoke to Jacob and changed his name to Israel saying, *"Your name will no longer be Jacob, but Israel, because you have struggled with God and with men and have overcome"* (Genesis 32:28 NIV).

Note: Out of desperation, Jacob turned to the Lord. He wrestled with God all night until the Lord blessed him. Jacob's struggle resulted in a spiritual life-changing experience for him. God changed his name from Jacob, which means "deceiver," to Israel. The name Israel has a double meaning and has been interpreted by different scholars as "prince with God," "one who struggles with God," "one who strives with God," "God rules," "God struggles," and "God strives."

Jacob's Encounter with Esau: (Genesis 33)

- Jacob met up with his brother, Esau, en route to Canaan. Esau was no longer upset with Jacob, so their encounter was peaceful.

- Twenty years had passed since the brothers had seen each other. They had an affectionate exchange of words, and Esau went on his way.

Jacob's Daughter, Dinah, Raped: (Genesis 34)

- Jacob's daughter, Dinah, was raped by a local ruler's son, who afterwards desperately wanted to marry her.

- When Jacob's sons, Levi and Simeon, heard about Dinah's defilement, they were enraged and wanted revenge. They deceived the local ruler, telling him that his son could marry Dinah if all the town's men agreed to be circumcised.

- The local ruler agreed. After every man had been circumcised and was in a weakened state, Levi and Simeon killed them.

- Jacob's other sons helped Levi and Simeon loot the town. Jacob was irate about what his sons had done and chastised them for their lack of judgment.

God Confirms His Covenant with Jacob: (Genesis 35)

- Jacob moved on to Bethel of Canaan. While there, God visited him and confirmed the covenant He had originally made with Abraham, his grandfather.

- Jacob and his household left Bethel and journeyed towards Bethlehem of Canaan.

- While en route, Rachel gave birth to Benjamin, Jacob's twelfth son. She died in childbirth. Rachel was buried in Bethlehem.

- Reuben, Jacob's oldest son, later slept with Bilhah, his father's concubine.

- Jacob traveled on towards Hebron. He finally reached his father's hometown and settled there.

- Isaac died at the age of 180. Esau and Jacob buried him.

RECOMMENDED BIBLE READING

Genesis 27:1–39	**Jacob's Deception**
Genesis 28:1–22	**Jacob's Dream**
Genesis 32:1–32	**Jacob's Name Changed to Israel**
Hebrews 11:8–20	**Abraham and Isaac's Faith**

SECTION 4: JOSEPH

Joseph Sold and Taken to Egypt: (Genesis 37)

- Jacob had twelve sons; however, his favorite was Joseph, the first son born to him by Rachel whom he loved more than Leah.

- Jacob once gave Joseph a colorfully decorated coat and seemed to show him more love than the others. This caused Joseph's brothers to become jealous.

- When Joseph was about seventeen years old, he had two dreams and shared them with his brothers. According to Joseph's dreams, his brothers would one day bow down before him, and Joseph would reign over them.

- When Joseph's brothers heard about his dreams, they became angry. One day while the brothers were caring for their father's flocks, they discussed killing Joseph. Reuben talked the brothers into throwing him into a pit instead.

- Judah suggested they get Joseph out of the pit and sell him, so the brothers sold Joseph for twenty pieces of silver to some merchants who were traveling to Egypt.

- The brothers then smeared goat's blood on Joseph's coat and took it to their father.

- When Jacob saw the bloody coat, he thought Joseph had been killed by a ferocious animal. He was grief-stricken over the loss of his son.

- Meanwhile in Egypt, the merchants sold Joseph to a man named Potiphar, who was one of Pharaoh's captains.

Perez and Zerah, Judah's Sons with Tamar: (Genesis 38)

- Judah moved away for a while and married a woman who gave birth to three of his sons.

- Judah's first son died and in accordance with tradition, Judah gave his second son in marriage to Tamar, his first son's widow.

- Then Judah's second son died, but Judah did not give his third son to Tamar in marriage. In the meantime, Judah's wife died.

- Tamar, Judah's daughter-in-law, tricked him into thinking she was a prostitute, and the two slept together. Tamar conceived and gave birth to twin boys, Perez and Zerah.

 Note: This story about Judah and Tamar provides information about the circumstances of Perez's birth. Jesus Christ was a descendent of Perez.

Joseph Imprisoned in Egypt: (Genesis 39)

- Potiphar noticed that everything Joseph did was blessed by God with success, so he made Joseph his assistant and put him in charge of his household.

- Joseph was a handsome man. Potiphar's wife soon became attracted to Joseph and tried to seduce him.

- When Joseph refused her advances, Potiphar's wife lied and told her husband that Joseph had tried to rape her.

- Potiphar became angry when he heard his wife's story and had Joseph imprisoned.

- God continued to bless Joseph. He became the warden's assistant and was given a wide-range of responsibilities inside the prison.

Joseph Interprets Pharaoh's Dream: (Genesis 40–41)

- While in prison, Joseph successfully interpreted dreams for the chief baker and chief cupbearer, two of Pharaoh's servants.

- A couple of years later, Pharaoh had a disturbing dream that greatly troubled him. He wanted to know its meaning, but no one was able to interpret the dream.

- After a while, Pharaoh's chief cup bearer remembered that Joseph, who was still in prison, had the gift of interpreting dreams and told Pharaoh about it. When Pharaoh heard about Joseph, he sent for him.

- Pharaoh told Joseph his dream, and God divinely revealed its meaning to Joseph.

- Joseph explained to Pharaoh that *"Seven years of great abundance are coming throughout the land of Egypt, but seven years of famine will follow them"* (Genesis 41:29–30a NIV).

- After hearing the interpretation, Pharaoh wisely made Joseph his second-in-command and put him in charge of all of Egypt's food supplies.

- Sure enough, just as Joseph had said, there were seven years of abundance. During this time, Joseph stored excess food in warehouses.

- Famine struck immediately after the seven years of abundance. Joseph made the food in the warehouses available to all who could afford to buy it.

- The famine was devastating and so widespread that other countries came to Egypt to buy food.

Joseph's Encounter with His Brothers: (Genesis 42–45)

- Canaan was experiencing a severe food shortage. When Jacob heard that Egypt still had food, he sent his sons there to buy grain.

- Jacob's sons met with Joseph in Egypt. Joseph recognized them, but they did not know they were buying food from the brother they had sold into slavery.

- They bought grain from Joseph several times. Each time Joseph tested their integrity and family loyalty. Judah, the one who had suggested the brothers sell Joseph, was the one who demonstrated genuine sacrificial love.

- When Joseph finally revealed himself to his brothers, they were terrified and feared what he would do in retaliation.

- Joseph assured them there was no malice in his heart and that everything happened as part of God's plan.

- Joseph said to his brothers, *"God sent me on ahead of you to keep your families alive and to save you in this wonderful way. After all, you weren't really the ones who sent me here—it was God . . ."* (Genesis 45:7–8 CEV).

- Pharaoh told Joseph's family they could come and live in Egypt, so Joseph arranged the move.

Jacob and His Household Migrate to Egypt: (Genesis 46–47)

- Jacob and his household gathered their belongings and made the pilgrimage from Canaan to the land of Goshen in Egypt, where they lived as herdsmen and farmers.

- Seventy people in all journeyed to Egypt, thus fulfilling God's prophetic words spoken to Abraham years earlier, *"your descendants will be strangers in a country not their own"* (Genesis 15:13a NIV).

Jacob Blesses His Sons and Then Dies: (Genesis 48–50)

- Some years later Jacob became ill and called for Joseph. He blessed Joseph's two sons, Manasseh and Ephraim, and prophetically stated that Ephraim (who was the younger) would someday become a greater nation than Manasseh.

- Jacob lived in Egypt for seventeen years. When he was 147 years old and nearing death, Jacob gathered all of his sons around him and blessed each of them. The blessings included prophecies about the future.

- Judah, Jacob's fourth son, received the greatest blessings. Jacob said, *"Judah, your brothers will praise you; your hand will be on the neck of your enemies; your father's sons will bow down to you. You are a lion's cub, O Judah . . . The scepter will not depart from Judah, nor the ruler's staff from between his feet, until he comes to whom it belongs and the obedience of the nations is his"* (Genesis 49:8–10 NIV).

> Jacob prophetically declared, "the scepter will not depart from Judah." A scepter is a wand used by kings as a symbol of authority. Jacob was implying that kings would come from Judah's descendants. This prophecy foreshadowed the coming of the Messiah, Jesus Christ, a descendant of Abraham, Isaac, Jacob, and Judah through whom all nations on earth would be blessed!

- When Jacob died, his sons took his body back to Canaan and buried him in the same place his grandfather, Abraham, and his father, Isaac were buried. Joseph's brothers feared that he would retaliate now that their father was dead.

- Joseph told his brothers again that they had nothing to fear saying, *"You intended to harm me, but God intended it for good to accomplish what is now being done, the saving of many lives"* (Genesis 50:20 NIV).

> God used Joseph as a savior. God arranged for Joseph to be in Egypt at the right time and to come into power. God gave Joseph wisdom and insight so He could use him to administer His grace and mercy to save and protect the nation of Israel.

- When Joseph was old and close to death, he gathered the sons of Israel (Jacob's descendants) and declared that God would someday bring them out of Egypt and send them back to Canaan, the land that had been promised to their forefathers.

- Joseph made them promise to carry his body with them on their journey back to Canaan. Joseph was 110 years old when he died.

RECOMMENDED BIBLE READING

Genesis 37:1–36 **Joseph Sold and Taken to Egypt**

Genesis 41:1–44 **Joseph Interprets Pharaoh's Dream**

Genesis 45:16–46:7 **Jacob and His Household Migrate to Egypt**

Hebrews 11:21–22 **Jacob and Joseph's Faith**

Romans 5:1–11 **Faith Gives Us Peace with God**

SECTION 5: JOB

Job's First Test of Faith: (Job 1)

- Job was a righteous man who lived in the land of Uz. Everything Job did was honorable and pleasing to the Lord.

- Job was also a very wealthy man. He owned a large number of sheep, cattle and other livestock. He had seven sons and three daughters and employed numerous servants.

- One day a discussion took place in heaven between God and Satan. God pointed out to Satan that Job was a man of outstanding integrity. God also told Satan that Job reverenced the Lord and was the most righteous man in the world.

- Satan responded saying Job was righteous and revered the Lord because he had been blessed in every way.

- Satan added that Job would curse God to his face if his riches were taken away. In a test of Job's faith, God allowed Satan to destroy all of Job's possessions, but would not allow him to harm Job's physical body.

- Job then experienced one disaster after another until everything he owned—including his children—were gone.

- Job was devastated and grief-stricken, but continued to honor God saying, *"The LORD gave me what I had, and the LORD has taken it away. Praise the name of the LORD"* (Job 1:21b).

Job's Second Test of Faith: (Job 2)

- Another discussion took place in heaven between God and Satan. God was pleased to inform Satan that Job was still serving Him even though he had lost all his earthly possessions.

- Satan's reply was that Job would curse God to his face if his physical body were harmed. In response to Satan's accusation, God allowed Satan to afflict Job's physical body, but would not allow him take Job's life.

- Job was stricken with a terrible disease that caused an outbreak of boils all over his body. Job's suffering was so great that his wife advised him to give up, curse the Lord, and die.

- Job's reply to his wife was that her words were foolish. He asked, *"Shall we accept good from God, and not trouble?"* (Job 2:10 NIV).

- Job's three friends, Eliphaz, Bildad and Zophar, heard about his affliction and came to comfort him. When they saw Job, they hardly recognized him because boils covered his entire body.

- Eliphaz, Bildad and Zophar were grief-stricken. Job's condition was so grave that they sat with him for seven days and nights without saying a word.

Job's Friends Explain His Suffering: (Job 3–31)

- Job finally spoke and cursed the day of his birth. Job said it would have been better to have never been born.

- Job's comments opened the door for his friends to respond. In a series of speeches, they each tried to explain the reason for his suffering.

- Job's friends concluded his suffering was the result of sin. They told Job that experience had taught them God always blesses the righteous and punishes the unrighteous. They advised Job to acknowledge his sin to God.

- Job insisted he had not sinned. Job said from his perspective, it appeared God treats the righteous and the unrighteous the same.

- Job recognized his need for a mediator saying, *"God is not a mortal like me, so I cannot argue with him or take him to trial. If only there were a mediator between us, someone who could bring us together"* (Job 9:32–33).

 Job's concept of a mediator is what we have in Jesus Christ. Jesus is our perfect Mediator, the One who identifies with our suffering and stands before God as our Advocate. He is willing and able to reconcile us with God if we put our faith in Him as our Savior.

- Job's friends criticized him for complaining about his suffering and continued to accuse him of sin.

- One of his friends went so far as to say Job deserved to suffer even more than he had. Another friend insisted Job had to be guilty of *something*. He said surely Job had refused to give water to the thirsty or food to the hungry.

- Job responded saying his friends did not know what they were talking about. Job told them they were supposed to be comforting him, but instead they were mocking him with accusations and insults.

- In the midst of agony and great pain, Job declared that God had wronged him. He begged for an opportunity to argue his case before God. He accused his friends of persecuting him, and his family of forsaking him.

- Although Job felt that his suffering was unjust, he reaffirmed his faith in God saying, *"But as for me, I know that my Redeemer lives, and he will stand upon the earth at last. And after my body has decayed, yet in my body I will see God"* (Job 19:25–26).

 Jesus Christ is our Redeemer, the One who took on our sins, stood in our place, and paid the price with His blood to set us free from the power of sin. We are redeemed when we accept Jesus Christ as our Lord and Savior.

Elihu's Response: (Job 32–37)

- Job's three friends finally refused to speak to him any further because he would not admit that he had sinned.

- A younger man named Elihu was also present with Job and his three friends. Elihu had remained silent out of respect for his elders, but finally began to speak.

- Elihu was upset with Job's friends for failing to adequately respond to Job's complaints. He was also angry with Job for saying that his suffering was unjust.

- Elihu reminded Job that God can do no wrong. God is sovereign, all-powerful, and always in control. Elihu also pointed out that God uses various situations to teach and correct us.

God Responds: (Job 38–42)

- Job had previously asked for a meeting with God, so the Lord graciously obliged. Speaking from a whirlwind God said to Job, *"Who is this that questions my wisdom with such ignorant words? Brace yourself like a man, because I have some questions for you, and you must answer them"* (Job 38:2–3).

- God then proceeded to ask Job one question after another in rapid succession. Each question highlighted the frailties and limitations of man in comparison to the awesomeness of God.

- Job humbly acknowledged God's sovereignty and repented for calling his suffering unjust.

- God expressed his displeasure with Job's friends and told them to ask Job to intercede for them in prayer.

- After Job prayed for his friends, God restored his health and blessed him with more wealth than he had before.

Note: The book of Job addresses the problem of pain and suffering, but does not explain or provide an answer for it. The message of Job is that God is sovereign and not all suffering is the result of sin. God uses adversity to help us grow spiritually and to glorify Himself. God wants us to trust Him.

RECOMMENDED BIBLE READING

Job 1:1–2:13	**Job's Tests of Faith**
Job 38:1–41	**God Responds**
Job 42:1–17	**Job Is Restored**
Romans 8:18–39	**Nothing Can Separate Us from God's Love**

MEDITATION & PRAYER

A Psalm of praise to the Lord God, Who saves and protects:

"I love the LORD, because He has heard
    My voice and my supplications.
Because He has inclined His ear to me,
    Therefore I will call upon Him as long as I live.

The pains of death surrounded me,
    And the pangs of Sheol laid hold of me;
    I found trouble and sorrow.
Then I called upon the name of the LORD:
    "O LORD, I implore You, deliver my soul!"

Gracious is the LORD, and righteous;
    Yes, our God is merciful.
 The LORD preserves the simple;
    I was brought low, and He saved me."

(Psalm 116:1–6 NKJV)

Dear God Almighty,

You are El Shaddai, the All-Powerful and All-Sufficient One. Your mercy and loving kindness are un-ending. You are my Friend, my Comforter, my Protector and Savior. You are my Everything and my All-in-All at all times! Strengthen me and increase my faith. It is my desire to follow You with childlike faith in all circumstances.

Amen

REVIEW QUESTIONS

1. How did Abraham demonstrate his faith in God? How did God reward his faith?

_____

_____

_____

_____

_____

_____

2. We all have character flaws and the patriarchs were no exception. What did Abraham do that was of questionable character? What about Jacob, Joseph and Job? Why do you think God continued to bless them in spite of their flaws?

_____

_____

_____

_____

_____

_____

3. It is important to remember that spiritual growth is a process. What did Abraham do that demonstrated spiritual growth? What about Jacob, Joseph, Job?

_____

_____

_____

_____

_____

_____

4. Joseph's brothers sold him into slavery. According to Joseph, his brothers' action was evil, but God used the situation for good. How did God turn Joseph's bad situation into good?

_____

_____

_____

_____

_____

_____

5. Which of Jacob's sons received God's covenant blessings, originally made with Abraham, that all nations of the earth would be blessed through his offspring? Before Jacob died, what did he say to this son as part of his blessing?

_____

_____

_____

_____

_____

_____

6. What parallels do you see between Joseph's life and Jesus' life?

_____

_____

_____

_____

_____

_____

7. Summarize the story of Job in a few sentences. Why did the author include Job's story in this chapter of the study?

_____

_____

_____

_____

_____

_____

Personal Reflections

8. Why did God reaffirm His covenant with Abraham so many times? What does this tell you about God?

_____

_____

_____

_____

_____

_____

9. In what areas of your life would God like you to grow more spiritually? What steps can you take to improve in these areas and strengthen your relationship with God?

_____

_____

_____

_____

_____

_____

10. What did God reveal to you about faith? Of what importance is faith to God?

_____

_____

_____

_____

_____

_____

11. Name a bad situation you or someone you know experienced that God turned into good. In what ways was God working that were difficult for you to see at the time?

_____

_____

_____

_____

_____

_____

12. What did God reveal to you about pain and suffering from the story of Job? How can you use the story of Job to help you or someone else through a difficult time?

_____

_____

_____

_____

_____

_____

13. What did God reveal to you about His character through His Hebrew names, *El Shaddai and Jehovah-Jireh*?

_____

_____

_____

_____

_____

_____

CLOSING PRAYER

The Apostle Paul teaches that faith is the key to God's promise:

"For the promise that he should be the heir of the world came not to Abraham or to his seed through the law, but through the righteousness of faith. . . . Therefore it is of faith, that it might be given by grace to the end that the promise might be made sure to all the seed, not to that only which is of the law, but to that also which is of the faith of Abraham, who is the father of us all (as it is written: 'I have made thee a father of many nations'), in the presence of Him whom he believed, even God, who quickeneth the dead and calleth those things which are not, as though they were."

(Romans 4:13, 16–17 KJ21)

Heavenly Father,

You are Jehovah-Jireh, my Provider. You are the One Who takes care of my every need. You entered into a covenant with father Abraham long ago, promising to bless the entire world through his offspring. Jesus Christ is the fulfillment of that promise, and it is through Him that You provided for my redemption and salvation. Your promise was given as a free gift that anyone can receive if they have faith like Abraham's. Faith is the key! I thank You for Your provisions and Your promises. Help me to more fully embrace by faith Your promises, for they are to all who believe in Your Word.

Amen

CHAPTER 3

ESTABLISHING THE NATION

OPENING PRAYER

Lord God,

As I prepare to read about how the nation of Israel was established, I ask for spiritual wisdom and understanding. Open my ears and let me hear Your voice. Open my eyes and show me Your Truths. Help me identify life's lessons taught in Scripture and show me how to apply them in my life. Mold me and transform me. Make me holy as You are holy.

Amen

CHAPTER SUMMARY

ESTABLISHING THE NATION

(Exodus 1–34)

When the book of Exodus opens, 430 years have passed since Jacob and seventy members of his household migrated to Egypt. Each of Jacob's sons became the patriarch of a tribe. Joseph was patriarch of two tribes, named after his sons, Ephraim and Manasseh.

Over the years, Jacob's descendants had significantly increased in numbers to about two and a half million people. They were known as Hebrews or Israelites. They were still living in Egypt, but had been enslaved and were being oppressed. The Lord divinely empowered a man named Moses to deliver them from slavery and lead them out of Egypt to the land God had promised their forefathers, Abraham, Isaac and Jacob.

Exodus tells the story of how God delivered Israel from the Egyptians by performing a series of miracles. God's miracles included sending ten plagues that devastated Egypt, sparing Israel's firstborn sons from death in an event known as the Passover, and parting the Red Sea so the Israelites could walk across and escape from the Egyptians.

Exodus continues with an account of the Israelites' journey as they headed for Canaan. God provided their every need. The Lord guided them through the desert with a pillar of cloud by day and a pillar of fire by night. God fed them, protected them from disease, and fought their battles. Along the way, the Lord cultivated His relationship with the Israelites, giving them the Ten Commandments and teaching them how to live righteous and holy lives. Israel was the nation established and set apart by God to live for Him and to teach other nations about the One True God.

	Approximate Timeline	Location	Biblical Scriptures	Author
Exile in Egypt	1526 B.C.–1446 B.C.	Egypt	Exodus 1–2	Moses
The Call of Moses	1446 B.C.	Egypt	Exodus 3–11	Moses
The Passover Miracle	1446 B.C.	Egypt	Exodus 12	Moses
Out of Egypt	1446 B.C.	Sinai Desert	Exodus 13–19	Moses
The Ten Commandments	1445 B.C.	Sinai Desert	Exodus 20–34	Moses

MAP OF KEY LOCATIONS

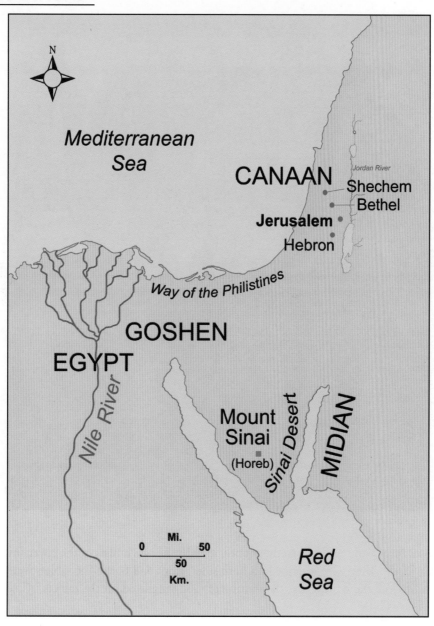

MOSES

"Moses turned and went down the mountain with the two tablets of the covenant law in his hands. They were inscribed on both sides, front and back. The tablets were the work of God; the writing was the writing of God, engraved on the tablets." (Exodus 32:15–16 TNIV)

Section 1: Exile in Egypt

Israel, from Joseph to Slavery in Egypt: (Exodus 1)

- About 430 years had passed since Jacob and his household of about seventy people migrated to Egypt to avoid famine.

- Jacob's twelve sons died, ending that generation, but their offspring rapidly multiplied. They were called "Hebrews" or "Israelites."

- There were now about two and a half million Israelites (descendants of Jacob) living in Goshen of Egypt, and their numbers were steadily increasing.

- While Joseph was alive, Egypt was a good place for the Israelites. However, another king came into power after Joseph's death who knew nothing about him and how he had helped Egypt.

- Pharaoh became concerned about such a large number of foreigners living in Egypt.

- Pharaoh feared the Israelites might align themselves with Egypt's enemies, conquer Egypt, and take over. To prevent this from happening, the Egyptians enslaved the Israelites.

- The Egyptians were brutal taskmasters, forcing the Israelites to work hard and long hours on Pharaoh's building projects; however, the more the Egyptians oppressed the Israelites, the more their numbers grew.

- In an effort to slow down the Hebrews' population growth, Pharaoh ordered all boys born to Israelites to be thrown in the river.

Moses, from Birth to Age Eighty: (Exodus 2)

- During this time, a boy was born to a couple who were descendants of Levi, Jacob's third son.

- To save her son, the baby's mother hid him for three months. She then put him in a basket and placed it along the bank of the river.

- Pharaoh's daughter found the baby. The baby's sister saw what happened and approached Pharaoh's daughter. She asked the princess if she needed a Hebrew mother to nurse the baby.

- The princess said yes and the baby's sister then arranged for the baby's own mother to nurse him.

- When the baby was older, his mother took him back to Pharaoh's daughter, who named him Moses and raised him as her own son.

- Years later when Moses had grown into adulthood, he went to visit his Hebrew family. While visiting his people, Moses saw an Egyptian beating a Hebrew slave.

- Moses looked around to see if anyone was watching and then killed the Egyptian. Although Moses had been cautious, someone saw him kill the Egyptian and the news soon spread.

- When Pharaoh heard about the murder, he ordered Moses' execution. However, Moses escaped and fled to Midian.

- Moses came to a well and sat down. Shortly afterwards, he saw several young girls who had come to the well for water. Some shepherds began harassing the girls and Moses came to their rescue.

- The girls later told their father about Moses' good deed and he invited Moses to join them for dinner.

- The girls' father, a priest in Midian, asked Moses to stay and become a member of his household. Moses accepted the offer and later married one of the priest's daughters, named Zipporah.

- Moses lived in Midian as a shepherd, tending his father-in-law's sheep for the next forty years.

- Meanwhile, the Israelites were still living in slavery and suffering in Egypt. They cried out to God for help.

- God was moved with compassion and began orchestrating plans for the Israelites' deliverance.

RECOMMENDED BIBLE READING

Exodus 1:1–2:25 **Slavery in Egypt**

Romans 9:1–5 **God's Chosen People**

SECTION 2: THE CALL OF MOSES

Moses Chosen to Deliver Israel: (Exodus 3–4)

- One day while Moses was tending sheep at Horeb (also called Sinai, the mountain of God), the Lord called out to him from a bush that was burning, but not consumed.

- The Lord told Moses that He (God) was sending him (Moses) to deliver Israel from slavery and lead them out of Egypt to Canaan.

- Moses was reluctant and objected to God's plan of deliverance, saying *"Who am I, that I should go to Pharaoh and bring the Israelites out of Egypt?"* God responded saying, *"I will be with you"* (Exodus 3:11–12 NIV).

- Then Moses said to God, *"Suppose I go to the Israelites . . . and they ask me, 'What is his (God's) name?'"* (Exodus 3:13 NIV).

- God told Moses that His name is *Yahweh,* which is translated, *"I am who I am. This is what you are to say to the Israelites: 'I AM has sent me to you'"* (Exodus 3:14 NIV).

Note: *Yahweh* is traditionally rendered "Jehovah." It is the Hebrew name of God usually translated "LORD" and appears in Scripture with an initial large capital letter followed by three small capital letters (LORD). The Hebrew name *Adonai* is also translated "Lord"; however, it appears in Scripture with only the first letter capitalized (Lord). Jehovah is the "Self-Existent One True God."

- Moses continued his protest asking, *"What if they do not believe me or listen to me . . . ?"* (Exodus 4:1 NIV). God gave Moses power to perform miracles so the Israelites would believe that the God of Israel had sent him.

- Finally Moses said to God, *"O Lord, I have never been eloquent . . . I am slow of speech and tongue . . . Please send someone else"* (Exodus 4:10, 13 NIV).

- At this point, God became angry with Moses and said to him, *"What about your brother, Aaron . . . He will speak to the people for you . . . But take this staff in your hand so you can perform miraculous signs with it"* (Exodus 4:14, 16, 17 NIV).

- Moses was about eighty years old when he went home, gathered his wife and children, and began the journey to Egypt, carrying the staff God had given him.

- Moses met up with Aaron along the way, and they traveled to Egypt together. Upon their arrival, they met with Israel's leaders and told them God was going to deliver the Israelites. Israel's leaders praised God for the message of deliverance.

Moses Confronts Pharaoh: (Exodus 5–6)

- Moses and Aaron met with Pharaoh and told him they were delivering a message from the God of Israel.

- Moses and Aaron said to Pharaoh, *"This is what the LORD, the God of Israel, says: Let my people go so they may hold a festival in my honor in the wilderness"* (Exodus 5:1b).

- God's message meant nothing to Pharaoh. He not only refused to let the Israelites go, but he increased their workload.

- The Israelites became discouraged as did Moses. God encouraged Moses and told him that all would soon see the power of the Lord, the God of their forefathers, Abraham, Isaac and Jacob.

God Sends Ten Plagues to Egypt: (Exodus 7–11)

- Moses and Aaron confronted Pharaoh numerous times demanding that he let the Israelites go free. With each encounter, Pharaoh stubbornly refused.

- Each time Pharaoh refused, the Lord sent a plague as a demonstration of His power. The plagues were devastating. God sent ten plagues before Pharaoh finally agreed to let the Israelites go.

THE TEN PLAGUES

- ✓ The water of the Nile River was turned to blood.

- ✓ Frogs took over the land.

- ✓ Gnats infested men and animals.

- ✓ Flies invaded Egypt, but not Goshen, where the Israelites lived.

- ✓ Egypt's livestock died, but not Israel's.

- ✓ Boils (sores) infected the Egyptians, but not the Israelites.

- ✓ Hail devastated Egypt, but not Goshen.

- ✓ Locusts destroyed everything left after the hail.

- ✓ Darkness covered Egypt, but not Goshen, for three days.

- ✓ Egypt's firstborn sons were killed, but Israel's were spared.

RECOMMENDED BIBLE READING

Exodus 3:1–4:20 **Moses Chosen to Deliver Israel**

Romans 9:6–24 **God's Sovereignty**

Section 3: The Passover Miracle

The Passover, Saved by the Blood: (Exodus 12)

- Before the tenth plague, God told Moses to tell the Israelites to slaughter a lamb—one that was perfect without defect—and smear its blood on the doorframes of their houses.

- Moses gave the people God's instructions, and they did just as they were told.

- At midnight, God's destroyer (angel of death) killed every one of the Egyptians' firstborn sons, including Pharaoh's oldest son. The Egyptians' firstborn animals were also killed.

- The angel of death passed over the houses with blood smeared on the doorframes, so the Israelites' firstborn were spared. This was the "Passover" miracle.

Passover is a Jewish holiday that is still celebrated annually. It is a reminder of how God delivered the Israelites from slavery in Egypt.

Passover foreshadowed the significance of blood for the remission of sins, *". . . without the shedding of blood there is no forgiveness"* (Hebrews 9:22b NIV).

Jesus was our Passover lamb, perfect without defect, who shed His blood for us. The Apostle Paul tells us that *". . . Christ, our Passover lamb, has been sacrificed"* (1 Corinthians 5:7b NIV).

- When Pharaoh realized what had happened, he told the Israelites to gather their belongings and leave Egypt at once.

- The Israelites left in such a hurry that they did not have time to let their bread rise. They took unleavened bread (a flat bread).

Note: Leavening (yeast) is often used in Scripture to represent sin, and unleavened bread is used to symbolize the removal of sin. For Scriptures that refer to yeast as sin, see Matthew 16:5–12; Mark 8:15; Luke 12:1; and Galatians 5:9. Today, the Feast of Unleavened Bread is celebrated as part of Passover. The unleavened bread symbolizes freedom from slavery.

Recommended Bible Reading

Exodus 11:1–12:30 **The Passover**

Hebrews 11:23–29 **Moses' Faith**

1 Corinthians 5:6–8 **Christ, Our Passover Lamb**

SECTION 4: OUT OF EGYPT

Miracle at the Red Sea: (Exodus 13–14)

- Moses led the Israelites out of Egypt through the desert towards the Red Sea. God guided them with a pillar of cloud by day and a pillar of fire by night.

- Following the pillar of cloud, the Israelites headed south towards Mount Sinai.

- God did not lead the Israelites through the region of the Philistines, which was the shortest route to Canaan; He knew they would lose a battle against the mighty Philistines.

 Note: The Philistines were an aggressive warring tribe. The Israelites, on the other hand, had been in slavery for years and were not trained or equipped for military battle. God knew they would lose a battle against the Philistines, and those who survived would retreat and return to Egypt.

- Moses and the Israelites carried Joseph's remains with them, for their ancestors had promised to bury Joseph in Canaan.

- Shortly after the Israelites' departure, Pharaoh became angry and changed his mind. He and his army went after Israel and caught up with them at the shore of the Red Sea.

- The Israelites were terrified when they saw Pharaoh and his army. Moses said to them, *"Do not be afraid. Stand firm and you will see the deliverance the LORD will bring you today"* (Exodus 14:13 NIV).

- Miraculously, God separated the waters of the Red Sea and the Israelites started walking across to the other side. The Egyptians followed the Israelites through the parted sea.

- The Egyptians were unable to make it to the other side because their chariots' wheels got stuck in the mud and came off, making them impossible to drive. The Egyptian army was thrown into a state of total confusion.

- After all the Israelites had crossed and were safe on the other side, God caused the waters to rush back into place, drowning Pharaoh's army.

> God used Moses as a savior. He was a deliverer, leader, and prophet. The parting of the Red Sea represented deliverance and is a picture of our deliverance from an old life separated from God to a new life in Christ.

The Lord's Provision, Protection, and Guidance: (Exodus 15–17)

- Moses led the Israelites from the Red Sea southward into the desert. Soon they began to complain because the water in the area was not safe to drink.

- God mercifully responded to their complaints, pointing out a tree branch to Moses. When Moses threw the branch into the water, it became safe to drink.

- God then told the Israelites that He would prevent them from getting sick and catching diseases if they would listen to Him and obey. God said, "I am *Jehovah-Rapha,*" which means "The LORD Who Heals" (Exodus 15:26).

Note: *Jehovah-Rapha* is a Hebrew name of God, the Great Physician and Healer.

- As the Israelites traveled onward, they complained about the lack of food. They were upset with Moses and blamed him for their situation.

- The people told Moses they would have been better off dead in Egypt. They grumbled saying, "at least there was food in Egypt."

- God mercifully responded again, sending quail for meat. The next morning, God provided a food substance they were to eat as bread.

- When the Israelites saw the food which formed on the ground each morning, they asked, "What is it?"

- Moses replied, saying it was bread. Moses also told them God would provide enough of this bread for them to eat each day. They called it *manna*, which means, "What is it?"

- As the Israelites journeyed farther, they began complaining about the lack of drinking water again. They were angry with Moses and demanded that he find water for them to drink.

- Moses cried out to the Lord in prayer, asking for help. Moses told the Lord that the people were so upset they were ready to stone him.

- The Lord pointed out a rock and told Moses to strike it with the staff of God. Moses obeyed the Lord, and drinking water came gushing out of the rock.

- The Amalekites, a nomadic group of people, later discovered that the Israelites were in the area and sent their warriors to fight against them. Moses called upon a young man named Joshua to lead the Israelites into battle.

- Joshua gathered men for battle, while Moses, Aaron and Hur (one of Moses' assistants) went to the top of a mountain, carrying the staff of God.

- As long as Moses held the staff of God in his hands and kept them raised, Joshua and his men were victorious. When Moses lowered his hands, the Israelites began to lose.

- The battle raged on for a long time. Moses finally grew weary and could no longer keep his hands raised, so Aaron and Hur held Moses' hands and kept them raised. The Israelites eventually won the battle against the Amalekites.

- Moses built an altar and called it *Jehovah-Nissi*, which means "The LORD Is My Banner" (Exodus 17:15).

 Note: *Jehovah-Nissi* is the Hebrew name of God as Conqueror. *Jehovah-Nissi* is the One Who Gives Victory Over the Enemy.

Advice on Delegating Authority: (Exodus 18)

- Jethro, Moses' father-in-law, having heard about the miracles God had performed, came to meet with Moses.

- Jethro soon noticed that everyone was coming directly to Moses for help with their individual problems.

- Jethro advised Moses to delegate authority to other capable leaders and to get involved only when issues were of high priority or when the delegated leaders needed his help.

- In this way, Jethro helped Moses organize a leadership structure for handling the people's social, moral, and religious issues.

Israel Arrives At Mount Sinai: (Exodus 19)

- Two months after the Israelites left Egypt, they came to Mount Sinai (the mountain of God) and set up camp.

- God told Moses to tell Israel they would be His treasured possession if they obeyed and kept His covenant.

- When Moses told the leaders of Israel what God had said, they responded in unison, *"All that the LORD has spoken we will do"* (Exodus 19:8a NKJV).

RECOMMENDED BIBLE READING

Exodus 13:1–14:31 **Miracle at the Red Sea**

Exodus 16:1–17:16 **The Lord's Provisions and Protection**

John 6:22–40 **Jesus is the Bread of Life**

SECTION 5: THE TEN COMMANDMENTS

God Gives Israel the Ten Commandments: (Exodus 20)

- God gave the people these commandments:

THE TEN COMMANDMENTS

1. *"You shall have no other gods before me."*

2. *"You shall not make for yourself an idol."*

3. *"You shall not misuse the name of the LORD your God."*

4. *"Remember the Sabbath day by keeping it holy."*

5. *"Honor your father and your mother."*

6. *"You shall not murder."*

7. *"You shall not commit adultery."*

8. *"You shall not steal."*

9. *"You shall not give false testimony against your neighbor."*

10. *"You shall not covet your neighbor's house . . . or anything that belongs to your neighbor."*

God Establishes Laws of the Covenant with Israel: (Exodus 21–24)

- In addition to the ten commandments, God gave Israel numerous other laws that covered social, moral, and religious issues such as:

  ✓ How slaves, widows, the poor and strangers were to be treated.

  ✓ How cases involving homicide, kidnapping, assault, stealing and property loss should be handled.

  ✓ How holidays and festivals were to be celebrated.

- God also gave Israel laws forbidding unrighteous conduct such as:

  ✓ Improper sex acts, idolatry, lying, cheating, deception and bribery.

  ✓ Making treaties with nations who worship idols.

- Moses read God's covenant laws to the people of Israel and again they responded in unison saying, *"All that the LORD has said we will do, and be obedient"* (Exodus 24:7b NKJV). Moses then sprinkled blood on the altar and on the people, sealing the covenant.

Under the covenant of the Old Testament, Israel would be God's treasured possession and in right standing with Him if they obeyed God's laws. The Old Testament covenant was sealed with animals' blood.

The covenant of the New Testament opens the door for anyone to be God's treasured possession. We are made righteous through faith in Jesus Christ. This covenant was sealed with the blood of Jesus Christ. (Matthew 26:28; Luke 22:20; Hebrews 9:13–15, 22)

- God later called Moses to the top of Mount Sinai for more detailed instructions.

- Moses took Joshua with him and left Aaron in charge at the base of the mountain. Moses spent forty days and forty nights in God's presence at the top.

God Gives Moses Plans for the Tabernacle and Priesthood: (Exodus 25–31)

- While at the top of Mount Sinai, God gave Moses detailed plans for building a tabernacle to be used as a place of worship. God also outlined procedures and plans for the priesthood.

- The Lord instructed Moses to tell the Israelites that they must observe the Sabbath, the seventh day of the week.

- God told Moses that the Sabbath is a sign of His covenant with Israel. Observing the Sabbath would help them remember that God is *Jehovah-Mekoddishkem*, which means, "The LORD Who Makes You Holy" (Exodus 31:13).

 Note: *Jehovah-Mekoddishkem* is the Hebrew name of God, The One Who Sanctifies. *Jehovah-Mekoddishkem* sets us apart and makes us pure for His sacred purposes.

Israel Worships an Idol: (Exodus 32–34)

- Meanwhile, Moses had been gone for such a long time that the people began to think he was not coming back. They went to Aaron and asked him to make an idol god for worship.

- Aaron listened to the people and made a golden calf, which the people worshiped with much rejoicing and celebration. This happened shortly after they had promised to obey the God of Israel.

- The Lord became so angered that He threatened to destroy the Israelites and make a great nation of Moses' descendants instead of the twelve tribes of Israel.

- Moses interceded for the Israelites, begging the Lord to forgive them. Moses reminded God of His covenant with their forefathers.

- Moses told the Lord that the Egyptians would mock them and say that the God of Israel led them into the desert and killed them.

- Moses continued pleading with God until He finally relented. The Lord renewed His covenant with Israel and admonished them to obey and not be led into idolatry again.

RECOMMENDED BIBLE READING

Exodus 20:1–17 **The Ten Commandments**
Exodus 32:1–35 **Israel Worships an Idol**
Exodus 33:1–34:14 **Moses Intercedes for Israel**
Galatians 3:15–29 **God's Law and God's Promises**
Romans 9:30–33 **Israel's Failure**

MEDITATION & PRAYER

Moses and Miriam sing after the Lord delivered Israel:

"Who among the gods is like you, Lord?

Who is like you—majestic in holiness, awesome in glory, working wonders? You stretch out your right hand, and the earth swallows your enemies. In your unfailing love you will lead the people you have redeemed. In your strength you will guide them to your holy dwelling."

(Exodus 15:11–13 TNIV)

Lord God Jehovah,

Who is like You? You are majestic in holiness and awesome in glory. You are everywhere and always present. Your love is immeasurable. You are all-powerful. Your strength is incomparable. You are all-knowing. Your wisdom is insurmountable. Lead me, as You did Israel, in Your unfailing love and guide me to Your Holy dwelling.

Amen

REVIEW QUESTIONS

1. Describe Moses' journey of spiritual growth from the burning bush to the Ten Commandments.

_____

_____

_____

_____

_____

_____

2. What parallels do you see between Moses' life and Jesus' life?

_____

_____

_____

_____

_____

_____

3. What miracles did God perform through Moses to demonstrate His power?

_____

_____

_____

_____

_____

_____

4. What is the story of Passover? What *Picture of Redemption* do you see in the story of Passover?

_____

_____

_____

_____

_____

_____

5. What event does the Feast of Unleavened Bread celebrate? How does unleavened bread provide a *Picture of Redemption*?

_____

_____

_____

_____

_____

_____

6. What provisions did God make for the Israelites as they journeyed to Mount Sinai?

_____

_____

_____

_____

_____

_____

7. God entered into a covenant with the nation of Israel at Mount Sinai. What was the Old Testament covenant and how was it sealed? God later entered into a covenant with all mankind. What is the New Testament covenant and how was it sealed?

_____

_____

_____

_____

_____

_____

_____

PERSONAL REFLECTIONS

8. Moses was reluctant to accept the mission God had for his life. In Moses' case, there was a burning bush to affirm God's presence. How do you know when God is calling you to action? What can you do to affirm God's call when there is no burning bush?

_____

_____

_____

_____

_____

_____

9. Moses' father-in-law, Jethro, advised him to delegate some of his authority to capable leaders. In what areas of your life do you need to delegate more authority? Think about how this applies to you at home, work, church, community, etc. What steps can you take that will enable you to delegate more?

_____

_____

_____

_____

_____

10. Aaron buckled under pressure and made a golden calf for the Israelites to worship. How do you respond when being pressured to please others? What about when you're being pressured to do something you know is wrong?

_____

_____

_____

_____

_____

_____

11. When God became angry with the Israelites for worshipping the golden calf, Moses interceded for them in prayer. Intercessory prayer is petitioning God's special favor for someone other than oneself. Why did Moses intercede for the Israelites in prayer instead of allowing God to kill them and make his (Moses') descendants a great nation? What did you learn from Moses about intercessory prayer?

_____

_____

_____

_____

_____

12. What did God reveal to you about His character through His Hebrew names: *Yahweh (Jehovah); Jehovah-Rapha; Jehovah-Nissi;* and *Jehovah-Mekoddishkem?*

_____

_____

_____

_____

_____

_____

13. What situation has God worked out for you recently? Write a message of thanks to God for His provision, protection, and guidance in your life.

_____

_____

_____

_____

_____

_____

CLOSING PRAYER

The author of Hebrews tells us that it is impossible to please God without faith:

"And it is impossible to please God without faith. Anyone who wants to come to him must believe that God exists and that he rewards those who sincerely seek him. . . . It was by faith that Moses left the land of Egypt, not fearing the king's anger. He kept right on going because he kept his eyes on the one who is invisible."

(Hebrews 11:6, 27)

Dear Lord Jehovah,

I thank You for all the mighty things You've done and are continuing to do for me. You are the One who gives me victory over my enemies. You are my Physician and the One who makes me holy. Help me as you did Moses to keep my eyes on You, the One who is invisible. Teach me to live in the fullness of Your presence. Strengthen my faith, for I want to be well-pleasing to You.

Amen

CHAPTER 4

ESTABLISHING LAW & WORSHIP

OPENING PRAYER

Dear Lord,

Prepare my heart and mind as I read about how You gave the nation of Israel Your laws and taught them how to worship and live holy. Help me understand the wisdom of Your laws. Enlighten me as only You can do. Teach me how to worship and glorify You. I reverence and honor Your Holy Name, for You are God and there is no other.

Amen

CHAPTER SUMMARY

ESTABLISHING LAW & WORSHIP

(Exodus 35–40; Leviticus, Numbers, Deuteronomy)

When the Israelites reached Mount Sinai, they stayed camped there for an entire year while God taught them how to serve Him. God spoke to them saying, *"I am the Lord who brought you up out of Egypt to be your God; therefore be holy, because I am holy"* (Leviticus 11:45 NIV). The nation was to be a righteous and holy people set apart to praise and worship God and to teach others about the One True God. Praise is thanking God for what He has done, while worship is glorifying God for who He is.

God talked to Moses face-to-face and gave Israel the Ten Commandments and more than 600 other laws to live by. The Lord provided plans for building the Tabernacle as a place of worship and for organizing the priesthood.

The Israelites built the Tabernacle and established procedures for worship according to God's instructions. They then left Mount Sinai and continued their journey to the promised land. Along the way, the people complained about God's provisions and questioned Moses' leadership on numerous occasions.

The Israelites finally reached the southern border of Canaan. However, when they heard reports that giants were living in Canaan, they became discouraged. Joshua and Caleb, leaders of their tribes, tried to convince the Israelites that God would fight their battles. The Israelites lacked faith and did not believe they could take the land God had promised to give them. As a result, God became angry and would not let the Israelites enter Canaan. The Lord made them wander in the desert for forty years until those who lacked faith died and a new generation emerged. Only Joshua and Caleb were allowed to enter the promised land.

Moses led Israel during these forty years until God was ready for His people to take possession of Canaan, their inheritance. Moses prepared the new generation, giving them God's instructions and encouraging them to obey God's laws. Moses told the Israelites they would be blessed for obedience and cursed for disobedience. Before they crossed into Canaan, Moses died and Joshua succeeded him as leader of the nation of Israel.

	Approximate Timeline	Location	Biblical Scriptures	Author
The Tabernacle	1446 B.C.–1445 B.C.	Desert in Sinai	Exodus 35–40	Moses
Law & Worship	1446 B.C.–1445 B.C.	Desert in Sinai	Leviticus 1–27	Moses
Disobedience	1446 B.C.–1445 B.C.	Desert in Sinai	Numbers 1–14	Moses
Wandering in the Desert	1445 B.C.–1406 B.C.	Desert in Sinai	Numbers 15–36	Moses
Preparing for Canaan	1406 B.C.	East of Canaan	Deuteronomy 1–34	Moses

MAP OF KEY LOCATIONS

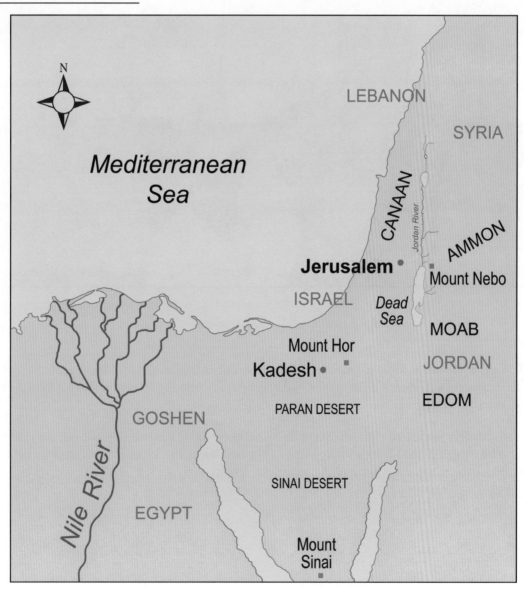

AARON

"The LORD told Moses:

Call together the twelve tribes of Israel and tell the leader of each tribe to write his name on the walking stick he carries as a symbol of his authority. Make sure Aaron's name is written on the one from the Levi tribe, then collect all the sticks.

Place these sticks in the tent right in front of the sacred chest where I appear to you. I will then choose a man to be my priest, and his stick will sprout. . . . The next day when Moses went into the tent, flowers and almonds were already growing on Aaron's stick." (Numbers 17:1–5, 8 CEV)

Section 1: The Tabernacle

The Tabernacle Built and Passover Celebrated: (Exodus 35–40)

- Moses started work on the Tabernacle according to the plans God had given him. The Tabernacle was also called the Tent of Meetings.

- The people donated more than enough supplies for the Tabernacle's construction, and the work began.

- The Tabernacle was completed one year after the Israelites left Egypt, in time for the first Passover celebration.

- Once completed, *"the glory of the LORD filled the Tabernacle"* (Exodus 40:34).

The Layout of the Tabernacle

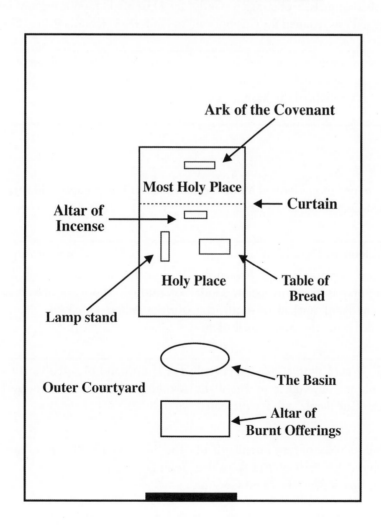

The Tabernacle, A Foreshadow of Jesus Christ

The Tabernacle: A mobile tent used as a sanctuary or a place of worship. It was also called the Tent of Meetings and was a constant reminder that God dwelt with the people. There were three main areas: the outer courtyard, the Holy Place, and the Most Holy Place.

The Outer Courtyard: The immediate grounds, surrounding the Tabernacle. It was an enclosed area about one quarter the size of a football field. The altar of burnt offering and the basin were located in the outer courtyard.

Old Testament Definition	New Testament Application
Altar of Burnt Offering - a brass or bronze platform used to sacrifice animals as offerings to God. The shedding of blood was required for redemption and access to God.	Jesus Christ is our sacrificial offering to God. Jesus shed His blood for our redemption, giving us access to God. (See Hebrews 9:11–12)
The Basin - a brass or bronze wash bowl used by priests to cleanse their hands and feet before entering the Holy Place. It symbolized the washing away of sin.	We are cleansed by the blood of Jesus, which purifies and washes away our sins. (See Hebrews 9:13–15)

The Holy Place: The first of two rooms located inside the Tabernacle. Only priests could enter the Holy Place. It had an altar for burning incense, a lamp stand, and a table.

Old Testament Definition	New Testament Application
The Altar of Incense - a platform used to burn incense, symbolizing prayers rising up before God. While the outer courtyard smelled of death, the Holy Place was filled with the sweet smell of incense.	Incense provided a picture of Christ as our Intercessor, through whom our prayers rise up to God. (See Revelation 5:6–8; 8:3–5)
The Lamp stand - a gold post, which supported seven lamps that burned olive oil to provide light for the Tabernacle. The lamp stand represented God's guidance.	The lamp stand pictured Christ as the Light of the World, guiding mankind to the Truth of God. (See John 8:12)
The Table of Bread - a piece of furniture that held twelve loaves of bread for each of Israel's twelve tribes, symbolizing Israel's dependence on God for life.	The Bread pictured Christ as the Bread of Life. (See John 6:35)

The Most Holy Place: It was where God's presence resided. The Most Holy Place was a separate room located inside the Holy Place, which housed the Ark of the Covenant.

Old Testament Definition	New Testament Application
The Curtain - a cloth room divider, which separated the Holy Place from the Most Holy Place. Only the High Priest was allowed behind the curtain and into the Most Holy Place; and only once a year, on the Day of Atonement, to offer a sacrifice of atonement for his sins and the sins of the people.	When Jesus died, the curtain was torn in two, symbolically showing that Jesus, our High Priest and perfect sacrifice, atoned for our sins once and for all through His death. We can enjoy spiritual restoration and peace with God because of the blood Jesus shed for us.
The Most Holy Place symbolically reminded the people that they were spiritually separated from God and in need of atonement and spiritual restoration.	We are no longer separated from God when we accept Jesus as our Lord and Savior. We can boldly enter into God's presence. (See Matthew 27:50–51; Hebrews 9:7–8; 10:19–22)
The Ark of the Covenant - the sacred chest, located inside the Most Holy Place, where God's presence resided. It contained the stone tablets of the Ten Commandments (God's laws), a pot of manna (God's provision), and Aaron's staff that budded (God's will for the priesthood).	Jesus lives in us when we accept Him as our Lord and Savior. Jesus is the embodiment of God's laws, God's provision and God's will. (See Romans 8:9–11; Galatians 2:20)
The Ten Commandments - God's covenant laws with Israel, which were kept inside the Ark of the Covenant. Written by God, these laws commanded the people to love the Lord and to love their fellow human beings. Under the old covenant, Israel was made right with God by obeying His laws.	Under the new covenant, we are made right with God by accepting Jesus Christ as our Lord and Savior. God puts His laws in our hearts and His Spirit indwells us. (See Hebrews 10:8–10, 16; 1 Corinthians 6:19–20)

RECOMMENDED BIBLE READING

Exodus 36:1–7 **Supplies for the Tabernacle**

Exodus 40:1–38 **The Lord's Glory Filled the Tabernacle**

Hebrews 8:1–13 **Jesus, High Priest of the New Covenant**

SECTION 2: LAW AND WORSHIP

Five Types of Offerings to God: (Leviticus 1–7)

- The book of Leviticus provides a record of God's instructions on living a life of worship and righteousness.

- While Israel was still camped at Mount Sinai, God gave specific procedures for five types of offerings.

 Five Types of Offerings, A Foreshadow of Jesus Christ

Sacrifice	Old Testament Definition	New Testament Application
Burnt Offering	An animal sacrifice to make restitution for individual sin and to express devotion to God. All sacrificial animals had to be without defect.	Jesus, who was perfect and without defect, paid for our sins with His death on the cross. (See Hebrews 10:1–7)
Grain Offering	A gift of flour or grain to God to acknowledge God as the Giver and Sustainer of life. The very best of one's flour or grain was offered and burned in reverence to God.	Jesus, God's very best, gave His life for us. (See John 3:16; Hebrews 9:14)
Fellowship (Peace) Offering	An animal sacrifice to express one's desire for peace and fellowship with God.	Jesus provides peace and fellowship with God. (See Ephesians 2:13–14, 18)
Sin Offering	An animal sacrifice to purify and cleanse one's unintentional sins.	Jesus purifies and cleanses us of all our sins. (See 1 John 1:7)
Guilt Offering	An animal sacrifice to make restitution for injuries against others and sins against God.	Jesus satisfied God's demand for justice and is our restitution. (See Romans 3:23–26)

The Duties of the Priesthood: (Leviticus 8–10)

- God gave Moses specific instructions on the duties of the priesthood to be performed exclusively by Aaron and his sons.

- Moses ordained Aaron and his sons as priests. They were responsible for making offerings and sacrifices to God for the people.

- Two of Aaron's sons were killed while performing the duties of the priesthood because they disobeyed God and offered "unauthorized fire."

Laws for Cleanliness and Purification: (Leviticus 11–15)

- God gave Moses specific instructions for the people on hygiene, cleanliness, and purification to prevent the spread of disease and death.

- These included laws regarding the people's diet, childbirth, infectious skin diseases, contaminated houses, and bodily discharges.

The Day of Atonement and the Sanctity of Blood: (Leviticus 16–22)

- God gave procedures for a National Day of Atonement or "reconciliation." On this day, all the people would confess their sins.

- The High Priest would then enter the Most Holy Place and make atonement for himself and the people.

- God prohibited the people from eating animals' blood saying, *"for the life of a creature is in the blood"* (Leviticus 17:11a NIV).

- God gave the people laws for righteous living, forbidden sexual practices, and moral conduct. There were also numerous laws for the priesthood.

The Holy Days, Feasts, and Festivals: (Leviticus 23–25)

- Sabbath was observed every seven days as a sacred day of rest. No work was performed.

- Sabbath Year was observed every seven years to allow the land to rest. No crops were planted.

- Year of Jubilee occurred every fifty years to celebrate restoration. All property was to be returned to its original owner.

- Passover was observed as a reminder of Israel's deliverance out of Egypt.

- Unleavened Bread was to be observed as a reminder of the exodus from slavery.

- First Fruits (First Harvest) was observed in a celebration of the first grains of the barley harvest.

- Weeks (Harvest, later called Pentecost) was observed in a celebration of the end of barley harvest and the beginning of the wheat harvest.

- Feast of Trumpets (later called Rosh Hashanah) was to be observed in a sacred gathering to present offerings to the Lord for the New Year.

- Day of Atonement (Yom Kippur) was to be observed in a sacred gathering to make atonement for the nation's sins. Sacrifices were to be made to cleanse the priests, people, tabernacle, and the altar.

- Feast of Tabernacles (Shelters or Booths) was observed as a reminder of God's protection and provisions while Israel was in the desert.

Blessings for Obedience and Punishment for Disobedience: (Leviticus 26–27)

- God admonished Israel to keep His commandments and laws. The people would be blessed for obedience and punished for disobedience.

- Israel received instructions on how to redeem gifts dedicated to God, which emphasized the importance of keeping vows made to God.

Recommended Bible Reading

Leviticus 9:1–10:11 **The Priests Begin Their Duties**

Hebrews 9:1–28 **Old and New Covenants Contrasted**

SECTION 3: DISOBEDIENCE

Israel's Departure from Mount Sinai: (Numbers 1–10)

- The book of Numbers gives an account of the Israelites' departure from Mount Sinai and their journey through the desert en route to Canaan.

- Before leaving Mount Sinai, God instructed Moses to take a census of those who would serve in Israel's army.

- Moses excluded the Levites from this count because they were to serve as priests and caretakers of the Tabernacle. A separate census was taken of the Levites.

- Each tribe was assigned a specific position in the marching order for when they were traveling and specific locations in camp for when they were stationary.

- The Levites were responsible for moving the Tabernacle. They were given specific duties and instructions on how to serve God.

- Israel left Mount Sinai with a pillar of cloud guiding them by day and a pillar of fire by night.

Israel's Complaints about God's Provisions: (Numbers 11–12)

- As the people traveled through the desert, they began to complain about their hardships.

- The Israelites' complaints made God so angry that He sent a raging fire into their camp, which killed thousands of people. Moses prayed to the Lord, and the fire stopped.

- Soon the people complained again. This time they grumbled, saying they were tired of eating manna and wanted meat to eat.

- They grumbled so much that Moses became distraught and cried out to the Lord, saying the people were too much for him to manage.

- In response to Moses' cries, the Lord sent quail for meat. However, God punished the Israelites for complaining about His provisions with a plague that killed a great number of people.

- Miriam and Aaron (Moses' sister and brother) complained that Moses' wife, a Cushite, was not Jewish and questioned his right to lead Israel.

- Their criticism angered the Lord. As a result, Miriam became ill with leprosy. Moses prayed for her and she was healed.

Israel Lacks Faith and Rebels Against God: (Numbers 13–14)

- When Israel reached Kadesh in the Desert of Paran, Moses sent twelve spies—one from each tribe—to explore the land of Canaan.

- When they returned forty days later, all twelve spies agreed the land was very fertile and desirable, *"a land flowing with milk and honey"* (Exodus 3:8).

- Ten of the spies reported that Israel would never be able to conquer the people living in Canaan because they were giants.

- However, Joshua from the tribe of Ephraim and Caleb from the tribe of Judah were convinced God would protect Israel and give them the land.

- The people listened to the ten spies who came back with a negative report and blamed God for their troubles. They plotted against Moses, rejecting him as their leader and saying they wanted to go back to Egypt.

- The people's disobedience and lack of faith angered God. Once again the Lord threatened to annihilate the people and establish a new nation through Moses' descendants.

- Moses interceded for the people and the Lord forgave them. However, as punishment for their lack of faith, God would not let anyone twenty years old or older (with the exception of Joshua and Caleb) enter Canaan.

- When Moses informed the people of these consequences, they tried to move forward into Canaan without God's blessing and were severely defeated by their enemies.

- The Lord made the Israelites wander in the desert for forty years until the disobedient and unfaithful generation died out and a new one emerged.

RECOMMENDED BIBLE READING

Numbers 13:1–14:45 **Israel's Lack of Faith**

Hebrews 10:1–39 **Jesus Christ, the Perfect Sacrifice**

SECTION 4: WANDERING IN THE DESERT

Rebellion and More Complaints: (Numbers 15–20)

- God gave the Israelites more laws relating to offerings. The Lord had previously made the Levites responsible for the Tabernacle, but the power of the priesthood had been given to Aaron and his descendants.

- Korah, who was a Levite and Aaron's cousin, conspired with 250 other leaders and led a rebellion against Moses and Aaron.

- Korah complained that others were just as capable as Aaron and his descendants to perform the more prestigious duties of the priesthood.

- Korah's accusations angered the Lord. The ground suddenly gave way and swallowed him and his followers who were standing nearby.

- Meanwhile, Korah's other followers were offering incense in the Tabernacle when fire jumped from the altar and killed them.

- When this happened, the Israelites became upset with Moses and Aaron, complaining that they had killed God's people.

- Once again, God became angry with the people; again Moses and Aaron interceded on their behalf.

- God had each of the twelve tribes bring a staff to Him. Overnight, the Lord caused Aaron's staff to grow a flower blossom, which was the sign God said would confirm Moses and Aaron's right to lead Israel.

- Aaron and his descendants continued as heads of the priesthood, with the Levites responsible for assisting them in the Lord's service.

 Moses' life paralleled that of Jesus Christ in that he was threatened at birth by a decree that all baby boys were to be killed; his own people rejected him, yet he interceded for them, asking God to forgive them.

- The people began complaining again about the lack of water. God told Moses to speak to a rock and water would come forth.

- Instead of speaking to the rock, Moses angrily hit the rock twice with the staff of God and water gushed forth.

- God then said to Moses and Aaron, *"Because you did not trust in me enough to honor me as holy in the sight of the Israelites, you will not bring this community into the land I give them"* (Numbers 20:12).

- Moses dishonored God when he disobeyed and hit the rock. As a result, neither he nor Aaron would be allowed to enter Canaan.

Note: Moses was very upset with the Israelites, who had continually rebelled against him. In a fit of anger, Moses hit the rock with the staff of God. It might be difficult to understand why Moses' actions were wrong in God's sight. However, God looks at the heart and knows when our actions are motivated by sin. God said that Moses failed to trust and honor Him as holy.

- Israel was forced to turn around because the Edomites would not let them pass through their land. Aaron died shortly after this at Mount Hor.

Encounters with Israel's Enemies: (Numbers 21–24)

- As the Israelites traveled around the Edomites' territory, which lengthened their journey, they became discouraged and started complaining again.

- This time God disciplined the people by sending venomous snakes that killed many with their bites.

- Once again Moses interceded and the Lord instructed him to make a bronze snake and raise it to the top of a pole.

- Everyone bitten by a snake would live if they looked up at the bronze snake and believed that they would be healed.

 Jesus Christ later compared this incident to Himself, saying *"Just as Moses lifted up the snake in the desert, so the Son of Man must be lifted up, that everyone who believes in him may have eternal life"* (John 3:14–15 NIV).

- When Israel reached the territory of the Amorites, they requested passage through their land, but the Amorites refused and attacked them.

- Israel defeated King Sihon of the Amorites and King Og of Bashan, giving them possession of land east of the Jordan River.

- The Israelites journeyed on until they reached the plains of Moab. The Moabites were terrified, having heard of Israel's victories over the Amorites.

- Concerned that the Israelites were camped nearby, Balak, king of Moab, offered Balaam, a sorcerer, money to travel to Moab and put a curse on Israel.

- At first Balaam would not go to Moab, but later he decided to go. As Balaam traveled on his donkey to Moab, God became angry with him and sent an angel with a sword in hand to block the roadway.

- The donkey saw the angel on the road and came to a halt. Balaam could not see the angel, so he began beating the donkey to make her move forward.

- The Lord miraculously gave the donkey a speaking voice. The donkey asked Balaam, *"What have I done to you?"* (Numbers 22:28b NIV).

- The Lord then allowed Balaam to see the angel. The angel told Balaam that the donkey had saved his life. God had sent the angel to oppose Balaam.

- The angel told Balaam he could continue on to Moab, but he must speak only the words God would give him to say.

- When Balaam arrived, Balak, the Moabite king, greeted him. Balak was looking forward to seeing Israel cursed.

- However, every time Balaam opened his mouth to speak, he spoke the Lord's blessings for Israel instead of curses.

Balaam's final blessing is a prophecy about the coming of the Messiah, Jesus Christ, *". . . I see him, but not now; I behold him, but not near. A star will come out of Jacob; a scepter will rise out of Israel"* (Numbers 24:17 NIV).

Israel Sins: (Numbers 25–31)

- While camped, some of Israel's men slept with the local Moabite and Midianite women and eventually joined in their idol worship. This evoked God's wrath. Soon afterwards a deadly plague swept through Israel's camp.

- The plague killed a great number of people. It did not end until the priest made atonement for Israel's sins.

- When the plague ended, Moses took another census. He divided among the tribes the land to be inherited in Canaan.

- A man named Zelophehad from the tribe of Manasseh had daughters, but no sons, when he died; so Moses did not give his family an allocation of land in Canaan.

- Zelophehad's daughters later petitioned Moses, saying they should receive land in Canaan as part of their father's inheritance.

- Moses consulted God, and the Lord told him Zelophehad's daughters were right. The daughters should be given the land that would have been assigned to their father.

- Moses announced to the people that if a man dies and has no sons, his inheritance should be given to his closest relative.

- The Lord later instructed Moses to climb Mount Nebo and look over into the promised land.

- Moses was allowed to view Canaan, but he was not allowed to cross over into the land because of his prior disobedience.

- Moses asked God to appoint another capable man to lead the people into Canaan. The Lord commissioned Joshua, Moses' assistant and apprentice.

- The Lord gave Israel more instructions on offerings and festivals as well as more laws that stressed the importance of keeping vows made to Him.

 Note: At this point, the Bible tells us that Balaam (the sorcerer) was the one who had advised the local women to seduce Israel's men and invite them to join their idol worship. (Numbers 31:15–16)

- The Lord told Moses to take vengeance on the Midianites for causing Israel to sin. As the Lord instructed, Israel attacked the Midianites and won the battle.

Israel's Inheritance East of the Jordan and in Canaan: (Numbers 32–36)

- After the battle, the tribes of Reuben and Gad asked Moses to let them have as their inheritance the territories Israel had won in battles east of the Jordan, which included the lands taken from King Sihon and King Og.

- Moses was upset when he heard their request. He thought the other tribes might become discouraged by this and would decide not to cross the Jordan and fight for their inheritance in Canaan.

- The men of Reuben and Gad explained that they wanted to settle their families east of the Jordan. They would then cross the Jordan with their fellow Israelites and fight alongside them to conquer the land of Canaan.

- They promised to stay and help their fellow Israelites take possession of Canaan, the land God had given them as an inheritance.

- Moses agreed to their request, giving the territories Israel possessed east of the Jordan to the tribes of Reuben, Gad, and half of Manasseh's tribe.

- God described the boundaries of the land Israel was to inherit in Canaan. Each tribe appointed one leader to help allocate and distribute the land according to God's specific instructions.

- However, Israel would first have to fight and conquer the people already living in Canaan.

RECOMMENDED BIBLE READING

Numbers 16:1–17:12 **Korah's Rebellion and Aaron's Staff**
Hebrews 3:1–19 **Jesus, Our High Priest**

SECTION 5: PREPARING FOR CANAAN

Preparing For the Promised Land: (Deuteronomy 1:1–4:43)

- When the book of Deuteronomy opens, forty years had passed since the people listened to the ten spies' negative report instead of trusting God.

- As a result, the Israelites wandered in the desert until the generation that lacked faith died out and a new generation emerged.

- Deuteronomy records the speeches Moses delivered to this new generation of Israelites while camped east of the Jordan River. Each speech was designed to prepare the people for the journey ahead.

- In the first speech, Moses reviewed events of the past forty years, reminding the people of two important facts:

  ✓ The reason they had to wander in the desert was because of their lack of belief and disobedience.

  ✓ God still loved them and blessed them with provisions and protection every step of the way.

Moses Exhorts Israel to Obey God's Laws: (Deuteronomy 4:44–26:19)

- In the second speech, Moses reviewed the Ten Commandments (Deuteronomy 5) and God's other, more detailed laws.

- Moses exhorted the people to listen, learn, and obey the laws of the covenant established between God and Israel.

- Concerning the people already in Canaan, God told Israel in Deuteronomy 7:

  ✓ Go into Canaan fighting and continue until the entire land is conquered.

  ✓ Annihilate the people and destroy their altars and any other instruments used for idolatry.

  ✓ Do not form relationships with the Canaanites, or make deals, or intermarry with them, lest the Israelites be led into idolatry.

 Note: God commanded Israel to go into Canaan and annihilate the people living there. Israel was not to form relationships of any kind with the Canaanites. They were not to make deals or intermarry with them. The Canaanites practiced a perverted form of worship in which illicit sex and sacrificing children had become a routine part of their religion. It was an abomination to God, and His righteous judgment called for the Canaanites to be annihilated. Extermination would keep the Canaanites from leading Israel into idolatry. It should be noted that God told Abraham 700 years earlier that his descendants would live in Canaan after the sin of the Amorites had run its course. The Amorites were one of the Canaanite nations. God had mercifully given them plenty of time to repent, but He knew years earlier that they would not. (See Genesis 15:16)

- Moses revealed God would send another prophet to Israel.

> Moses' prophecy foreshadowed the coming of Jesus Christ. God said to Moses, *"I (God) will raise up for them a prophet like you from among their brothers; I will put my words in his mouth, and he will tell them everything I command him"* (Deuteronomy 18:18 NIV).

Blessings for Obedience and Curses for Disobedience: (Deuteronomy 27–28)

- Moses explained the terms of the covenant included blessings for obedience and curses for disobedience.

Joshua Commissioned as Israel's New Leader: (Deuteronomy 29–34)

- In Moses' third speech, he encouraged Israel to obey God and choose life rather than death.

- Joshua was commissioned as Israel's new leader. God predicted Israel would eventually disobey His commandments after Moses' death.

- In a farewell address, Moses gave Joshua some final instructions. He recited a song to remind Israel of the past and gave the people his final blessings.

- Moses then climbed to the peak of Mount Nebo where he was able to see across the Jordan into the land of Canaan. He died shortly afterwards at the age of 120.

RECOMMENDED BIBLE READING

Deuteronomy 31:1–29	**Joshua Commissioned as Israel's New Leader**
Deuteronomy 34:1–12	**Moses' Death**
Acts 3:17–26	**Peter's Speech about Moses' Prophecy**
Acts 7:1–38	**Stephen's Speech about God's Chosen People**

MEDITATION & PRAYER

A Psalm about how God blesses those who obey His commands:

"Praise the LORD!

How joyful are those who fear the LORD
    and delight in obeying his commands.
Their children will be successful everywhere;
    an entire generation of godly people will be blessed.
They themselves will be wealthy,
    and their good deeds will last forever.
Light shines in the darkness for the godly."

(Psalm 112:1–4a)

Holy Father,

You are the One who makes us holy and sets us apart for Your sacred purposes. I delight in obeying Your commands, for I know You are the key to my success and happiness. You will never leave or forget about me. When I am in trouble and in great distress, Your light will break through the darkness and shine on me.

Amen

REVIEW QUESTIONS

1. How did the Tabernacle foreshadow *God's Plan of Redemption*?

_____

_____

_____

_____

_____

_____

2. When Jesus Christ died on the cross the curtain in the Temple was supernaturally torn in two. What was the significance of this event?

_____

_____

_____

_____

_____

_____

3. How did the various offerings & sacrifices foreshadow *God's Plan of Redemption*?

_____

_____

_____

_____

_____

_____

_____

4. How did the role of the priesthood foreshadow *God's Plan of Redemption*?

_____

_____

_____

_____

_____

_____

_____

5. Why did God punish Israel and make them wander in the desert for forty years? What happened at Kadesh Barnea?

_____

_____

_____

_____

_____

_____

6. Moses delivered several important speeches to the new generation of Israelites while camped east of the Jordan. What did Moses tell them in these speeches and why?

_____

_____

_____

_____

_____

_____

7. What very important command did God give Israel for when they reached Canaan?

_____

_____

_____

_____

_____

_____

_____

PERSONAL REFLECTIONS

8. Moses faced numerous obstacles along the way to the Promised Land. What obstacles are you facing? What frustrates you?

_____

_____

_____

_____

_____

_____

_____

9. What steps can you take to more effectively handle conflict with your spouse or family members? Church members? Coworkers? Your boss or authority figures?

_____

_____

_____

_____

_____

_____

_____

10. What did God teach you about leadership while studying this lesson? In your opinion, why was Joshua the right person to take over leadership of the Israelites?

_____

_____

_____

_____

_____

11. What role should you play when someone else is leading and you are the one following? How can you apply what you've learned in your life?

_____

_____

_____

_____

_____

CLOSING PRAYER

The author of Hebrews tells us that the Lord will put His laws in our minds and write them on our hearts:

"But God found fault with the people and said:
'The time is coming, declares the Lord,
when I will make a new covenant
with the house of Israel
and with the house of Judah.
It will not be like the covenant
I made with their forefathers
when I took them by the hand
to lead them out of Egypt,
because they did not remain faithful to my covenant,
and I turned away from them, declares the Lord.
This is the covenant I will make with the house of Israel
after that time, declares the Lord.
I will put my laws in their minds
and write them on their hearts.
I will be their God,
and they will be my people.'"

(Hebrews 8:8–10 NIV)

Dear God Most High,

Thank you for the new covenant You so faithfully kept and continue to keep with mankind. You said You would put Your laws in our minds and write them on our hearts. Help me to remember Your laws and keep them close to my heart. You are God Most High and I belong to You!

Amen

CHAPTER 5

LIVING IN THE PROMISED LAND

OPENING PRAYER

Heavenly Father,

As I read this chapter about living in the Promised Land, teach me to live in the fullness of Your promises. Help me to comprehend the depths of Your love and the certainty of Your Word. I know Your promises will come to pass because You are faithful and true. I will glorify You and praise Your Holy Name all the days of my life.

Amen

CHAPTER SUMMARY

LIVING IN THE PROMISED LAND

(Joshua & Judges)

The book of Joshua covers about thirty years of Israel's history and Judges covers about 330 years. A major portion of the book of Joshua tells of the military battles Israel fought to take possession of Canaan from the various peoples already living there. Joshua had been Moses' assistant during Israel's journey through the desert and was a respected military leader from the tribe of Ephraim. God divinely appointed Joshua to succeed Moses and lead the people into Canaan.

Israel crossed the Jordan and fought major military battles for possession of the land for seven years under Joshua's leadership. Joshua captured vast territories, but did not conquer all of Canaan before allocating land to the tribes. Each tribe was given a portion of land as an inheritance, with the understanding that they would continue fighting for the remaining unconquered territories and eventually drive all the Canaanites out. *Canaanite* was a general term used to reference all the various peoples living in Canaan.

We discover in the book of Judges that Israel never completed their mission. They did not totally drive the Canaanites out of the land as God had commanded. As a result, the Canaanites influenced Israel and led them into idolatry.

Judges covers Israel's history from Joshua's death to just prior to the appointment of Israel's first king. It describes a very dark period of moral decay. The people vacillated between serving God and abandoning Him to worship idols. Israel's enemies oppressed them and they would cry out to God for help. God would divinely empower a judge (a leader) to help Israel overcome their oppressors. Once freed from oppression, Israel would serve God for a while and then fall back into idolatry. This cycle was repeated over and over again during the period of the judges. The last verse in the book of Judges sums up the period and the problem, *"In those days Israel had no king; all the people did whatever seemed right in their own eyes"* (Judges 21:25).

	Approximate Timeline	Location	Biblical Scriptures	Author
Possessing the Land	1406 B.C.–1398 B.C.	Canaan	Joshua 1–12	Joshua
Allocating the Land	1398 B.C.–1375 B.C.	Canaan	Joshua 13–24	Joshua
The Judges (Part 1)	1375 B.C.–1122 B.C.	Canaan, later called Israel	Judges 1:1–10:5	Unknown, possibly Samuel
The Judges (Part 2)	1122 B.C.–1055 B.C.	Canaan, later called Israel	Judges 10:6–16:31	Unknown, possibly Samuel
Israel's Moral Failures	During the Period of the Judges 1375 B.C.–1050 B.C.	Canaan, later called Israel	Judges 17–22	Unknown, possibly Samuel

MAP OF KEY LOCATIONS

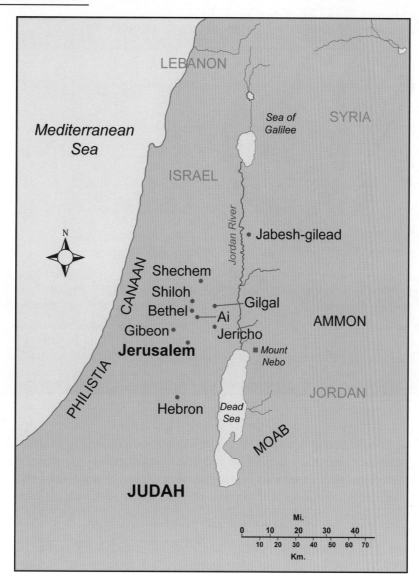

GIDEON

"The LORD said, 'Gideon, your army is too big. I can't let you win with this many soldiers. The Israelites would think that they had won the battle all by themselves and that I didn't have anything to do with it. So call your troops together and tell them that anyone who is really afraid can leave Mount Gilead and go home.' Twenty-two thousand men returned home, leaving Gideon with only ten thousand soldiers. 'Gideon,' the LORD said, 'you still have too many soldiers.'" (Judges 7:2–4a CEV)

Section 1: Possessing the Land

From Moses to Joshua: (Joshua 1)

- Joshua assumed leadership after Moses' death and prepared to lead Israel into Canaan.

 Joshua's name was *Hoshea*, meaning "Salvation," until Moses changed it to *Joshua*, meaning "The Lord is Salvation." The name Joshua in Hebrew is the same as *Jesus* in Aramaic. God used Joshua as a savior, victoriously leading Israel into battle for the land God had promised them.

- God strengthened Joshua spiritually and encouraged him to be strong and courageous. The Lord told Joshua that He would not leave or fail him.

- God exhorted Joshua to do all things in accordance with the laws of Moses and told him obedience to the law would result in success.

- Joshua prepared the people, telling them to get ready to cross the Jordan and fight for possession of Canaan. The people responded, saying they would obey everything Joshua commanded.

 Note: The Canaanites' religion was a perverted form of worship and was an abomination to God.

Joshua Sends Spies to Jericho: (Joshua 2)

- Joshua sent two men to spy on Jericho, a city just east of the Jordan River. When the men got there, they met a woman named Rahab, a prostitute living at the entrance to the city.

- When the king of Jericho heard that Israelites were at Rahab's house, he ordered her to bring them to him, but instead Rahab helped them escape. She had heard of the miracles the Lord had performed for Israel and had faith in their God.

- In return for Rahab's faith and kindness, the spies promised to save Rahab and her family when Israel attacked Jericho.

- The spies told Rahab to hang a scarlet (red) cord from her window to identify her house. The cord would be a sign to the Israelites that Rahab was the one who had helped them and she should not be killed.

Israel Crosses the Jordan into Canaan: (Joshua 3–4)

- God told Joshua how Israel was to cross the Jordan River. Joshua gave the people God's instructions and they faithfully obeyed.

- The priests walked in front—carrying the Ark of the Covenant—and the people followed behind them.

- The river was overflowing its banks. However, when the priests stepped into the river, the waters were suddenly blocked upstream and a dry path was created for them.

- The priests walked further until they were in the middle of the Jordan. They stood, holding the Ark of the Covenant, until all the people had crossed safely to the other side.

- Joshua then instructed one man from each of the twelve tribes to pick up a stone from the river. He used the stones to build a memorial to serve as a reminder of the miracle God had performed there for Israel.

- Joshua ordered the priests to cross the river. As soon as they were safe on the other side, the river began to flow again.

 Note: The miracle at the Jordan River validated Joshua's position as Israel's leader, affirmed God's presence, strengthened Israel's faith, and terrified Israel's enemies.

Israel Circumcised and Passover Celebrated: (Joshua 5)

- Israel camped at Gilgal, which was located on the west bank of the river. There God told Joshua to circumcise all the men.

- Circumcision was a sign of God's covenant with Abraham; however, none of the men had been circumcised since Israel left Egypt. Joshua obeyed the Lord and circumcised all of Israel's men.

- Israel then celebrated Passover and ate food they had gathered in Canaan. God's provision of manna suddenly ceased and from that day forward the people ate food from the land of Canaan.

- As Joshua approached the city of Jericho, he met a man who said he was the Commander of the Lord's Army.

- Joshua fell facedown in reverence to the Commander of the Lord's Army, who said to Joshua, *"Take off your sandals, for the place where you are standing is holy"* (Joshua 5:15b NIV).

Note: Who was the Commander of the Lord's Army? Scripture does not provide a definitive answer. Some Bible scholars believe the Commander was a high-ranking angel, while others believe the Commander was Jesus, God in human form.

God Gives Israel Victory at Jericho: (Joshua 6:1–21)

- God gave Joshua His plan for how Jericho would be conquered. Joshua announced the plan to Israel and they carried it out.

- Once each day for six consecutive days, Israel marched in silence around the city of Jericho as the priests blew their trumpets.

- On the seventh day, Israel marched around the city seven times. On the seventh time around, with the priests blowing their trumpets, Joshua ordered the people to shout.

- At the sound of the people's shouts, the walls around the city of Jericho collapsed, allowing Israel to easily take the city.

Rahab and Her Family Saved: (Joshua 6:22–27)

- Joshua honored Israel's agreement with Rahab. The two men who had spied on Jericho found the scarlet cord and escorted Rahab and her family safely out of the city.

 The scarlet (red) cord saved Rahab and her family. Rahab had faith in the God of Israel and God rewarded her faith. The scarlet cord saved Rahab just as the red blood of the Passover lamb had saved Israel's first born in Egypt. Rahab is noted in Hebrews 11:31 for her faith.

Rahab was in King David's lineage and an ancestor of Jesus Christ. (See Ruth 4:22; Matthew 1:5)

- Israel completely burned the city and everything in it as an offering to the Lord. They did not burn the precious metals, which were for the house of God.

Israel Defeated at Ai: (Joshua 7)

- A man named Achan disobeyed God and took some of the items that were to be set aside for the Lord.

- After conquering Jericho, Israel's next battle was for possession of the city of Ai. Joshua sent men to spy on the town.

- When the spies returned, they told Joshua that the city was small and could be easily captured with a few soldiers.

- Listening to this report, Joshua went into battle with a few men and ended up suffering a great defeat at Ai. Israel was forced to retreat.

- Joshua and Israel's leaders were panic-stricken and sought answers from the Lord.

Note: Joshua consulted the Lord for guidance before the battle of Jericho. He followed God's instructions and the Israelites were victorious with very little effort on their part. When strategizing for the next battle, Joshua failed to seek the Lord's guidance. He consulted men rather than God and suffered a major defeat.

- Joshua cried out to God, and the Lord told him there was sin in the camp.

- Joshua set out to find the guilty party. He soon discovered that Achan had disobeyed God and kept for himself some of the sacred items found in Jericho. Achan had stolen from the Lord.

- Joshua and all of Israel consecrated the camp in accordance with God's law. They stoned Achan and his family to death.

Note: In ancient times, the family head represented his entire family. The family head and his household were treated as one. Achan was punished for violating God's sacred command and his household suffered the consequences of their family head's actions. This was not uncommon for the time period. The Israelites stoned Achan to rid the camp of sin.

God Gives Israel Victory at Ai: (Joshua 8)

- Now that Achan's sin had been addressed, the Lord instructed Joshua to attack the city of Ai again but with the entire army this time.

- God encouraged Joshua and told him to set an ambush behind the city.

- Following the battle strategy the Lord gave Joshua, Israel successfully captured and defeated the city of Ai.

- After the battle, Joshua built an altar and presented offerings to God. He copied the laws God gave Moses and read them to everyone in a sacred ceremony.

Israel's Failure With the Gibeonites: (Joshua 9)

- The kings in the area heard about Israel's victories. All except the people of Gibeon quickly joined forces to fight against Israel.

- The Gibeonites feared Israel and did not want to fight them. They deceived Israel by telling them they were not Canaanites, but travelers from a foreign land.

- Joshua believed the Gibeonites and signed a peace agreement with them without asking the Lord for guidance.

- A few days later, the Israelites discovered Gibeon's deception and became furious with Joshua and the other leaders for signing the agreement.

- Nevertheless, Joshua and the other leaders would not kill the Gibeonites or break their peace agreement because it was an oath made before God.

- Instead they made the Gibeonites serve Israel and the house of the Lord by chopping wood and carrying water, an arrangement that continued for years.

God Gives Israel Victory in the Southern Region: (Joshua 10)

- Some time later, the kings of the southern region heard about Gibeon's peace agreement with Israel and united to attack Gibeon.

- The Gibeonites went to Israel to ask for help. They reminded them that the people of Gibeon were their servants and had an agreement with them.

- The Lord encouraged Joshua, letting him know that Israel would be successful in battle against these kings. Israel responded to Gibeon's call for help in a surprise attack against the people of the southern region.

- God blessed Israel and created a hailstorm that killed a great number of their enemies. When Joshua prayed for the sun to stand still so that Israel could continue fighting, daylight was miraculously extended.

- Israel fought and conquered all of these kingdoms in a single campaign before returning to their camp at Gilgal.

God Gives Israel Victory in the Northern Region: (Joshua 11–12)

- When the kings of the northern region heard about Israel's victory in the south, they rallied together and joined forces.

- Once again the Lord encouraged Joshua and told him that those preparing to attack Israel would be dead the next day.

- Israel fought the people of the northern region and completely destroyed their cities and killed the people.

- Altogether, Israel defeated two kings east of the Jordan and thirty-one kings west of the Jordan. Israel now possessed all the land these kings once ruled.

Recommended Bible Reading

Joshua 3:1–3:17   **Israel Crosses the Jordan**

Joshua 5:13–6:27   **God Gives Israel Victory at Jericho**

Joshua 10:7–10:15   **The Sun Stands Still for Israel**

Romans 10:1–15   **Saved by Faith**

MAP OF KEY LOCATIONS

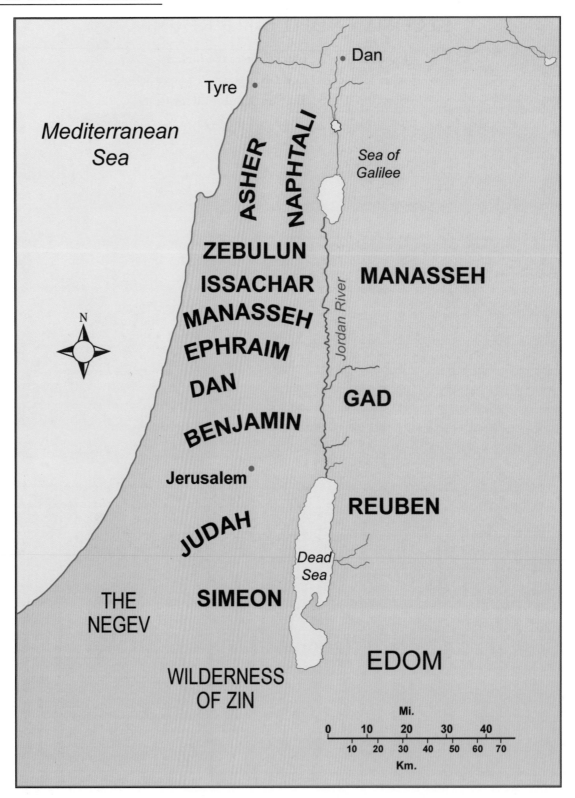

SECTION 2: ALLOCATING THE LAND

Joshua Allocates Land to Each Tribe as an Inheritance: (Joshua 13–19)

- Joshua was getting up in age. After seven years of fighting, the Lord told him to divide and allocate the land to each tribe.

- Some of the land promised to Israel still had not been conquered. God told Joshua to allocate the land anyway and He would help Israel conquer the remaining territories.

- The tribes of Reuben, Gad, and half of Manasseh's tribe received their inheritance east of the Jordan before Moses died, so nine and a half tribes remained that were to receive an inheritance west of the Jordan.

- The Levites were not given an allocation because they received the offerings sacrificed to God as their inheritance. However, they were assigned towns to live in and pastureland for their flocks and herds.

- Caleb reminded Joshua that more than forty-five years ago, Moses had promised him the city of Hebron.

CALEB'S TESTIMONY

"Now then, just as the LORD promised, he has kept me alive for forty-five years since the time he said this to Moses, while Israel moved about in the desert. So here I am today, eighty-five years old! I am still as strong today as the day Moses sent me out; I'm just as vigorous to go out to battle now as I was then. Now give me this hill country that the LORD promised me that day. You yourself heard then that the Anakites were there and their cities were large and fortified, but, the LORD helping me, I will drive them out just as he said."

(Joshua 14:10–12 NIV)

- Joshua honored the agreement and gave Hebron to Caleb. Since Caleb was from the tribe of Judah, Judah's allocation was in the same region as Hebron.

- The Israelites then gathered at Shiloh and set up the Tabernacle.

- The land was divided and the remaining tribes cast lots for each section. After all the land had been assigned, the Israelites gave Joshua a special section.

- Land was allocated to twelve tribes: East of the Jordan were Reuben, Gad, and half of Manasseh's tribe. West of the Jordan were Judah, Ephraim, Benjamin, Simeon, Zebulun, Issachar, Asher, Naphtali, Dan, and the other half of Manasseh's tribe.

 Note: The tribe of Levi did not receive a land allocation, but both of Joseph's sons (Ephraim and Manasseh) received land.

Joshua Designates Cities of Refuge and Towns for the Levites: (Joshua 20–21)

- The Lord told Joshua to designate cities of refuge so that anyone accused of murder would have a refuge for safety until a trial could be held.

- Once the accused reached a city of refuge, the victim's death could not legally be avenged. This protected those involved in an accidental killing and guaranteed them the right to a trial.

- Joshua designated three cities east of the Jordan and three cities west of the Jordan as cities of refuge. They were strategically located throughout the land. A person never had far to go to reach a city of refuge.

- Joshua then assigned Levites and priests to serve in forty-eight towns. They lived in these towns and ministered to the people.

The Tribes East of the Jordan Return Home: (Joshua 22)

- Finally, Joshua gathered the tribes of Reuben, Gad, and half of Manasseh's tribe and commended them for keeping their promise to help their brothers fight for possession of Canaan.

- Joshua blessed the tribes of Reuben, Gad, and half of Manasseh's tribe and told them to return home—east of the Jordan River.

- The tribes of Reuben, Gad, and half of Manasseh's tribe left, but on their way back they stopped and built an altar. This infuriated the tribes west of the Jordan because they thought the altar would be used to worship idol gods.

- The tribes west of the Jordan talked about going to war with Reuben, Gad, and half of Manasseh's tribe, but decided to send a delegation to discuss the matter first.

- The tribes east of the Jordan explained that the altar was not for idol worship, but was a memorial to serve as a reminder to their children that they were Israelites and related to the tribes west of the Jordan.

- The tribes of Reuben, Gad, and half of Manasseh's tribe were concerned that as years passed, the Israelites east of the Jordan and those west of the Jordan might forget they were both descendants of Abraham and served the same God.

- The Israelites west of the Jordan were happy to hear this, so discussions about going to war with the tribes east of the Jordan ceased.

God's Covenant with Israel Renewed: (Joshua 23–24)

- When Joshua was very old and close to death, he gathered the people of Israel together and delivered a farewell speech.

- Joshua encouraged the Israelites to be faithful and obedient to God and to carefully keep all the laws of Moses.

- He told them to be strong and courageous, reminding them of past victories and telling them God would continue blessing them with victories as long as they remained faithful to Him.

- He warned that God would certainly leave them and no longer fight their battles if they fell into idolatry.

- Joshua again reminded them that they were not to intermarry with the Canaanites or have any dealings with them whatsoever.

- Joshua told the people they must decide whether they were going to serve idol gods or the One True God. They could not serve both. If they were going to serve the One True God, they must get rid of their idol gods.

JOSHUA'S TESTIMONY

"Now fear the LORD and serve him with all faithfulness. Throw away the gods your forefathers worshiped beyond the River and in Egypt, and serve the LORD. But if serving the LORD seems undesirable to you, then choose for yourselves this day whom you will serve, whether the gods your forefathers served beyond the River, or the gods of the Amorites, in whose land you are living. But as for me and my household, we will serve the LORD."

(Joshua 24:14–15 NIV)

- The people promised to obey and live for the God of Israel. Joshua renewed God's covenant with Israel. Soon after this, Joshua died at the age of 110.

- Joseph's body, which Israel had carried with them when they left Egypt, was finally buried at Shechem, fulfilling Joseph's request that he be buried in Canaan.

- Israel served the Lord God throughout Joshua's lifetime and the lifetimes of those who witnessed the miracles God performed during Joshua's leadership.

RECOMMENDED BIBLE READING

Joshua 14:1–15 **Caleb Inherits Hebron**

Joshua 20:1–9 **Cities of Refuge**

Joshua 23:1–16 **Joshua's Farewell Address**

Hebrews 4:1–16 **God's Promise of Rest**

SECTION 3: THE JUDGES (PART 1)

Israel's Failure and Disobedience: (Judges 1:1–3:6)

- After Joshua's death, no one succeeded him as leader of Israel, so the nation was without a leader.

- The tribe of Judah was the first to fight the Canaanites living in unconquered territories of their inheritance. The tribe of Simeon fought as allies with Judah and together they were successful in battle.

- Caleb and those fighting with him attacked Hebron and conquered it. Caleb offered his daughter in marriage and a portion of land to anyone who helped him drive the Canaanites out of the rest of his land.

- Othniel, Caleb's nephew, responded to this challenge and was victorious.

- The tribe of Judah reciprocated Simeon's assistance and joined with them to drive their enemies out of their land.

- However, many of the tribes failed to drive the Canaanites out, leaving a large number of unconquered territories.

- An angel of the Lord delivered a message to Israel to let them know God was displeased. God had faithfully kept His covenant, but Israel had failed to uphold their part of the agreement.

- Israel had disobeyed God's command to totally drive out the Canaanites. As years passed by, the old generation died and a new one emerged that did not serve the Lord.

- This new generation of Israelites allowed the Canaanites to influence their way of life. As a result, Israel fell into idolatry.

Othniel, First Judge of Israel: (Judges 3:7–11)

- The Israelites had abandoned God, so the Lord allowed their enemies in Aram-naharaim (Mesopotamia) to oppress them. They were forced into servitude for eight years.

- Israel cried out to God and He mercifully responded. The Lord divinely empowered Othniel from the tribe of Judah to become Israel's first judge.

Note: What was a judge? "Judge" was the name Israel gave the people God empowered to perform His special work. Israel had no elected leader and there was no standing army. God used judges to accomplish His will and rescue Israel from their enemies. They functioned as rulers, deliverers, military leaders, saviors, liberators, administrators of justice, settlers of disputes, counselors, and much more.

- Othniel led Israel into battle against their enemies and was victorious. There was peace for forty years while Othniel served as Israel's judge.

THE PERIOD OF THE JUDGES

> **Israel's Disobedience and Great Failure:** The Israelites failed to obey God and drive all the Canaanites out of the land. They allowed the Canaanites to influence their religious life, which caused them to fall into idolatry.
>
> **Repeated Cycle of Oppression and Deliverance:** The Canaanites would oppress Israel and the Israelites would cry out to God for help. God would answer the Israelites' pleas by empowering a judge to deliver them.
>
> **Sin and Idolatry:** Each time Israel was delivered, they would serve God for a while and then fall back into the sin of idolatry.

Ehud and Shamgar, Judges of Israel: (Judges 3:12–31)

- Israel turned away from God again and started doing all kinds of evil. The Lord allowed their enemies, led by King Eglon of Moab, to oppress them for eighteen years.

- Israel cried out to God for help, and the Lord divinely empowered Ehud, from the tribe of Benjamin, to deliver Israel from their enemies.

- Ehud had been delegated to take a tax payment for Israel to King Eglon. When Ehud arrived with the taxes, he met privately with the king and killed him.

- Ehud then rallied a band of Israelites, attacked, and defeated their enemies. There was peace for eighty years while Ehud served as Israel's judge.

- After Ehud, Shamgar became a judge and rescued Israel from the Philistines.

Deborah with Barak, Judge of Israel: (Judges 4–5)

- After Ehud's death, the Israelites returned to their wicked ways and the Lord once again allowed their enemies to oppress them.

- This time their enemies were King Jabin and the Canaanites. The commander of the Canaanite army, Sisera, had been exceptionally cruel to Israel for twenty years, so Israel cried out to the Lord for help.

- Deborah, a prophetess who had been serving as a judge in Israel, received a special revelation from the Lord.

- She told Barak that God had commanded him to gather warriors from the tribes of Naphtali and Zebulun and attack King Jabin.

- The Lord had promised Barak the victory; however, Barak would not go without Deborah. Deborah went into battle with Barak and Israel's warriors. They were victorious just as God had promised.

- All the Canaanite warriors were killed except Sisera, who escaped but was later killed by a brave woman named Jael, a descendant of Moses' brother-in-law.

- Afterwards, Deborah and Barak sang a song about their victory. Israel then had peace for forty years.

Gideon, Tola, and Jair, Judges of Israel: (Judges 7:1–10:5)

- Israel again turned away from God and became a wicked nation of ungodly people. The Lord allowed the Midianites to oppress them for seven years.

- The Midianites were ruthless marauders who completely vandalized Israel, stealing their crops and livestock and leaving them with nothing to eat.

- Facing starvation, Israel cried out to God for help and the Lord commanded them to stop worshipping idols.

- God sent an angel to a man named Gideon, who was from the tribe of Manasseh. The angel appeared to Gideon and told him that God was going to empower him to rescue Israel from the Midianites.

- Gideon did not realize he was in the presence of an angel, so he questioned what the angel said. Gideon's self-esteem was very low and he could not see himself—a nobody—rescuing Israel.

- The angel told Gideon that the Lord God would fight the battle. Gideon then hurried home to prepare a meal and returned with meat and bread. The angel instructed Gideon to put the food on a rock. Gideon did as he was told.

- The angel touched the food with his staff and fire suddenly appeared, totally consuming the meat and bread. The angel then disappeared.

- Gideon suddenly realized he had been in the presence of an angel. He built an altar to the Lord and named it *Jehovah-Shalom*, which means "The LORD is Peace" (Judges 6:24).

 Note: *Jehovah-Shalom* is the Hebrew name of God, The One Who Gives Peace. *Jehovah-Shalom* frees us from stressful or oppressive thoughts and gives us peace of mind and tranquility.

- The Lord then commanded Gideon to destroy all the instruments of idol worship in the town and build a proper altar to the God of Israel. Gideon obeyed, but did it at night because he was afraid of the people.

- When the people discovered Gideon had destroyed the idols, they wanted to kill him, but Gideon's father defended his son.

- Shortly after, Israel's enemies united and positioned themselves for battle. God empowered Gideon and he was able to build an army of 32,000 warriors.

- Gideon then asked God for a sign to prove the Lord was really going to give him the victory.

- First, Gideon put a fleece on the ground and asked God to make the fleece wet with dew, but keep the ground dry overnight. God made it happen just as Gideon had asked.

- Then Gideon asked the Lord to make the ground wet with dew, but keep the fleece dry overnight. Again God made it happen.

- These miracles strengthened Gideon's faith. Having received assurance of victory from the Lord, Gideon was now ready for battle.

- However, the Lord told Gideon he had too many men. If Gideon fought with such a large number of warriors, the people would think they had won through their own strength and not the Lord's.

- God made Gideon reduce his army from 32,000 warriors to a mere 300 men.

- Gideon and his 300 men marched into the enemies' camp blowing trumpets and breaking clay jars. They created such a panic that their enemies became confused and killed each other.

- A few escaped, but Gideon and his men caught up with them and killed them.

- Israel asked Gideon to rule over them, but Gideon refused. Instead, Gideon asked each of them for a piece of gold, which they gladly gave him.

- Gideon took the gold and made an ephod, a garment worn by priests. Sadly, the people began to worship it as an idol god.

- There was peace in Israel for forty years. Then Gideon died, leaving seventy sons to mourn his death.

- One of Gideon's sons, Abimelech, zealous to take over his father's legacy, killed all of his brothers except one who escaped.

- The people in Shechem put Abimelech in power and he ruled Israel for three years. Finally, the people revolted and Abimelech was killed, but not before he and his troops destroyed the city of Shechem.

- After Abimelech's death, Tola from the tribe of Isaachar rescued Israel from their enemies and served as judge for twenty-three years before he died.

- Then a man named Jair from Gilead, east of the Jordan, served as judge of Israel for twenty-three years before he died.

RECOMMENDED BIBLE READING

Judges 2:1–23	**Israel's Failure and Disobedience**
Judges 4:1–24	**Deborah with Barak, Judge of Israel**
Judges 6:1–7:25	**Gideon, Judge of Israel**
Hebrews 2:1–10	**Warning Against Drifting Away from God**

SECTION 4: THE JUDGES (PART 2)

Jephthah, Ibzan, Elon, and Abdon, Judges of Israel: (Judges 10:6–12:15)

- Again, Israel failed to serve the One True God and began worshipping idols. The Lord allowed Israel's enemies to oppress them for eighteen years.

- Israel's enemies, the Philistines and the Ammonites, overtook Israel and created havoc on both the east and west sides of the Jordan River.

- Finally, Israel cried out to God saying, *"We have sinned against you, forsaking our God and serving the Baals (idol gods)"* (Judges 10:10b NIV).

- The Israelites got rid of their idols and began serving the One True God.

- The Lord had mercy on Israel and empowered a man named Jephthah to lead the Israelites into battle against the Ammonites.

- Before going into battle, Jephthah vowed that if he were victorious, he would sacrifice the first to greet him upon his return. God was with Jephthah and Israel conquered their enemies.

- When Jephthah returned home, his young daughter, an only child, was the first to greet him. Jephthah was grief-stricken, but he kept his vow and sacrificed his daughter to the Lord.

- Warriors from the tribe of Ephraim later became angry with Jephthah and accused him of not giving them an opportunity to help fight against Israel's enemies.

- Jephthah refuted the Ephraimites' allegations, saying that he had called them, but they did not come.

- The dispute became so intense that Jephthah went to war against the Ephraimites and killed a great number of them. Jephthah was judge of Israel for six years.

- After Jephthah, Ibzan, who lived in Bethlehem, served as judge for seven years and then he died.

- Elon, from the tribe of Zebulun, served as judge for ten years and then died. After Elon, Abdon served as judge for eight years and then died.

Samson, Judge of Israel: (Judges 13–16)

- Again the Israelites fell into idolatry and abandoned God. The Lord allowed the Philistines to oppress Israel for forty years.

- An angel appeared to a woman—whose husband's name was Manoah—and told her she would soon have a child.

- The angel said the child was to be dedicated to God as a Nazarite and the child would rescue Israel from the Philistines.

Note: What was a Nazarite? A Nazarite was one who had taken a vow to dedicate his life to God's service for either a specific period of time or for a lifetime in accordance with the laws outlined in Numbers 6:1–21. In Samson's case, his parents took the Nazarite vow for him. A Nazarite could not drink alcoholic beverages, cut his hair, or touch a dead body.

- Later, the angel appeared to the woman and her husband, Manoah who was from the tribe of Dan, and confirmed to both of them what he had told her.

- Just as the angel said, they had a son and named him Samson. The Spirit of the Lord was with Samson as he grew into manhood.

- Samson told his parents he wanted to marry a Philistine woman. His parents strongly objected because the Philistines were their enemies.

- Samson's parents begged him to find a nice Israelite girl to marry, but Samson insisted on having the Philistine woman as his wife.

- Samson's parents relented and made arrangements for him to marry the Philistine woman.

- During the wedding celebration, Samson made a bet with the Philistine men that they could not solve one of his riddles.

- For several days the Philistine men tried but were unable to solve the riddle. Finally, they went to Samson's wife and told her to get the answer from him.

- Samson's wife was able to get the answer from him. She gave it to the Philistine men, who were then able to solve Samson's riddle.

- Samson became so irate that he went back to his parents' home without his wife. After Samson left, his wife's father gave her in marriage to Samson's best man.

- Samson returned and learned the woman was no longer his wife. He became angry and burned the Philistine's fields.

- When the Philistines discovered the reason for Samson's rage, they killed the woman and her father, thinking it would appease Samson. This made Samson angrier than he was before.

- Samson went on a rampage and started killing the Philistines. They retaliated by attacking the tribe of Judah.

- When the men of Judah discovered the Philistines were attacking them because of Samson, they found him and handed him over to the Philistines.

- The Philistines were unable to restrain Samson. He broke free and killed thousands of Philistines using a donkey's jawbone as a weapon.

- Samson later fell in love with a Philistine woman named Delilah.

- The Philistine leaders went to Delilah and promised to pay her if she found out the source of Samson's strength so they could capture him.

- Delilah repeatedly asked Samson what made him so strong, but each time Samson would tell her a lie about his strength.

- Delilah was persistent. Finally Samson told her his strength was in his hair, which had never been cut.

- Delilah realized Samson had told her the truth. She waited until he fell asleep and called a man to shave Samson's head.

- When Samson awoke, all of his strength was gone. The Philistines were able to easily capture him. They put out his eyes and imprisoned him.

- During a festival, Samson was taken to the Philistines' temple so they could make fun of him.

- Samson, by then blind, asked one of the servants to put his hands on the pillars of the temple so he could rest.

- Samson then prayed to the Lord and his strength returned.

- Samson was able to apply enough force against the pillars to knock the entire temple structure down, killing all the people inside, including himself.

- Samson killed more Philistines at his death than he did during his entire life. Samson had served as judge of Israel for twenty years.

SUMMARY OF ISRAEL'S REPEATED CYCLE OF SIN

Judge(s)	Enemies	Scriptures
Othniel	Mesopotamians	Judges 3:7–11
Ehud/Shamgar	Moabites, Philistines	Judges 3:12–31
Deborah/Barak	Canaanites	Judges 4:1–5:31
Gideon/Tola/Jair	Midianites	Judges 6:1–10:5
Jephthah/Ibzan/ Elon/Abdon	Ammonites	Judges 10:6–12:15
Samson	Philistines	Judges 13:1–16:31

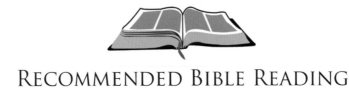

RECOMMENDED BIBLE READING

Judges 16:1–31 **Samson, Judge of Israel**
Romans 1:18–32 **The Sinfulness of Mankind**

SECTION 5: ISRAEL'S MORAL FAILURES

The Tribe of Dan Steals an Idol for Worship: (Judges 17–18)

 Note: These final chapters of Judges provide a picture of the moral state of decline in Israel during this period.

- A man named Micah was given an idol as a gift from his mother. He used it to set up a shrine and hired a Levite to serve as his personal priest.

- Meanwhile, the tribe of Dan was searching for land to settle because they had never conquered the Canaanites living in the territory they had inherited.

- While scouting for land, a few Danites stopped at Micah's house and noticed his shrine.

- The Danites left Micah's house and found a town inhabited by peace loving people. They decided the town would be easy to attack and conquer.

- The tribe of Dan went back to Micah's house, stole his shrine, and took the Levite who served as his priest. They attacked the peaceful town, killed all the people, then rebuilt and settled the town.

- The tribe used Micah's shrine for pagan worship, and Micah's Levite served as their priest. They never again worshiped the One True God at the Tabernacle in Shiloh.

The Tribes Go to War against Benjamin: (Judges 19–22)

- A Levite was traveling with his concubine (mistress) when he decided to stop and rest in a town where people from the tribe of Benjamin resided. An old man living there invited the Levite to stay at his house overnight.

- Later that evening, some wicked men from the town came to the old man's house and demanded that he give them the Levite so they could have sex with him.

- The old man begged them not to do such an evil thing, but they would not go away. The Levite's concubine was given to the wicked men instead. They raped and abused her all night until she died.

- Afterwards the Levite summoned all of Israel together. They met and listened to the Levite's story. After hearing what had happened, all of Israel was outraged.

- Israel's leaders demanded that the tribe of Benjamin hand over the men who had done this terrible act, but they would not.

- All of Israel went to war against the tribe of Benjamin and killed all of them except 600 men, who escaped.

- Afterwards, all of Israel grieved for the tribe of Benjamin because one of their tribes was almost extinct. Only 600 Benjamite men were left, and they needed wives to replenish the tribe.

- Israel's leaders were determined to find wives for these men, but most of Israel had taken an oath that they would not allow their daughters to marry a Benjamite.

- Israel's leaders discovered the men of Jabesh-gilead had not fought and taken the oath against the Benjamites as all of Israel had been commanded.

- The leaders sent warriors to Jabesh-gilead to kill all the people except the virgins, who were to be given as wives to the Benjamite men.

- After doing this, there still were not enough women for the Benjamite men. Israel's leaders told the remaining Benjamites to steal and marry some Israelite girls who would soon be attending an annual festival.

- Israel's leaders decided this would be the right thing to do.

- They rationalized it, saying the Benjamites would have wives; these girls' fathers would not be breaking their oath because they were not willingly giving their daughters to the Benjamites.

"In those days Israel had no king; all the people did whatever seemed right in their own eyes."

(Judges 21:25)

RECOMMENDED BIBLE READING

Judges 18:1–31 **The Tribe of Dan Steals an Idol for Worship**

Romans 2:1–16 **God's Judgment Against Sin**

MEDITATION & PRAYER

God exhorts Joshua to be strong and courageous and gives him the formula for success:

"Be strong and courageous, because you will lead these people to inherit the land I swore to their forefathers to give them. Be strong and very courageous. Be careful to obey all the law my servant Moses gave you; do not turn from it to the right or to the left, that you may be successful wherever you go. Do not let this Book of the Law depart from your mouth; meditate on it day and night, so that you may be careful to do everything written in it. Then you will be prosperous and successful . . . Do not be terrified; do not be discouraged, for the Lord your God will be with you wherever you go."

(Joshua 1:6–8, 9b NIV)

Dear LORD of Peace,

According to Your Word, obedience to Your commandments and laws is the key to success. Strengthen me as I meditate on Scripture and help me commit Your commandments and laws to memory. In times of trouble or great distress, I will not be discouraged. You are Jehovah-Shalom and will give me peace. I will be strong and courageous, knowing that You are with me wherever I go.

Amen

REVIEW QUESTIONS

1. What is a major portion of the book of Joshua about?

_____

_____

_____

_____

_____

_____

2. What does Joshua's name mean? How did God prepare Joshua for leadership?

_____

_____

_____

_____

_____

_____

_____

3. The Ark of the Covenant was in front of the people in the Jordan River miracle. What was its significance?

_____

_____

_____

_____

_____

_____

4. Who fought the Battle of Jericho and how?

_____

_____

_____

_____

_____

_____

5. Who was Rahab? What role did she play in *God's Plan of Redemption*?

_____

_____

_____

_____

_____

_____

6. What purpose did the cities of refuge serve?

_____

_____

_____

_____

_____

_____

7.   What was a judge? What role did judges play in Israel's history?

_____

_____

_____

_____

_____

_____

8.   What was the repeated cycle described in the Book of Judges?

_____

_____

_____

_____

_____

_____

_____

PERSONAL REFLECTIONS

9. What spiritual growth lessons did God point out to you while reading about Joshua's life? How can these lessons be applied in your life?

_____

_____

_____

_____

_____

_____

10. Judges 21:25 states, *"In those days Israel had no king; all the people did whatever seemed right in their own eyes."* What does this verse mean? Are there any similarities between Israel's attitude towards moral issues and people's attitude today? If so, what are they?

_____

_____

_____

_____

_____

11. What spiritual growth lessons did you learn from the period of the Judges?

_____

_____

_____

_____

_____

_____

12. Gideon built an altar to Jehovah-Shalom, which means *The LORD is Peace*. Do you want to be freed from stressful or oppressing thoughts? Write a prayer to God, Jehovah-Shalom, asking Him for peace of mind and tranquility.

_____

_____

_____

_____

_____

_____

13. Re-read Joshua and Caleb's testimonies in Section 2 of this chapter. What did you learn about Joshua through his testimony? What did you learn about Caleb? What did you learn about God?

_____

_____

_____

_____

_____

_____

14. Write your own personal testimony about what God has done in your life.

_____

_____

_____

_____

_____

_____

CLOSING PRAYER

The Apostle Paul reminds us that we too were foolish and disobedient:

"At one time we too were foolish, disobedient, deceived and enslaved by all kinds of passions and pleasures. We lived in malice and envy, being hated and hating one another. But when the kindness and love of God our Savior appeared, he saved us, not because of righteous things we had done, but because of his mercy. He saved us through the washing of rebirth and renewal by the Holy Spirit, whom he poured out on us generously through Jesus Christ our Savior, so that, having been justified by his grace, we might become heirs having the hope of eternal life."

(Titus 3:3–7 NIV)

Lord God,

I thank you for Your love, Your mercy, and Your grace. I admit that I, too, have been foolish and disobedient. I fall short of Your glory. Please forgive me and help me overcome the spirit of disobedience. Teach me to guard my heart and actions. Reveal Yourself to me and renew me with Your Spirit. You are my hope for eternal life.

Amen

CHAPTER 6

ESTABLISHING THE KINGDOM

OPENING PRAYER

Heavenly Father,

Prepare my mind and heart as I begin to read about the kingdom of Israel and how it was established. Through Your Spirit, give me a better understanding of Your Word; help me to remember what I've read; point out the lessons You would like me to learn; and give me the wisdom, humility, and fortitude to apply those lessons in my life.

Amen

CHAPTER SUMMARY

ESTABLISHING THE KINGDOM

(Ruth, 1 & 2 Samuel, 1 Kings, and 1 & 2 Chronicles)

Ruth lived during the period of the Judges when Israel had no king. Israel had turned away from God and fallen into idolatry during this period. Some people, however, continued to serve the Lord, and Ruth's Jewish mother-in-law, Naomi, was one of them. Ruth was a Moabite who learned about the God of Israel from Naomi. Her tremendous love and respect for Naomi led her to the Lord. God rewarded Ruth's faith, blessing her to become an ancestor of both King David and Jesus Christ.

Samuel, the last judge of Israel, was also a priest and prophet. He ministered to Israel and led the nation back to the Lord. During the latter years of Samuel's life, the people asked him to appoint a king to rule over Israel. Although Samuel was disappointed by their request, God instructed him to anoint Saul as king. Samuel counseled Saul on God's ways, but Saul would not obey the Lord and so God's Spirit soon left him.

The Lord then instructed Samuel to anoint David as the next king of Israel. When Saul realized God's Spirit was with David, he became jealous and was afraid David would take the kingdom away from him. Saul repeatedly tried to kill David, but God protected David. Saul finally died in a battle against the Philistines and David became king.

David loved the Lord and was a man after God's own heart. He made mistakes, but was quick to ask the Lord for forgiveness. David fought Israel's enemies on every side and was victorious. The kingdom was now firmly established under David's leadership. God entered into a covenant with David, promising him a kingdom that would last forever. This covenant was fulfilled through Jesus Christ, a descendant of King David, whose kingdom is forever.

David's son, Solomon, succeeded him as king. Solomon ruled during a time of peace. The Lord blessed him with wisdom, wealth, and fame. Solomon built a temple for the Lord. He married hundreds of women from other nations and allowed them to bring their pagan practices with them to Israel. Solomon's wives eventually led him into idolatry.

	Approximate Timeline	**Location**	**Biblical Scriptures**	**Author**
Ruth	Sometime between 1375 B.C.–1050 B.C.	Moab & Bethlehem	Ruth 1–4	Unknown
Samuel	1105 B.C.–1050 B.C.	Israel	1 Samuel 1–10	Possibly Samuel
King Saul	1050 B.C.–1010 B.C.	Israel	1 Samuel 11–31 Chronicles 10	Possibly Samuel Ezra
King David	1010 B.C.–970 B.C.	Israel	2 Samuel 1–24 1 Kings 1–2 1 Chronicles 11–29	Unknown Unknown Ezra
King Solomon	970 B.C.–930 B.C.	Israel	1 Kings 2–11 2 Chronicles 1–9	Unknown Ezra

MAP OF KEY LOCATIONS

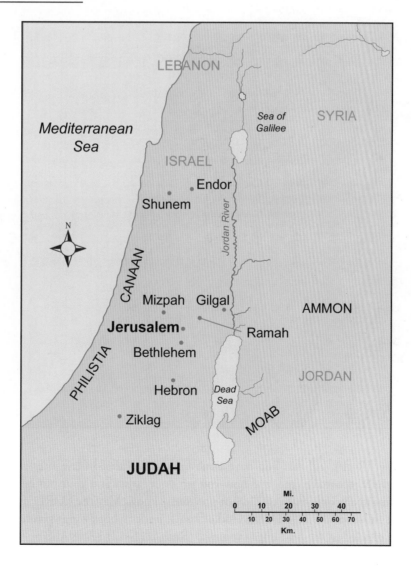

RUTH

"Boaz replied to her (Ruth), 'All that you have done for your mother-in-law after the death of your husband has been fully reported to me, and how you left your father and your mother and the land of your birth, and came to a people that you did not previously know. May the LORD reward your work, and your wages be full from the LORD, the God of Israel, under whose wings you have come to seek refuge.' . . . So she gleaned in the field until evening." (Ruth 2:11–12, 17a NASB)

SECTION 1: RUTH

Naomi and Ruth: (Ruth 1)

- During the period of the Judges, a man named Elimelech moved with his wife, Naomi, and their two sons from a famine in Bethlehem of Judah to Moab.

- Elimelech died after moving to Moab. His sons married Moabite women whose names were Orpah and Ruth. Both sons later died.

 Note: The Moabites were descendants of Lot, Abraham's nephew.

- When the widowed Naomi heard that the famine in Bethlehem had come to an end, she decided to return home. Along with her daughters-in-law, Naomi began the journey back to Bethlehem.

- While on the road, Naomi thought it would be best for her two daughters-in-law to go home to their parents.

- They did not want to leave Naomi, but she insisted. Finally, Orpah kissed Naomi goodbye and went back home to her people, but Ruth stayed.

- Ruth said to Naomi, *"Don't urge me to leave you or to turn back from you. Where you go I will go, and where you stay I will stay. Your people will be my people and your God my God"* (Ruth 1:16 NIV).

- Naomi soon realized Ruth was determined to stay and stopped insisting that she return home. The two women traveled to Bethlehem, arriving in time for the harvest season.

Ruth Meets Boaz: (Ruth 2)

- Poor and in need of food, Ruth asked Naomi for permission to glean in the fields. Naomi said yes.

 Note: Poor people would glean (pick up grain left behind by harvesters) for food.

- Ruth gleaned in the field of a wealthy man named Boaz. He was a relative of Naomi's late-husband, but Ruth did not know this at the time.

- Boaz learned Ruth was Naomi's daughter-in-law. He introduced himself and insisted that she glean only in his fields. Boaz was kind to Ruth and gave her extra food and protection.

- When Ruth told Naomi about Boaz, she was pleased and said, *"That man is our close relative; he is one of our kinsman-redeemers"* (Ruth 2:20b NIV).

 What is a kinsman-redeemer? According to Jewish law, if an Israelite became poor and had to sell his property, his close relative should pay the price to redeem or recover it. Naomi was letting Ruth know that Boaz was a close relative who could redeem her late-husband's property.

"If one of your countrymen becomes poor and sells some of his property, his nearest relative is to come and redeem what his countryman has sold" (Leviticus 25:25 NIV).

Jesus is our kinsman-redeemer. As our kinsman, He shared in our humanity and redeemed us, paying the price to set us free from sin.

"For this reason he (Jesus) had to be made like his brothers in every way, in order that he might become a merciful and faithful high priest in service to God, and that he might make atonement for the sins of the people" (Hebrews 2:17 NIV).

- Ruth continued to glean in Boaz's field through the barley and wheat harvest.

The Kinsman-Redeemer: (Ruth 3–4)

- Naomi cared about Ruth's welfare. She knew it would be best for her daughter-in-law if Boaz redeemed her late husband's property.

- Naomi counseled Ruth and told her how to determine if Boaz was willing to redeem their property. Ruth faithfully did everything Naomi told her to do.

- Boaz was indeed willing to redeem Naomi's late husband's property. However, there was a closer relative, who was first in line to redeem the property.

- Boaz met with the closer relative and asked him if he wanted to buy Naomi's late husband's property.

- The closer relative agreed to redeem the land. Boaz then told the closer relative that Ruth had to be included with the deal so the dead man's name would be kept with the property.

- When the closer relative heard Ruth was part of the deal, he changed his mind and relinquished his rights.

- The closer relative said acquiring Ruth *"might endanger my own estate"* (Ruth 4:6 NIV).

- Boaz was now next in line. He bought Naomi's late husband's property. He also acquired and married Ruth.

- Boaz and Ruth had a son named Obed, who was the father of Jesse, who was the father of King David, all of whom were ancestors of Jesus Christ.

 Ruth was King David's great-grandmother and an ancestor of Jesus Christ. (Ruth 4:22; Matthew 1:5).

RECOMMENDED BIBLE READING

Leviticus 25:25–55   **The Law of the Kinsman-Redeemer**

Ruth 1:1–4:20   **The Story of Ruth**

Hebrews 2:11–18   **Jesus, Our Kinsman-Redeemer**

SECTION 2: SAMUEL

The Birth of Samuel: (1 Samuel 1–2)

- Elkanah, a man from Ramah, had two wives. One had children but the other wife, Hannah, was childless.

- Hannah prayed fervently for a child. She called out to *Jehovah-Sabaoth*, which means "The LORD of Hosts" (1 Samuel 1:11), and promised to give that child to Him if He blessed her with one.

Note: *Jehovah-Sabaoth* is the Hebrew name of God, The One Who Has Multitudes In His Service. *Jehovah-Sabaoth* is Sovereign Ruler of all heavenly and earthly hosts (armies) and delivers those who are feeling overwhelmed and powerless.

- The Lord answered Hannah's prayers and blessed her with a child whom she named Samuel.

- Hannah kept her promise to the Lord and gave her child to Eli, the high priest, to minister in the Tabernacle.

- Eli's two sons were very wicked. They took portions of the meat sacrifices that belonged to God and slept with women serving at the Tabernacle.

- Although Eli talked to his sons about their wickedness, they did not listen and Eli did nothing to stop them.

- One day, the Lord sent a man to Eli who told him God was displeased with his failure to restrain his sons.

- The man prophesied that both of Eli's sons would die on the same day and his other male descendants would die early deaths.

Samuel, God's Chosen Spiritual Leader: (1 Samuel 3–10)

- One night while Samuel was lying down, the Lord called him. Samuel thought Eli was calling him, so he got up and ran to Eli.

- Eli told Samuel that he had not called. Samuel went back to bed and the Lord called him again. This happened three times before Eli realized the Lord was calling the boy.

- Eli said to Samuel the next time this happens, say, *"Speak, Lord, for your servant is listening"* (1 Samuel 3:9b NIV).

- Samuel followed Eli's instructions. The Lord told him Eli's family would be judged for his sons' wickedness and his failure to restrain them.

- The next morning Samuel was afraid to tell Eli what God had said, but Eli insisted. So Samuel told him.

- Samuel grew up, and God was with him as he ministered throughout Israel.

- Israel later suffered a great defeat in a battle against the Philistines. The Israelites decided the Ark of the Covenant should be with them in the next battle.

- When Israel's troops were again mobilized to fight the Philistines, Eli's two sons carried the Ark into camp. The battle was fought, and Israel suffered an even greater defeat.

- The Philistines seized the Ark. Eli's two sons were both killed on the same day, just as the man of God had prophesied. When Eli heard the news about the Ark, he fell backward and died.

- After capturing the Ark, the Philistines took it to the temple where their idol god was housed. Each morning when they entered the temple, the Philistines found their god had fallen facedown on the ground in front of the Ark.

- The Philistines of that city became afflicted with tumors. Many died, so they moved the Ark to another Philistine city. The people there also became sick and died.

- Several Philistine leaders insisted the Ark be taken back to its own people, so they sent the Ark back to Israel.

- As the Israelites were carrying the Ark, seventy men looked inside it and died. It was finally taken to an Israelite named Eleazar, who was consecrated to guard it.

- The Ark was in Eleazar's care for twenty years before Israel repented and turned to the Lord under Samuel's leadership.

- Samuel told the people to get rid of their idols and to gather at Mizpah, where he would pray for them.

- When the Philistines heard the Israelites were at Mizpah, they attacked, but God answered Samuel's prayers and the Philistines were defeated.

- Samuel continued as judge, prophet, and priest in Israel. Throughout his lifetime, the Philistines were subdued.

 God used Samuel as a savior. He was one of Israel's greatest judges and was also a prophet and a priest. Samuel led Israel back to God.

- Samuel grew old and appointed his sons as judges, but they were not faithful to the Lord.

- The elders met with Samuel and said, *". . . you are now old, and your sons are not like you. Give us a king to judge us like all the other nations have"* (1 Samuel 8:5).

- Their request displeased Samuel, but the Lord told him the people were not rejecting him (Samuel), but were rejecting God as their King. The Lord told Samuel to do what the people asked and give them a king.

- The Lord instructed Samuel to anoint Saul, who was from the tribe of Benjamin, to be Israel's leader and king.

- Samuel gathered the people together and announced that God had chosen Saul to be their king. Some of the people gave Saul their allegiance, but others resisted his leadership.

RECOMMENDED BIBLE READING

1 Samuel 1:1–28 **The Birth of Samuel**
1 Samuel 3:1–21 **Samuel, God's Chosen Spiritual Leader**
Romans 2:17–29 **Jews and the Law**

Section 3: King Saul

Saul, King of Israel: (1 Samuel 11–15)

- The Ammonites captured a town in Israel and threatened to gouge out the right eye of everyone living there.

- Saul was outraged and launched a surprise attack. It was a great military victory for Saul. Afterwards, all of Israel supported Saul as their king.

- Samuel led Israel in a sacred ceremony to reaffirm Saul as king and to encourage the people to obey and serve the Lord God always. Saul was thirty years old when he became king and he reigned for forty-two years.

- Saul's son, Jonathan, attacked and captured a Philistine outpost. When the other Philistines heard the news, they were outraged. Saul quickly mobilized Israel's warriors in preparation for battle.

- The Philistines rallied their troops. They had so many men that Israel's army became terrified and some ran away.

- Samuel told Saul to wait for him before going into battle so he could offer sacrifices to the Lord.

- Saul waited for seven days, but when he saw each day that more and more of his men were running away, he decided to offer the sacrifices himself.

- Samuel arrived just as Saul was finishing the offering. Saul explained his actions. He said Samuel was late, his men were abandoning him, and the Philistines were ready for battle.

- Samuel told Saul he had acted foolishly by disobeying God's command for only priests were to offer sacrifices.

- Furthermore, Samuel told Saul that if he had obeyed, his kingdom would have been established forever. Instead, it would come to an end.

- Meanwhile, Jonathan crossed over into a Philistine outpost with his armor-bearer and killed about twenty men.

- The Philistines panicked. Suddenly, an earthquake created more confusion. Saul and his men, taking advantage of the confusion, rushed in and killed a great number of Philistines.

- Saul's men grew weary because Saul made them vow to not eat until his full vengeance had been taken against the Philistines. Jonathan was not aware of this vow and ate some honey.

- When Jonathan heard about his father's oath, he told the men his father had crippled Israel. They would have been able to kill more Philistines if they had not been hungry.

- Later that night, Saul decided to launch another attack against the Philistines. The priest advised Saul to ask the Lord for guidance first. When he did, there was no response from the Lord.

- Saul believed the Lord did not respond because there was sin in the camp. He vowed to kill whoever had committed the sin.

- When Saul learned Jonathan had eaten some honey, he decided Jonathan had sinned. Jonathan's sin was preventing Saul from hearing God.

- Saul planned to kill his own son, but the soldiers stopped him. They said Jonathan had fought valiantly and won the battle for Israel that day.

- One day, Samuel delivered a message from the Lord to Saul. Samuel said God was ready to punish the Amalekites for their wickedness.

- God wanted Saul to lead an attack against the Amalekites and to completely destroy them and all of their animals.

- Saul attacked and was victorious, but he did not fully obey the Lord. He and his army took the Amalekite's king alive and kept the best of their livestock for themselves.

- Samuel went to talk to Saul, but he was not at the outpost. Saul was busy arranging for a monument to be erected in his own honor.

- Samuel finally found Saul and chastised him for disobeying the Lord. Saul blamed the soldiers. He said the soldiers took the best of the Amalekites' livestock to offer a sacrifice to the Lord.

- Samuel responded to Saul saying, *"What is more pleasing to the LORD: your burnt offerings and sacrifices or your obedience to his voice? Listen! Obedience is better than sacrifice, and submission is better than offering the fat of rams"* (1 Samuel 15:22).

- Saul finally admitted his guilt and begged for forgiveness. Samuel told him God was displeased and was taking the kingdom away from him.

- Samuel then killed the Amalekite king and left. Although Samuel continued to mourn for Saul, he never met with Saul again during his lifetime.

Samuel Anoints David: (1 Samuel 16)

- The Lord instructed Samuel to go to Bethlehem to anoint one of Jesse's eight sons to be the next king of Israel.

- When Samuel arrived in Bethlehem, he naturally assumed God had chosen one of Jesse's older sons.

- God said to Samuel, *". . . Looks aren't everything. Don't be impressed with his looks and stature. I've already eliminated him. GOD judges persons differently than humans do. Men and women look at the face; GOD looks into the heart"* (1 Samuel 16:7 MSG).

- God chose Jesse's youngest son David, a mere shepherd boy, to be the next king of Israel. Samuel obeyed the Lord and anointed young David.

Note: Although Samuel anointed David as the next king of Israel, Saul was still the reigning king. God was preparing David for his future assignment. David did not become king until much later when the people crowned him as their king. (2 Samuel 2:1–4; 5:1–5)

- Meanwhile, God's Spirit had left Saul. He was often tormented with bouts of depression. Some of Saul's servants suggested music might help. They told Saul about Jesse's son, David, who played the harp.

- Saul sent for David. Whenever a spirit of depression troubled him, David would play his harp. The music calmed Saul and made him feel better.

David Kills Goliath: (1 Samuel 17)

- The Philistines again gathered for battle against Israel. The Philistines were on one hill and the Israelites were gathered on the opposite hill.

- Goliath was a giant Philistine who stood over nine feet tall. He taunted Israel and challenged them to send out a man to fight with him one-on-one.

- Goliath said that if Israel's challenger won, the Philistines would serve Israel; if he won, Israel would serve the Philistines.

- Saul and his men were terrified when they heard this challenge. Goliath came out every day and every evening for forty days, ready to fight anyone in Israel who would take the challenge.

- One day, Jesse sent young David to take food to his older brothers, who were in Saul's army on the battlefield. David heard about Goliath's challenge and told Saul he would fight the giant.

- Saul thought David was too young. David insisted, so Saul relented.

- When David came out, Goliath sneered and cursed in the name of his gods. David replied saying he was fighting in the name of the God of Israel.

- David ran out and hit Goliath in the forehead with one stone from his slingshot. Goliath fell and died, giving David and Israel the victory.

Saul Tries to Kill David: (1 Samuel 18–20)

- David later met Jonathan, Saul's son, and the two became friends.

- Saul made David a commander in his army. When the women of Israel began to praise David for his valor, Saul became jealous and outraged.

- On several occasions when David was playing the harp, Saul became enraged. Like a madman, he threw a javelin at David.

- In the meantime, Saul's daughter, Michal, fell in love with David. When Saul learned this, he offered Michal's hand in marriage to David if he would kill one hundred Philistines.

- Saul's offer was really a plan to get rid of David. Saul thought the Philistines would certainly kill David. David and his men succeeded in killing the Philistines, so Saul gave Michal to David as his wife.

- As time went on, Saul became more and more jealous and afraid of David, so he made plans to have David assassinated. One day Saul sent troops to David's house with orders to kill him, but Michal helped David escape.

- David told Jonathan his father was trying to kill him, but Jonathan did not believe him. Jonathan realized David was telling the truth when his father hurled a spear at him (Jonathan) for showing kindness to David.

- Jonathan told David to go in peace. The two made a vow to always be friends. They entrusted each other and each other's children to the Lord.

David Runs From Saul: (1 Samuel 21–27)

- David left and was on the run, hiding in caves from Saul. David was soon joined by his relatives and others who were discontent with Saul.

- Saul and his army pursued David as he and his men roamed the countryside, hiding and running away from Saul.

- On several occasions, David had an opportunity to kill Saul, but he would not because David respected Saul as God's anointed one.

- Finally, David and his men moved their hiding place to a Philistine city. He knew Saul would not cross into Philistine territory to search for him. David was right. Saul stopped his pursuit.

The Death of Saul: (1 Samuel 28–31; 1 Chronicles 10)

- The Philistines gathered a large army for war against Israel.

- In the meantime, Samuel died. The nation of Israel mourned his death.

- When Saul saw the large Philistine army, he was gripped with fear. He decided to consult a medium even though he, himself, had banned sorcery and divination.

- Saul found a medium in the town of Endor and told her to bring Samuel from the dead.

- The medium conjured up Samuel's spirit. Samuel informed Saul that the Philistines would defeat Israel in the upcoming battle. Samuel said Saul and his sons would die the next day.

- The following day, the Philistines attacked Israel and slaughtered them. Jonathan and his brothers were killed in the battle and Saul was wounded. Saul did not want to be captured by the Philistines, so he fell on his own sword and died.

RECOMMENDED BIBLE READING

1 Samuel 11:1–15	**Saul Reaffirmed as Israel's King**
1 Samuel 13:1–15	**Samuel Chastises Saul**
1 Samuel 15:1–34	**God's Spirit Leaves Saul**
Romans 3:1–20	**Sin and the Law**

SECTION 4: KING DAVID

David, King of Israel: (2 Samuel 1–6; 1 Chronicles 11–16)

- When David learned of Saul's and Jonathan's deaths, he grieved for them.

- The tribe of Judah made David their king in Hebron. Ish-bosheth, Saul's son, became king over the other tribes of Israel.

- Seven years later, Ish-bosheth was assassinated and the people made David king over all the tribes of Israel.

- David fought the Jebusites for possession of Jerusalem and won. After his victory, he moved the capital from Hebron to Jerusalem.

- David later had the Ark of the Covenant moved to Jerusalem. As the Ark came into the city, all of Israel celebrated as David danced before the Lord.

God's Covenant With David: (2 Samuel 7–10; 1 Chronicles 17–19)

- During a time of peace, David called Nathan, the prophet, and told him that he wanted to build a temple for the Ark of the Covenant.

- Nathan told David to go ahead, but the Lord spoke to Nathan and told him David was not to build the Temple. David's job was to fight and establish the nation. One of David's sons would build the Temple.

 Note: We learn in 1 Chronicles 28:3 that God did not want David to build the Temple because he was a warrior and had caused much bloodshed.

- God told Nathan that He would establish a covenant with David. The Lord promised David would have a dynasty and a kingdom forever.

 God's covenant with David was fulfilled with the birth of Jesus Christ, who was a descendant of King David and whose kingdom is everlasting.

"... I will raise up your offspring to succeed you, who will come from your own body, and I will establish his kingdom ... and I will establish the throne of his kingdom forever" (2 Samuel 7:12, 13 NIV).

- When Nathan told David about God's covenant, David humbled himself before the Lord and gave God the glory and the praise.

- David fought many battles against the Philistines and Israel's other enemies. He sought the Lord's advice and won his battles. Israel's borders were greatly expanded as a result of David's victories.

- David was a just king. He was also very gracious to Jonathan's crippled son, Mephibosheth. He returned all of Saul's property to Mephibosheth and arranged for him to eat at the king's table like one of his own sons.

David Commits Adultery with Bathsheba: (2 Samuel 11–12)

- When Israel went to war against the Ammonites, David chose to stay in Jerusalem rather than fight on the battlefield. David sent Joab, the army commander, to lead Israel's troops into battle.

- One day, as David strolled on the palace rooftop, he saw a beautiful woman named Bathsheba, who was married to a man named Uriah. David sent for Bathsheba and slept with her.

- When David learned Bathsheba was pregnant with his child, he sent for Uriah, Bathsheba's husband, who was out on the battlefield. David wanted Uriah to sleep with his wife, but Uriah would not go home out of respect for the other men who were still on the battlefield.

- David sent Uriah back to camp with a note instructing Joab to put Uriah on the front line, where the fighting was intense.

- Joab did just as David requested, and Uriah died in battle. Afterwards, David married Bathsheba. A son was born to them, but God was not pleased.

- David had committed adultery and arranged for Uriah to be killed. According to Jewish law, both acts were punishable by death. Nathan, the prophet, confronted David and said his family would be in constant turmoil because of his sin.

- Nathan told David that the Lord God said, *"And now, because you treated God with such contempt and took Uriah the Hittite's wife as your wife, killing and murder will continually plague your family . . ."* (2 Samuel 12:10 MSG).

- David confessed. The Lord forgave him, but there were consequences. Soon afterwards, the child born to David and Bathsheba became sick and died.

David's Son, Absalom, Rebels Against Him: (2 Samuel 13–20)

- David's son, Amnon, raped Tamar, his half-sister. When David heard about the incident, he was upset but did nothing about it.

- Meanwhile, another of David's sons, Absalom, who was Tamar's full brother, waited for an opportunity to avenge his sister.

- Two years later, Absalom hosted a dinner for his brothers, David's sons. While there, Absalom had his men kill Amnon and then he left Jerusalem. David mourned for Amnon.

- David never tried to get in touch with Absalom. Joab, David's army commander, finally arranged for Absalom's return, but David refused to see him. Joab interceded again and the two were seemingly reconciled.

- Four years later, Absalom led a rebellion against David, forcing David and those loyal to him to leave the palace. Absalom took over the kingdom and slept with his father's concubines.

- As David's men prepared for battle against Absalom and Israel's army, David instructed his commanders to spare Absalom's life.

- During the battle, Absalom's long hair got caught in a tree. While he was dangling in the air, Joab ignored David's instructions and killed Absalom.

- David mourned bitterly for Absalom. He returned to Jerusalem and was eventually reinstated as king.

David's Final Years: (2 Samuel 24; 1 Kings 1:1–2:12; Chronicles 21–29)

- David took a census, which displeased the Lord. Afterwards, he confessed his sin and the Lord forgave him, but not without consequences.

 Note: The Bible does not tell us why the census was displeasing to God. David's actions might have been prideful, arrogant, or lacked faith in God's sight. God looks at the heart and knows our thoughts.

- Because of David's sin, God sent a plague that killed 70,000 people. Then, the Lord told David to buy a threshing floor and build an altar there. David did as he was told, and the plague ended.

- David decided the Temple should be built at the same place where the altar had been erected, which had previously been a threshing floor.

- David told his son, Solomon, God wanted him (Solomon) to build the Temple during a time of peace. Although Solomon would later build the Temple, David made all the preparations.

- David donated large quantities of gold and other materials for construction of the Temple and arranged for skilled men to perform the work. He outlined the duties of the Levites and priests and gave Solomon his plans for the Temple.

- David was getting up in age, so his attendants found a beautiful young girl named Abishag to serve as his nurse.

- Adonijah, one of David's sons, decided he should be the next king. Adonijah tried to take over the kingdom from his aged father.

- Nathan, the prophet, and Bathsheba spoke to David about his plans for a successor. David officially named Solomon as the next king of Israel.

- David was seventy years old when he died. He had reigned for forty years: seven years as king of Judah and thirty-three years as king of Israel.

 God used David as a savior. David fought numerous battles and saved Israel from their enemies. The kingdom of Israel was firmly established under his leadership. David is credited with writing 73 of the 150 Psalms recorded in the Bible. Psalms were written as poetry to be sung as an expression of praise, worship, supplication, thanksgiving, and confession to God. David wrote many Psalms while he was running from Saul.

Some of David's Psalms included prophecies about Jesus Christ. In Psalm 23, one of his most recognized psalms, David called God, *Jehovah-Raah*, which means, *The LORD Is My Shepherd*. Jesus is the Good Shepherd (John 10:11); the Great Shepherd (Hebrews 13:20); and the Head Shepherd (1 Peter 5:4).

Note: "Jehovah-Raah" is the Hebrew name of God as Shepherd. Jehovah-Raah is the One who takes care of all the needs of His flock. He feeds, calms, leads, renews, guides, accompanies, protects, comforts, befriends, invites, welcomes, and much more.

RECOMMENDED BIBLE READING

2 Samuel 7:1–27 **God's Covenant with David**

2 Samuel 11:1–12:24 **David Commits Adultery with Bathsheba**

1 Chronicles 22:1–18 **Preparations for the Temple**

Hebrews 11:30–40 **Israel's Faith**

SECTION 5: KING SOLOMON

Solomon, King of Israel: (1 Kings 2:13–4:34; 2 Chronicles 1)

- After Solomon took over the kingdom, Adonijah wanted Solomon to give him Abishag, David's young nurse, as his wife. Adonijah asked Bathsheba to make the request for him.

- When Solomon heard the request, he had Adonijah put to death because he thought Adonijah was plotting to take the throne away from him.

- One night, the Lord appeared to Solomon in a dream and told him to ask for whatever he wanted. Solomon asked the Lord for wisdom and understanding to govern the people.

- God was pleased Solomon asked for wisdom. He granted Solomon's request and gave him great riches and honor as well.

Solomon Builds the Temple: (1 Kings 5–8; 2 Chronicles 2–7)

- Israel was at peace during Solomon's reign. Solomon implemented his father's plans and built the Temple in seven years. He also built a palace for himself, completing it in thirteen years.

- When the Temple was finished, Solomon instructed the priests to carry the Ark of the Covenant into the Temple's Most Holy Place.

- Solomon gathered the people in front of the altar and dedicated the Temple in a prayer to the Lord. Then Solomon and the people offered sacrifices to God and celebrated.

- God again appeared to Solomon and told him that his prayers at the Temple had been heard. God consecrated the Temple and admonished Solomon to obey and serve the Lord always.

Solomon's Greatness and Downfall: (1 Kings 9–11; 2 Chronicles 8–9)

- After the Temple and the palace were built, Solomon focused on other building projects and commerce. He also built numerous alliances with other nations.

- Solomon became well known in other countries for his wisdom. On one occasion the Queen of Sheba made a pilgrimage to Jerusalem to see if Solomon was as wise as she had heard.

- She asked plenty of tough questions and he answered them all. She soon discovered the reports about Solomon's wisdom were true.

- Solomon was blessed with great riches, and he accumulated vast amounts of wealth.

- Solomon married women from pagan nations even though God had warned about such marriages. He had 700 wives and 300 concubines, most of whom served idol gods.

- Solomon allowed his wives to bring idolatry with them to Israel. Eventually they turned him away from God. He even worshiped their idol gods.

- The Lord was displeased with Solomon. He told him the kingdom would be taken away from him and that he would be left with only one tribe for David's sake.

- During the later years of Solomon's reign, he had several enemies. A man named Jeroboam, who had been in charge of Solomon's workforce, rebelled against him.

- Solomon tried to kill Jeroboam, but he fled to Egypt and stayed there until after Solomon's death.

- Solomon was king of Israel for forty years and then he died. His son, Rehoboam, succeeded him as king.

 Solomon's wisdom personified that of Jesus Christ, *"in whom are hidden all the treasures of wisdom and knowledge"* (Colossians 2:3). Solomon wrote Proverbs, a compilation of words of wisdom for daily living; Ecclesiastes, a book in which Solomon expresses how empty and futile life is without God; and *Song of Solomon* (Song of Songs), a love story about the joys of love in marriage.

RECOMMENDED BIBLE READING

2 Samuel 7:1–27 **God's Covenant with David**

1 Kings 8:22–66 **Solomon Dedicates the Temple**

1 Kings 11:1–13 **Solomon Turns Away from God**

Romans 3:21–31 **All Have Sinned**

MEDITATION & PRAYER

David wrote Psalm 51 after Nathan confronted him about committing adultery with Bathsheba:

"Have mercy on me, O God,
  because of your unfailing love.

Because of your great compassion,
  blot out the stain of my sins.

Wash me clean from my guilt.
  Purify me from my sin.

Create in me a clean heart, O God.
  Renew a loyal spirit within me.

Do not banish me from your presence,
  and don't take your Holy Spirit from me.

Restore to me the joy of your salvation,
  and make me willing to obey you."

(Psalm 51:1–2; 10–12)

O Lord My God,

Have mercy on me! Shower me with Your unfailing love. Cleanse me and make me pure in Your sight. Refine my rough edges and help me to walk upright before You. Don't remove me from Your presence or take Your Spirit from me. Restore my joy. I will rejoice in You, O Lord, always!

Amen

REVIEW QUESTIONS

1. The Book of Ruth tells the story of the kinsman-redeemer. What is a kinsman-redeemer? Who is our kinsman-redeemer?

_____

_____

_____

_____

_____

_____

2. How was Ruth related to Jesus Christ?

_____

_____

_____

_____

_____

_____

3. God chose Samuel to be Israel's spiritual leader during the latter years of the period of the judges. What role did Samuel play in Israel's history?

_____

_____

_____

_____

_____

_____

4. Saul was Israel's first king. What was his downfall? What sins did he commit?

_____

_____

_____

_____

_____

_____

5. David was Israel's second king. Describe his character and accomplishments.

_____

_____

_____

_____

_____

_____

6. What sin(s) did David commit? What were the consequences of his sin(s)?

_____

_____

_____

_____

_____

_____

7. Solomon was Israel's third king. What were his accomplishments and downfall?

_____

_____

_____

_____

_____

_____

_____

PERSONAL REFLECTIONS

8. Samuel told Saul that obedience to God is far better than sacrifice. Why is it better to obey God than to sacrifice? How does God view our good deeds and services when we fail to obey Him?

_____

_____

_____

_____

_____

_____

9. Saul pursued David with a vengeance, but David prevailed. What did you learn from David about handling tough times?

_____

_____

_____

_____

_____

_____

10. What problems existed between David and his sons? How could David have improved his relationship with his son(s)?

_____

_____

_____

_____

_____

11. How are your relationships with family members? Are any in need of improvement? What steps can you take to improve your relationships with family members?

_____

_____

_____

_____

_____

12. Read Ecclesiastes 1:1–18. Solomon says that everything is meaningless. How would you respond to Solomon if he were living today? What would make your life more meaningful? What steps can you take today towards experiencing a more meaningful life?

_____

_____

_____

_____

_____

_____

_____

13. What did God reveal to you about His character through His Hebrew names, *Jehovah-Sabaoth and Jehovah-Raah*?

_____

_____

_____

_____

_____

_____

_____

CLOSING PRAYER

The Apostle Paul reminds us to put on the full armor of God:

"Finally, be strong in the Lord and in his mighty power. Put on the full armor of God so that you can take your stand against the devil's schemes. For our struggle is not against flesh and blood, but against the rulers, against the authorities, against the powers of this dark world and against the spiritual forces of evil in the heavenly realms. Therefore put on the full armor of God, so that when the day of evil comes, you may be able to stand your ground, and after you have done everything, to stand."

(Ephesians 6:10–13 NIV)

Heavenly Father,

You are Jehovah-Raah, the Great Shepherd, who takes care of all my needs. I want to be strong in You and well-protected. Reveal Yourself to me and teach me to put on the full armor of God so that I can stand against the devil's strategies and schemes. Strengthen me in my weaknesses and help me to persevere. Show me the areas in my life that are vulnerable to attack. I want to be fully equipped and ready so that when temptations come, I will be able to stand my ground.

Amen

CHAPTER 7

THE DIVIDED KINGDOM

OPENING PRAYER

Dear God,

Teach me through Your Spirit as I read about how the kingdom of Israel was divided and then came to an end. I pray for unity, harmony, and peace around the world. I pray for spiritual awakening and renewal. I pray that our leaders will look to You for guidance, wisdom, and understanding. Keep us safe and well-protected with our minds and hearts focused on You.

Amen

CHAPTER SUMMARY

THE DIVIDED KINGDOM

(1 Kings 12–22, 2 Kings 1–16, 2 Chronicles 10–27)
(Isaiah, Hosea, Joel, Amos, Obadiah, Jonah, Micah, Nahum, and Zephaniah)

After King Solomon's death, his son Rehoboam succeeded him as king. Soon afterwards, the people asked Rehoboam for relief from the heavy taxes imposed by his father. He refused. As a result, ten tribes revolted and two separate nations were formed. The ten revolting tribes joined together and were called the Northern Kingdom of Israel with Jeroboam as their king. Jeroboam was a former palace official who rebelled against Solomon. The tribes of Judah and Benjamin kept Rehoboam as their king and were known as the Southern Kingdom of Judah.

Jeroboam, the first king of the Northern Kingdom, introduced idolatry to Israel early in his reign to keep his subjects from traveling to Jerusalem for worship. All of Israel's kings after Jeroboam were ungodly and continued to uphold the practice of idolatry. There were twenty kings and nine dynasties in the Northern Kingdom of Israel over a period of about 200 years.

The Southern Kingdom of Judah had twenty kings over a period of about 300 years, but only one dynasty. All were descendants of King David. A few of Judah's kings served the Lord God, but many of them were ungodly and led the people of Judah into idolatry.

Despicable forms of idolatry, which included prostitution, sex orgies, and child sacrifice as part of religious worship, were eventually introduced in Israel and in Judah. Both nations became entrenched in these evil practices, and the people lost their sense of morality and decency. God sent prophets again and again to urge the people to turn away from idolatry and come back to the Lord. Sadly, the people refused to listen to the prophets.

	Approximate Timeline	Location	Biblical Scriptures	Author
Division and Early Years	930 B.C.–848 B.C.	Israel & Judah	1 Kings 12– 2 Kings 2 2 Chronicles 10–20	Unknown Ezra
Idolatry Judged	848 B.C.–835 B.C.	Israel & Judah	2 Kings 2–11 2 Chronicles 21–23	Unknown Ezra
Call to Righteousness	835 B.C.–750 B.C.	Israel & Judah	2 Kings 12–14 2 Chronicles 24–25	Unknown Ezra
Israel's Final Years	750 B.C.–722 B.C.	Israel & Judah	2 Kings 15–17 2 Chronicles 26–28	Unknown Ezra
Judah's Final Years	721 B.C.–608 B.C.	Judah	2 Kings 18–23 2 Chronicles 29–35	Unknown Ezra

MAP OF KEY LOCATIONS

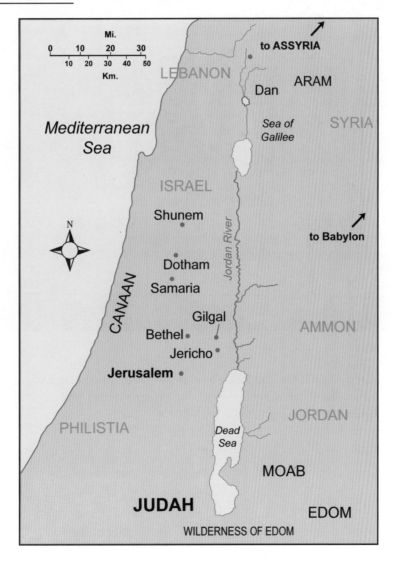

ELIJAH

"It was almost time for the LORD to take Elijah by a whirlwind up into heaven. . . . As they were walking and talking, a chariot and horses of fire appeared and separated Elijah from Elisha. Then Elijah went up to heaven in a whirlwind." (2 Kings 2:1, 11 NCV)

Section 1: Division & Early Years

Northern Kingdom Kings of Israel	Date B.C.	Southern Kingdom Kings of Judah	Date B.C.	Prophets	Date B.C.
Jeroboam I (Ungodly)	930–909	Rehoboam (Mostly Ungodly)	930–913		
Nadab (Ungodly)	909–908	Abijah (Mostly Ungodly) aka Abijam	913–910		
Baasha (Ungodly)	908–886	Asa (Mostly Godly)	910–869		
Elah (Ungodly)	886–885				
Zimri (Ungodly)	885				
Omri (Ungodly)	885–874				
Ahab (Most Ungodly)	874–853	Jehoshaphat (Godly)	872–848	Elijah	875–848
Ahaziah (Ungodly)	853–852				

Jeroboam Becomes King of Israel; Rehoboam Is King of Judah: (1 Kings 12–14; 2 Chronicles 10–12)

- During King Solomon's reign, the people were heavily taxed to pay for his numerous building and commercial projects. When Rehoboam succeeded his father as king, the people asked for tax relief.

- Rehoboam's response was a harsh refusal, so ten tribes revolted. They seceded from the kingdom, and two separate nations were formed.

- The ten revolting tribes became the Northern Kingdom of Israel and made Jeroboam, who rebelled against Solomon, their king.

- The other two tribes, Judah and Benjamin, remained loyal to Rehoboam and became the Southern Kingdom of Judah.

- After Jeroboam became king of the Northern Kingdom (Israel), he did not want his subjects worshiping at the Temple in Jerusalem, for fear they might change their minds and reunite with the Southern Kingdom (Judah).

- Jeroboam made two golden calves. He placed one in Bethel and the other in Dan, cities located in Israel. He then commanded his subjects to worship his man-made idols instead of worshiping at the Temple in Jerusalem.

- Jeroboam led Israel into idolatry. He is repeatedly referred to in Scripture as the man, who *". . . sinned and made Israel sin along with him"* (1 Kings 14:16).

- The Levites, priests, and people who remained faithful to God were forced to leave their homes in the Northern Kingdom (Israel) and move to Jerusalem.

- Solomon's son, Rehoboam of the Southern Kingdom (Judah), abandoned the Lord until Judah was attacked by the Egyptians.

- When the Egyptians attacked, Rehoboam humbled himself before God and the kingdom was spared. The Egyptians took many of the Temple treasures, but did not destroy Jerusalem.

- Rehoboam was king of Judah for seventeen years and then he died; Abijah, his son, became king.

Abijah Becomes King of Judah: (1 Kings 15:1–8; 2 Chronicles 13)

- Abijah became king of Judah while Jeroboam was still reigning as king of Israel. Rehoboam, Abijah's father, had battled with Jeroboam and Israel throughout his entire reign, so when Abijah succeeded his father as king, the fighting continued.

- Abijah was not fully devoted to the Lord, but during a battle with Israel in which his forces were outnumbered two to one, Abijah called on God for help. The Lord answered, and Judah won the battle.

- Abijah reigned for three years and then died. His son, Asa, became king of Judah.

Asa Becomes King of Judah; Nadab and Baasha Are Kings of Israel: (1 Kings 15:9–33; 2 Chronicles 14–16)

- When Asa became king, he destroyed the idol gods and led the people back to the Lord. He deposed his grandmother from her position as queen mother because she practiced idolatry.

- Jeroboam, king of Israel, died and his son, Nadab, succeeded him as king. Jeroboam had reigned in Israel for twenty-two years. Nadab was ungodly like his father. During his second year as king, Nadab was assassinated by a man named Baasha.

- Baasha took over the kingdom. When his position as king was secure, he killed Jeroboam's entire family. Baasha was another ungodly king of Israel.

- Baasha continued the battles against Judah during his reign. Eventually Asa, King of Judah, made a deal with Ben-Hadad, King of Aram. Ben-Hadad partnered with Asa and forced Baasha to withdraw.

 Note: The ancient land of Aram included what is now Lebanon, Syria, parts of Israel, and Jordan. The Arameans were for the most part enemies of both Israel and Judah.

- A prophet told Asa afterwards that the Lord was not pleased with him because he had relied on the king of Aram for help instead of fully trusting God. This angered King Asa, so he put the prophet in prison.

Elah, Zimri, and Omri, Kings of Israel: (1 Kings 16:1–28)

- Baasha reigned as king of Israel for twenty-four years and then he died. His son Elah succeeded him as king of Israel.

- Elah reigned two years and then was assassinated by Zimri, one of his officials. Zimri made himself king of Israel and proceeded to kill all the members of Baasha's family.

- Zimri was king for seven days when Omri, commander of Israel's army, was proclaimed king of Israel by those in his camp.

- Israel's army attacked the town where Zimri was living. When Zimri saw what was happening, he set the town on fire and died in the fire.

- Half the people of Israel wanted a man named Tibni to be king, but Omri's supporters prevailed. Omri became king of Israel and reigned for twelve years.

- King Omri bought the hill of Samaria and made it the capital city. He, as did all the kings of Israel, served idol gods and was evil in the sight of the Lord.

- When Omri died, his son, Ahab, succeeded him as king of Israel. Shortly afterwards, King Asa of Judah became ill.

- King Asa did not seek the Lord for his healing, but rather consulted with his physicians. Two years later, Asa died. His son Jehoshaphat succeeded him as king of Judah. King Asa had reigned in Judah for forty-one years.

Ahab, King of Israel: (1 Kings 16:29–34)

- King Ahab reigned over the Northern Kingdom from the city of Samaria. He was Israel's most wicked king. Ahab was married to Jezebel. Together they led Israel into Baal worship, one of the vilest forms of idolatry.

 Note: Israel continued to worship the golden idol calves that Jeroboam set up in Bethel and Dan. However, Ahab and Jezebel promoted worship to the idol god, Baal, and his goddess wife, Ashtoreth. Baal worship was a demoralizing form of idolatry. It incorporated prostitution and wild, group-sex parties as part of worship. Children were routinely killed in sacrifice to Baal.

God Sends the Prophet Elijah to Israel: (1 Kings 17–19)

- The Lord sent the prophet Elijah to denounce the practice of Baal worship.

The Role of the Prophet: God divinely chose prophets to remind the people of their covenant with Him. The Lord communicated with the prophets through visions, dreams, angels, and at times audibly. They delivered God's message to the people. There were numerous false prophets. Scripture tells us that a prophet is not from God if what he proclaims does not happen. We know *God* sent the prophets of the Bible because their prophecies always came true. (Deuteronomy 18:22; 2 Peter 1:20)

Prophets instructed the people to obey God's laws. They pointed out sin, urged the people to return to God, and warned about the consequences of sin. The prophet's job was difficult. His message was often not well received, and his life was in danger whenever the message became too distasteful.

The prophets are often categorized as major and minor prophets. It is important to keep in mind that the terms "major" and "minor" are a reference to the size of the prophet's book and not the significance of its content. Although the major prophets wrote more Scripture, the minor prophets' writings are equally important as those of the major prophets.

God often inspired the prophets to reveal future events. Many prophesied about the coming of the "Messiah," a Hebrew word which is translated as "Christ" in Greek, and "Anointed One" in English. These prophecies are referred to as Messianic Prophecies.

- The prophet Elijah told King Ahab there would be no rain in Israel until he (Elijah) declared it would rain again.

- After delivering God's message, Elijah left. He was fed by ravens and drank water from a brook. When the brook dried up, God instructed Elijah to go to a widow's house and ask for some bread.

- When Elijah arrived, the widow was down to her last cup of flour. The Lord miraculously increased her supply of flour so it never ran out.

- The widow's son died. He was miraculously brought back to life through the prophet Elijah's prayers.

- After three years, the drought and famine in Samaria had become severe, so God told Elijah it was time to confront Ahab.

- Elijah went to a man named Obadiah and told him to tell Ahab that he wanted to meet with him. Obadiah had hidden one hundred of God's prophets when Jezebel ordered they all be killed.

Note: It is unknown whether this Obadiah was the author of the book of Obadiah. Most references state the book of Obadiah was either written during the time period of the prophets Elijah and Elisha or sometime during the prophet Jeremiah's ministry.

- Elijah met with Ahab and challenged him to a contest that would determine who was most powerful—the idol god Baal—or the Lord God.

- Elijah said the god who set the altar on fire in response to prayer would be declared the One True God.

- Ahab accepted the challenge. The prophets of Baal prayed and did everything they could to get the idol god to answer, but there was no response.

- After the prophets of Baal had prayed all day long, Elijah began to mock them.

- Elijah told the people to pour water on the altar three times. He then prayed to God and immediately fire flashed down from heaven onto the altar.

- Elijah told the people to seize the prophets of Baal. When the prophets of Baal had been captured, Elijah killed them. Shortly afterwards, Elijah prayed for rain and it finally rained again throughout the land.

- When Ahab told Jezebel that Elijah had killed the prophets of Baal, she threatened to kill Elijah.

- Fearing for his life, Elijah ran away. He became very depressed and asked God to take his life.

- An angel of the Lord appeared to Elijah and gave him food. It strengthened Elijah, and he traveled to Mount Sinai, the mountain of God.

- There the Lord God spoke to Elijah and asked, *"What are you doing here, Elijah?"* (1 Kings 19:9b NIV).

- Elijah responded to the Lord, saying the people had killed all the true prophets of God and now he (Elijah) was the only one left.

- The Lord God spoke to Elijah in a gentle whisper and told him to anoint Hazael as king of Aram, anoint Jehu as king of Israel, and anoint Elisha as his assistant.

- The Lord told Elijah that these three, Hazael, Jehu, and Elisha, would execute His righteous judgment on Israel.

- Israel had become an abomination to God because of their practices of Baal worship and other forms of idolatry.

- God revealed to Elijah that there were 7,000 others in Israel who had never worshiped Baal.

- Elijah left and found Elisha, who became his traveling companion and faithful assistant.

Jehoshaphat, King of Judah: (1 Kings 22; 2 Chronicles 17–19)

- While Ahab reigned in Israel, Jehoshaphat was king of Judah. He was a good king who served the One True God.

- Jehoshaphat sent the Levites, priests, and other men of God throughout Judah to minister and teach the people on the laws of Moses.

- King Jehoshaphat made peace with Israel and arranged for his son to marry one of evil King Ahab's daughters. Later, he entered into an alliance with Ahab and they fought together against the nation of Aram.

- King Jehoshaphat was wounded in this battle. He called on the Lord, and God helped him. When Jehoshaphat returned to Jerusalem, a man of God chastised him for aligning himself with evil King Ahab.

- During this same battle, Ahab was wounded and died. His son, Ahaziah, took over his kingdom.

Ahaziah, King of Israel: (2 Kings 1)

- Shortly after Ahaziah became king of Israel, he fell and seriously injured himself. He wanted to know if he would recover, so he sent men to the temple of Baal to get the answer.

- Elijah met with King Ahaziah and asked why he was inquiring about this from Baal. Elijah asked Ahaziah, *"Don't you believe there's a God in Israel?"* (2 Kings 1:16 CEV).

- Elijah told Ahaziah he would not recover because of this sin. Shortly afterwards, King Ahaziah died. King Ahaziah had no sons, so his brother, Joram, became king of Israel.

King Jehoshaphat's Prayer: (2 Chronicles 20)

- One day, King Jehoshaphat of Judah learned the armies of Moab, Ammon, and Edom had declared war against him.

- Jehoshaphat called the people of Judah together and led them in a solemn prayer to the Lord.

- The Lord answered Jehoshaphat's prayers. God fought Judah's battle. When Judah's army reached the battlefield, they found their enemies had turned on each other and were all lying dead on the ground.

 Note: King Jehoshaphat's prayer is a model prayer that is well worth reading. It is recorded in 2 Chronicles 20:1–30.

- After this, Jehoshaphat's kingdom was at peace. He reigned for twenty-five years as one of the good kings of Judah, and then he died. His oldest son, Jehoram, succeeded him as king.

Elijah Taken Into Heaven: (2 Kings 2:1–18)

- Later, Elijah and Elisha were walking together when Elijah asked Elisha what he could do for him before God took him away. Elisha replied, *"Let me inherit a double portion of your spirit"* (2 Kings 2:9 NIV).

- Elijah told Elisha his request would be answered if he (Elisha) saw him (Elijah) when he was taken away.

- Suddenly, a chariot of fire hitched to horses of fire separated the two men. Elijah was carried up into heaven in a whirlwind.

- Elisha saw it and he became Elijah's successor as one of God's great prophets.

 The prophet Elijah: Elijah was sent as God's representative to confront and challenge Israel about Baal worship, a despicable form of idolatry practiced in Israel during the reign of King Ahab. Both Elijah and Jesus came to deliver God's message. They confronted sin and were rejected by the people.

RECOMMENDED BIBLE READING

1 Kings 18:1–19:22 **The Prophet Elijah**

Matthew 17:1–13 **Elijah Appears When Jesus Is Transfigured**

Romans 11:1–24 **God's Mercy for Israel**

SECTION 2: IDOLATRY JUDGED

Northern Kingdom Kings of Israel	Date B.C.	Southern Kingdom Kings of Judah	Date B.C.	Prophets	Date B.C.
Joram (Ungodly)	853–841	Jehoram (Ungodly)	848–841	Obadiah	855–840 (?)
		Ahaziah (Ungodly)	841	Elisha	848–797
Jehu (Mostly Ungodly)	841–814	Athaliah (Ungodly Queen)	841–835		

The Prophet Elisha's Miracles: (2 Kings 2:19–25, 4:1–5:19)

- The prophet Elisha performed numerous miracles for the needy. When men from Jericho came and told him the water in a nearby spring had become contaminated, Elisha miraculously purified the water.

- Next, a widow needed to pay her late-husband's debt. Elisha told her to take a flask of olive oil and pour the oil into as many jars as she could borrow. The widow did as Elisha said, and the oil in the flask miraculously multiplied.

- The widow filled many jars with more olive oil than originally in the flask. Elisha then told her to sell the oil and use the money to pay her debts.

- Elisha later wanted to show his gratitude to a woman from the town of Shunem who had been kind to him and his assistant.

- When Elisha heard the woman had no children, he told her she would soon have a child. The woman thought it was impossible, but she did have a son the following year just as Elisha had prophesied.

- The woman's son became ill and died. Elisha came and miraculously brought her son back to life.

- Elisha performed several miracles during a period of famine so people would have food to eat. He turned a pot of poison stew into edible food, and fed a number of people with a few loaves of bread.

- The commander of Aram's army was a man named Naaman, who was ill with leprosy. Naaman learned Elisha could heal him. He went to see the prophet.

- When Naaman arrived, Elisha sent a messenger to tell Naaman he should wash seven times in the Jordan River. Naaman thought this was absurd, but his officers convinced him to try it anyway.

- When Naaman washed in the Jordan River as Elisha had instructed, his skin was restored and he was healed.

Elisha and Aram's Army: (2 Kings 6:8–8:15)

- During this time period, the nation of Aram was at war with Israel; however, every time Aram's army mobilized to attack Israel, Elisha would warn Israel's king and frustrate the king of Aram's plans.

- When the king of Aram learned it was Elisha who was foiling his plans, he sent his army to the city where Elisha lived.

- Elisha's assistant became terrified when he saw Aram's army surrounding the city. Elisha prayed, and the Lord allowed Elisha's assistant to see the mighty (invisible) heavenly army prepared to fight on Elisha's side.

- Elisha prayed again and Aram's army became blind. Elisha led them to the king of Israel, who, following Elisha's instructions, sent them home.

- The king of Aram mobilized his army again and laid siege to Samaria so that no one could come or go. As a result of the siege, Samaria's food supply ran out and the people were starving to death.

- The king of Israel sent an officer to Elisha. When the officer arrived, Elisha told him there would be plenty of flour and grain available for sale at an inexpensive price in Samaria's marketplace by the same time the next day.

- The officer did not believe Elisha and said it was impossible. Elisha told the officer that he would live to see it happen, but would not eat any of it.

- Overnight, the Aramean army became confused and thought they were being attacked by multiple armies. They abandoned their camp and fled.

- When Israel's scouts went to see what had happened, they found the food and clothing the Arameans had left behind. They reported their findings, and the people of Samaria rushed out to plunder the abandoned camp.

- The officer in charge of the city gates was knocked down and trampled to death as the people rushed out to plunder the camp. It was the officer who had told Elisha that what he had said was impossible.

- Elisha's words had come true. Flour and grain were sold in Samaria at a low price that day. The officer lived to see it, but did not live to eat any of it.

- Afterwards, Ben-Hadad, King of Aram, was assassinated by Hazael, one of his officials. Hazael became the next king of Aram. This set in motion God's plan to execute judgment on Israel as God had revealed to Elijah.

 The Prophet Elisha: Elisha was Elijah's assistant. When Elijah was taken into heaven, Elisha succeeded him as a mighty prophet of God. Both Elisha and Jesus Christ came teaching the Word of God, helping the needy, and performing mighty miracles in the name of God.

Joram, King of Israel and Jehoram, King of Judah: (2 Kings 3:2, 8:16–24; 2 Chronicles 21)

- Joram was king of Israel while Jehoram was king of Judah. Joram ruled for twelve years and was evil, but not as evil as his parents, Ahab and Jezebel.

- Jehoram, Jehoshaphat's son, did not follow the Lord as his father did.

- Jehoram was married to Ahab's daughter. His reign was like that of Israel's ungodly kings. When his position as king was secure, he killed all his brothers and led Judah into idolatry.

- During King Jehoram's reign, the nation of Edom was part of the kingdom of Judah. However, the Edomites revolted against Judah and became a free nation with their own king.

 Note: The Edomites were descendants of Esau and inhabited an area that is now southern Israel and parts of Jordan.

- Although the Edomites were related to Israel and Judah through Jacob's brother, Esau, they constantly feuded with the Jews. The Lord sent the prophet Obadiah to deliver a message to the Edomites.

The Prophet Obadiah: The time period of Obadiah's ministry is uncertain. However, Biblical scholars believe that it was either during the period of Jehoram's reign in about 845 B.C. or much later during Jeremiah's ministry in about 590 B.C. Obadiah delivered to the people of Edom God's message that He was not pleased with their constant attacks against the Jews. Also, Edom had become proud as they feuded with Israel and Judah. Obadiah pronounced God's judgment against Edom for their pride and harassment of the Jews.

The Book of Obadiah is the shortest book in the Old Testament and records God's judgment against Edom. Both Obadiah and Jesus Christ delivered God's message of judgment against sin.

- Jehoram was king of Judah for eight years. Then he died from an intestinal disease. His son Ahaziah succeeded him as king.

Ahaziah, King of Judah: (2 Kings 8:25–9:29; 2 Chronicles 22:1–9)

- Ahaziah's mother was Athaliah, daughter of Ahab and Jezebel. He heeded Ahab's family's advice and continued the practice of idolatry in Judah.

- The prophet Elisha arranged for one of his fellow prophets to anoint Jehu, a commanding officer in Israel's army, to be king of Israel.

- The prophet found Jehu and told him God had called him (Jehu) to kill every member of Ahab's family. Jehu would then become king of Israel.

- The Lord had previously told both Elijah and Elisha that his righteous judgment would be executed through Jehu. King Hazael of Aram would finish the job in accordance with God's Word.

- Jehu found Joram, king of Israel, and killed him. Joram had reigned in Israel for eleven years. Jehu then killed King Ahaziah of Judah who was visiting Joram at the time.

Jehu Executes God's Judgment and Becomes King of Israel: (2 Kings 9:30–10:36)

- Jehu had Jezebel and all seventy of Ahab's sons killed. He then killed all of Ahab's relatives, friends, priests and assistants.

- Jehu killed all the prophets and worshipers of Baal. He destroyed the altar of Baal, the temple of Baal, and all traces of Baal worship in Israel.

- Jehu became king of Israel, but did not destroy the golden calves that King Jeroboam had placed in Bethel and Dan. While Jehu destroyed Baal worship, he continued to worship the idol calves instead of the One True God.

Athaliah, Queen of Judah: (2 Kings 11; 2 Chronicles 22:10–23:21)

- King Ahaziah of Judah reigned for one year before Jehu killed him.

- When Ahaziah's wicked mother, Athaliah, learned that her son was dead, she killed Ahaziah's sons (her grandsons) and took the throne of Judah for herself.

- Ahaziah's sister, who was married to Jehoiada the priest, hid Ahaziah's infant son, Joash, so Athaliah could not kill him.

- Joash remained hidden for six years. Then Jehoiada the priest organized a rebellion, and the wicked Queen Athaliah was killed.

- Joash, only seven years old, became king of Judah. Jehoiada the priest served as his advisor.

- Jehoiada the priest had the idol god Baal destroyed. He restored worship of the One True God in Judah.

RECOMMENDED BIBLE READING

2 Kings 4:1–7:20 **The Prophet Elisha's Miracles**
Luke 4:16–30 **Prophets Rejected in Their Own Hometown**

SECTION 3: CALL TO RIGHTEOUSNESS

Northern Kingdom Kings of Israel	Date B.C.	Southern Kingdom Kings of Judah	Date B.C.	Prophets	Date B.C.
Jehoahaz (Ungodly)	814–798	Joash (Godly - Changed to Ungodly)	835–796	Joel	835–796 (?)
Jehoash, aka Joash (Ungodly)	798–782	Amaziah (Mostly Godly)	796–767		
Jeroboam II (Ungodly)	793–753	Uzziah,	792–740	Jonah	793–753
		aka Azariah (Mostly Godly)		Amos	760–750
				Hosea	753–715

Joash, King of Judah: (2 Kings 12; 2 Chronicles 24)

- When Joash became king of Judah, King Jehu was still reigning in Israel.

- King Joash started his reign as one of the good kings of Judah. He ordered the renovation of the Temple in Jerusalem, which had been desecrated with Baal worship during the years wicked Queen Athaliah reigned in Judah.

- As long as Jehoiada the priest was living, Joash served the Lord.

- When Jehoiada died, the leaders of Judah convinced Joash to abandon God. They eventually led Joash and the nation of Judah into idolatry.

- When Jehoiada's son, Zechariah, warned the people about turning away from the Lord, King Joash ordered Zechariah's execution, even though Zechariah's father had been kind to Joash throughout his entire lifetime.

- King Joash's own officers assassinated him for ordering Zechariah's death.

- Joash reigned over Judah for forty years. His son Amaziah succeeded him as king.

- Judah became materially prosperous, but suffered spiritually from the ills of idolatry, immorality, and complacency.

- The Lord sent the prophet Joel to minister to the people.

The Prophet Joel: The time period of Joel's ministry is uncertain. However, scholars believe it most likely occurred from 835 B.C. to 796 B.C. If these dates are correct, Joel ministered in Judah during King Joash's reign. The Book of Joel was written to admonish the people of Judah about their complacency and to warn them about the impending Day of the Lord's Judgment. Joel urged the people to repent and come back to the Lord. He told them God is merciful and long-suffering. If they returned to God, they would be blessed and not punished.

Joel also prophesied that one day God's Spirit would be poured out on all people. Many years later, after Jesus' death and resurrection, the Apostle Peter addressed a crowd of people in Jerusalem on the Day of Pentecost. Peter told the crowd that the Holy Spirit had come just as Jesus promised, in fulfillment of the Scripture as written by the prophet Joel: *". . . In the last days, God says, I will pour out my Spirit on all people"* (Joel 2:28b; Acts 2:17 NIV).

Jehoahaz and Jehoash, Kings of Israel: (2 Kings 13)

- Jehu was king of Israel for twenty-eight years. His son, Jehoahaz, succeeded him. Jehoahaz continued the practice of idolatry in Israel just as his forefathers had before him.

- Throughout most of King Jehoahaz's reign, Israel was under heavy attack by King Hazael of Aram. King Hazael was harsh, making this a time of severe oppression in Israel.

- King Jehoahaz ruled seventeen years and then died. His son, Jehoash, became the next king of Israel. Jehoash was another ungodly king. During his reign, King Hazael of Aram died, bringing relief in Israel from the army of Aram.

- King Jehoash recovered several towns in Israel that had been captured by King Hazael of Aram. During this time, the wealthy in Israel were oppressing the poor.

Amaziah, King of Judah: (2 Kings 14:1–22, 2 Chronicles 25)

- Amaziah, King Joash's son, was king of Judah while King Jehoash reigned as king of Israel. King Amaziah served the Lord God, but not wholeheartedly.

- When Amaziah's position as king was secure, he killed the men who assassinated Joash, his father. After winning a major battle against the Edomites, Amaziah arrogantly challenged King Jehoash of Israel to a battle.

- King Jehoash of Israel mobilized his troops and captured King Amaziah. Jehoash went on to demolish a great section of the wall of Jerusalem and carried off gold and silver from the Temple.

- Jehoash reigned in Israel for sixteen years and he died. His son, Jeroboam II, became the next king of Israel.

Jeroboam II, King of Israel: (2 Kings 14:23–29)

- King Jeroboam II was another evil king of Israel who reigned while Amaziah was king of Judah. The prophets Jonah, Amos, and Hosea ministered during his reign.

 The Prophet Jonah: Jonah ministered while Jeroboam II was king of Israel. During this time, Assyria became a powerful and wicked nation. God told Jonah to go to Nineveh, the capital of Assyria, and tell the people to repent.

Jonah did not want to give the Assyrians an opportunity to repent because they were one of Israel's most dreaded enemies, so Jonah ran away in the opposite direction. The Lord had a way of getting Jonah's attention. God caused Jonah to be swallowed by a very large fish. Jonah was in the fish's belly for three days and three nights. Later, Jesus compared Jonah's experience to His own, saying, *"for as Jonah was three days and three nights in the belly of a huge fish, so the Son of Man will be three days and three nights in the heart of the earth . . . and now one greater than Jonah is here"* (Matthew 12:40, 41c NIV).

Jonah prayed. God delivered him from the fish's belly. Jonah went to Assyria and delivered God's message. The Assyrians repented and the Lord forgave them. God's message of mercy and grace was the same then as it is today. The Lord will forgive anyone who accepts His Plan of Redemption through Jesus Christ.

Note: Assyria was located in an area called Mesopotamia near the Tigris and Euphrates Rivers. The Mesopotamian region was located in modern day Iraq, eastern Syria, and southeastern Turkey. After Jonah delivered God's message, the Assyrians were repentant for a short time but then returned to their evil ways.

- King Amaziah reigned in Judah for twenty-five years and then he died. His son Uzziah became king of Judah while King Jeroboam II was reigning in Israel.

 The Prophet Amos: Amos was a shepherd in Judah whom God called to minister during the time of Jeroboam II's reign in Israel and Uzziah's reign in Judah. Amos boldly delivered God's message of impending judgment primarily to the nation of Israel. However, Amos started his book denouncing Israel's neighbors—the unrighteous nations of Aram, Philistia, Tyre, Edom, Ammon, and Moab. Then he turned his attention to the Jews, mightily pronouncing God's judgment on both Israel and Judah. Amos was relentless as he told Israel and Judah they had not learned from their past. He explained the reason for God's judgment was their failure to obey and serve the Lord God. Amos called upon the people to repent. He warned they would be captured and exiled by their enemies if they did not turn to God.

The message of the Book of Amos is that God requires righteousness and will judge unrighteousness. Nevertheless, the Book of Amos ends with hope as Amos tells of God's mercy and proclaims the eventual restoration of God's people. Our restoration has been made possible through Jesus Christ.

 The Prophet Hosea: Hosea began his ministry in Israel at a time when the nation was prospering outwardly but was in a state of serious moral decline under King Jeroboam II. The story of the prophet Hosea dramatically parallels the story of God's persistent love and compassion for the wayward nation of Israel. God commanded Hosea to marry a prostitute he knew would be unfaithful. Hosea's wife eventually left him. Hosea found his wife, paid for her release, and brought her back to live with him again. Just as Hosea redeemed his wife, Jesus Christ has redeemed us. He stands ready to reconcile us to God if we come to Him with a repentant heart.

The message of the Book of Hosea is that God is not pleased with sin, so judgment against sin is certain. God gives us ample opportunity to walk away from unrighteousness and follow Him. He pursues His people and is always ready to accept those whose hearts are repentant.

RECOMMENDED BIBLE READING

Jonah 1:1–4:11 **The Prophet Jonah**

Matthew 12:38–42 **Sign of the Prophet Jonah**

Romans 11:25–36 **God's Mercy for All People**

SECTION 4: ISRAEL'S FINAL YEARS

Northern Kingdom Kings of Israel	Date B.C.	Southern Kingdom Kings of Judah	Date B.C.	Prophets	Date B.C.
Jeroboam II (Ungodly)	793–753	Uzziah, aka Azariah (Mostly Godly)	792–740	Micah Isaiah	740–687 740–681
Zechariah (Ungodly)	753	Jotham (Godly)	750–735		
Shallum (Ungodly)	752				
Menahem (Ungodly)	752–742	Ahaz (Ungodly)	732–715		
Pekahiah (Ungodly)	742–740				
Pekah (Ungodly)	752–732				
Hoshea (Ungodly)	732–722				

Uzziah, King of Judah: (2 Kings 15:1–7; 2 Chronicles 26)

• Uzziah was king of Judah for fifty-two years. During the early years of his reign, Uzziah pleased the Lord. He became successful and powerful. This bolstered his ego, causing him to become prideful in later years.

• One day, Uzziah went into the Temple. Instead of letting the priests perform their sacred duty of burning incense at the altar, Uzziah did it himself. When confronted by the high priest, Uzziah became furious.

• Uzziah broke out with leprosy and had to be removed from the Temple. Uzziah lived in isolation for the rest of his life. His son, Jotham, was put in charge of the kingdom.

• King Uzziah had leprosy until the day he died; then Jotham became the next king of Judah. During this time, Isaiah was ministering in Judah.

Zechariah, Shallum, Menahem, Pekahiah, Pekah, Kings of Israel: (2 Kings 15:8–31)

• Jeroboam II was king for forty-one years and then he died. His son Zechariah became the next king of Israel.

• King Uzziah was reigning in Judah when Zechariah took the throne in Israel. Zechariah practiced idolatry, as did the other kings of Israel. He reigned for only six months when Shallum assassinated him.

• Shallum became the next evil king of Israel. He reigned for one month before Menahem assassinated him. Menahem took the throne and ruled as another ungodly king of Israel for ten years.

• During Menahem's reign, the king of Assyria became a powerful force and mobilized his army to attack Israel.

• In response, Menahem imposed a special tax on Israel and sent a payment to the king of Assyria. The Assyrians called off their attack on Israel. Menahem died and his son, Pekahiah, became the next king of Israel.

• Pekahiah ruled in Israel while Uzziah was king of Judah. When Pekahiah had ruled Israel for two years, Pekah, the commander of his army, assassinated him.

• Pekah is thought to have co-reigned with Menahem and Pekahiah. He ruled in Israel for twenty years and was another evil king.

• During Pekah's reign, the Assyrians attacked Israel again. They captured several cities and took numerous people to Assyria as captives.

- A man named Hoshea assassinated King Pekah and became the last and final king of Israel.

Jotham and Ahaz, Kings of Judah: (2 Kings 15:32–16:20; 2 Chronicles 27:1–28:27)

- Jotham was Uzziah's son, who ruled in Judah after Uzziah was stricken with leprosy. He was a good king and reigned while Pekah was king of Israel. Jotham was successful because he was obedient to God.

- Jotham reigned in Judah for sixteen years and then died. His son Ahaz became king of Judah. Ahaz did not follow in his father's footsteps. He reinstituted Baal worship in Judah and even sacrificed his own sons to Baal.

- During Ahaz's reign, King Pekah of Israel and the king of Aram declared war against Judah. God allowed the King of Aram to win battles against Judah and exile many people to Aram as slaves.

- Israel also defeated Judah in battles and planned to enslave those they had captured. When a prophet of God told Israel it was not right to enslave their own relatives, they released their prisoners from Judah.

- The Edomites later attacked Judah. Instead of calling on the Lord for help, King Ahaz sent silver and gold to the king of Assyria and asked him to help Judah fight against their enemies.

- The Assyrians conquered the people of Aram in Damascus. Afterwards, the Arameans were no longer a threat to Israel or Judah.

- The Assyrians turned against Judah and began to oppress them, but King Ahaz refused to call on the Lord for help. Instead, he closed down the Temple in Jerusalem and set up more pagan shrines for idol worship.

- King Ahaz reigned for sixteen years and then died. His son Hezekiah became king of Judah. During this time, Micah was ministering in Judah.

The Prophet Micah: Micah ministered during the reigns of Jotham, Ahaz, and Hezekiah. Micah carefully presented God's case against Israel and Judah. He pronounced judgment on their sinful acts of fraud, stealing, cruelty, oppression, hypocrisy, idolatry, corruption, money-gouging, murder, etc. Micah prophesied about Israel and Judah's captivity and chastised the false-prophets for saying that it would never happen. Micah urged the people to return to the Lord. He also prophesied about God's promise of future restoration through the coming Messiah, Jesus Christ.

Micah's Messianic Prophecies: Micah told us the Lord himself would guide us (Micah 2:13), and the Messiah would be born in Bethlehem Ephrathah (Micah 5:2). Jesus Christ came to guide us and was born in Bethlehem Ephrathah.

Israel Captured and Exiled to Assyria (2 Kings 17)

- After assassinating King Pekah, Hoshea became king of Israel and ruled the nation for nine years while Ahaz reigned as king of Judah.

- Hoshea was ungodly, but he was not as bad as some of the other kings of Israel.

- During this period, the Assyrians were a well-established ruling power, having conquered many of the nations in their surrounding area.

- The Assyrians had attacked Israel several times during the reigns of Israel's last two kings. They returned during King Hoshea's reign and demanded annual payments from Israel.

- Instead of calling on the Lord for help, King Hoshea refused to send payments. He asked the king of Egypt to join in his protest against Assyria.

- When the king of Assyria realized King Hoshea was rebelling, he put Hoshea in prison and attacked Israel for the third and final time.

- The Assyrians laid siege to Samaria, Israel's capital, for three years. They conquered the city in 722 B.C. The Assyrians captured the people of Israel and exiled them to various areas in Babylonia and Assyria.

Note: Babylonia and Assyria were both located near the Tigris and Euphrates Rivers in Mesopotamia. Assyria was in the northern half of Mesopotamia and Babylonia was in the southern half. The Mesopotamian region was located in modern day Iraq, eastern Syria, and southeastern Turkey.

- The people of Israel allowed their kings to lead them in the evil practice of idolatry for more than 200 years.

- God sent prophets again and again to urge the people to come back to the Lord, but they refused to listen.

- Israel chose to worship worthless idol gods instead of serving the One True God. The Lord finally executed judgment against their sin of idolatry.

- God allowed the Assyrians to destroy Samaria as punishment for Israel's disobedience.

- After the king of Assyria exiled the Israelites—forcing them out of Samaria—he resettled the city with foreigners from Babylonia and other areas.

- The foreigners who resettled Samaria soon learned from a local priest how to worship the One True God of Israel. The priest had been exiled, but had been ordered to return and teach the people to worship God.

- Although the foreigners began to worship God, they also worshiped the idol gods of their various pagan nations and continued this practice over the years.

Note: The foreigners who resettled Samaria eventually intermarried with poor Jews left behind during the exile. Their descendants continued to practice Judaism mixed with various forms of pagan worship. As a result, the Samaritans were looked down on and despised by the Jews because they were not racially, culturally, or religiously pure. This attitude towards the Samaritans continued over the years and was present during Jesus' time on earth. Jesus taught that this kind of prejudice is wrong through his parable about the Good Samaritan in Luke 10:30–37 and the story of the Samaritan woman at the well in John 4:7–26.

RECOMMENDED BIBLE READING

2 Kings 17:1–41	**The Fall of Samaria**
Isaiah 53:1–12	**One of Isaiah's Messianic Prophecies**
Micah 5:1–5	**Micah's Prophecy about Bethlehem**
Matthew 2:1–6	**Micah's Prophecy Fulfilled**
Romans 12:1–21	**Living and Holy Sacrifice**

Section 5: Judah's Final Years

Southern Kingdom Kings of Israel	Date B.C.	Prophets	Date B.C.
Hezekiah (Very Godly)	715–686	Micah	742–687
		Isaiah	740–681
Manasseh (Most Ungodly Changed to Godly)	697–642	Nahum	663–654
Amon (Most Ungodly)	642–640		
Josiah (Very Godly)	640–609	Zephaniah	640–621

Hezekiah, King of Judah: (2 Kings 18–20; 2 Chronicles 29–32; Isaiah 36–39)

- After evil King Ahaz died, his son Hezekiah succeeded him as king of Judah. Hezekiah was not like his father. He was obedient to the Lord.

- Hezekiah fully trusted God. One of his first acts as king was to reopen the Temple. It had been shut down for years by his father, evil King Ahaz.

- After the priests and Levites cleansed the Temple, King Hezekiah dedicated it in a solemn ceremony and reinstituted worship.

- Hezekiah organized a Passover celebration for the Jews in both Israel and Judah. It was the first Passover to be commemorated in years.

- Hezekiah sent messengers throughout Israel and Judah, inviting people to come to Jerusalem to celebrate the Passover.

- Most of those left in Israel after the exile laughed at the messengers, but some were touched by the invitation and decided to attend.

- The response from the people of Judah was more positive. They removed the pagan altars from Jerusalem to help get the city ready for the event.

- The Passover celebration was the greatest in Jerusalem since the days of King Solomon. King Hezekiah gave a large number of his own animals as an offering for the sacrifices.

- Hezekiah led the people back to serving the Lord and commanded them to start tithing again.

- After King Hezekiah's religious reforms had been implemented, the Assyrians invaded Judah.

- Hezekiah prepared the people to defend Jerusalem. He told them God would fight their battle.

- The King of Assyria threatened Hezekiah and mocked the Lord God. He arrogantly said the gods of other nations could not defeat the mighty Assyrians and neither could the God whom Hezekiah served.

- King Hezekiah cried out to the Lord in prayer as did the prophet Isaiah. God answered their prayers, dispatching an angel to the Assyrian's camp. In a single night 185,000 Assyrian soldiers were killed.

- When the King of Assyria woke up the next morning and saw the dead bodies lying everywhere, he called off his attack. He returned home and was assassinated by his own sons.

- Hezekiah later became ill. The prophet Isaiah visited Hezekiah and told him to get his affairs in order because he was going to die.

- When Hezekiah heard this, he cried out to the Lord in prayer and wept bitterly.

- The Lord God heard Hezekiah's cry. He sent Isaiah back to let Hezekiah know an additional fifteen years would be added to his life.

- Soon afterwards, ambassadors from Babylon came to visit Hezekiah. He welcomed them and took great pride in showing them all the wealth of his kingdom.

- Isaiah was greatly troubled when he learned that Hezekiah had shown the Babylonian ambassadors the treasures of the kingdom.

- Isaiah told Hezekiah the Babylonians would return someday, conquer Jerusalem, and take everything of value. Isaiah also prophesied that Hezekiah's descendants would be captured and taken to Babylon as slaves.

 Note: During Hezekiah's reign, the Assyrians were the ruling power. In about 612 B.C., the Babylonians rebelled against Assyria and conquered the capital city of Nineveh. The Assyrian Empire fell in 605 B.C.; the Babylonians replaced them as the ruling power. The Babylonians invaded Judah three times between 605 B.C. and 586 B.C., taking captives and temple treasures with them each time. Isaiah's prophecy to King Hezekiah came true.

- Hezekiah reigned in Judah for twenty-nine years and then died; his son Manasseh became the next king of Judah.

- Manasseh did not walk in his father's footsteps. He was the most ungodly of all the kings of Judah.

The Prophet Isaiah: Isaiah began ministering as a prophet during King Uzziah's reign in Judah and continued through the reigns of Jotham, Ahaz, and Hezekiah. Although Isaiah's messages were to Israel and other nations, he spoke primarily to the people of Judah. He urged them to return to the Lord God and warned them about God's impending judgment.

Isaiah was King Hezekiah's friend and advisor. Hezekiah was obedient to the Lord and listened to Isaiah. According to tradition, Isaiah was sawn in two by Hezekiah's son, evil King Manasseh.

Isaiah's Messianic Prophecies: The Book of Isaiah is filled with references to Jesus Christ, the coming Messiah. Isaiah spoke about the Messiah more than any other prophet of the Old Testament. Isaiah prophesied that God would send a Messiah to save His people (Isaiah 9:6–7), and that the Messiah would be born of a virgin (Isaiah 7:14). Isaiah told us the Messiah would come to serve the needy (Isaiah 61:1–2), and would perform miracles (Isaiah 35:5–6). Isaiah described the Messiah as One who would suffer, be rejected, and would die as a perfect sacrifice for sin (Isaiah 53). Isaiah also told us the Messiah would swallow up death forever (Isaiah 25:8). These prophecies and more were fulfilled through Jesus Christ.

Manasseh, King of Judah: (2 Kings 21:1–18; 2 Chronicles 33:1–20)

- King Manasseh rebuilt the pagan altars his father had torn down and reintroduced idolatry. He worshiped the forces of nature, the sun, and the moon.

- Manasseh practiced sorcery and consulted mediums and psychics. He murdered innocent people and was responsible for much bloodshed.

- Manasseh re-instituted the despicable practice of Baal worship and set up idols inside the Temple. He even sacrificed his own sons.

- King Manasseh was more evil than the Canaanites who had previously lived in the land. He led the people of Judah into more evil than was practiced in pagan nations.

- God pronounced judgment on the people of Judah. They would be captured and exiled like their relatives in Israel had been years earlier.

- The Assyrian army eventually came and took Manasseh prisoner to Babylon. While in prison and in deep distress, Manasseh cried out to God.

- According to 2 Chronicles, King Manasseh humbled himself before the Lord in prayer, and God was moved with compassion. The Lord allowed Manasseh to return to his kingdom in Jerusalem.

- King Manasseh now understood there was only One True God, so he began to worship the Lord God.

- Manasseh encouraged the people of Judah to do the same, but it was too late. They refused to listen and continued to practice idolatry.

- Manasseh reigned in Jerusalem for fifty-five years and then died. His son Amon became the next king of Judah.

Amon, King of Judah: (2 Kings 21:19–26; 2 Chronicles 33:21–25)

- Amon did not follow the example his father had set after returning from prison in Babylon, but did all the evil things Manasseh had done earlier.

- Amon was king of Judah for two years. His own servants assassinated him in the palace. King Amon was succeeded by his son Josiah.

Josiah, King of Judah: (2 Kings 22:1–23:30; 2 Chronicles 34–35)

- Josiah, on the other hand, was a good king and was fully committed to the Lord. He began to seek the Lord at an early age and started a campaign to rid the nation of idolatry.

- King Josiah ordered the restoration of the Temple and assigned priests to supervise the long overdue repairs.

- One day while the Temple was under construction, the high priest found a copy of the Book of the Law, which contained the laws God had given to Moses while Israel was in the desert at Mount Sinai.

- King Josiah had the Book of the Law read aloud. He was overcome with sadness when he began to realize how far Judah had strayed away from the Lord.

- After the book had been read, the king humbled himself before God in sorrow.

- A prophetess of God sent a message to Josiah saying the Lord had indeed heard his cries and was moved with compassion. She told Josiah Jerusalem would not be destroyed until after his death.

- After hearing this message from the Lord, King Josiah gathered the people of Judah together and read the entire Book of the Law to them. In a solemn ceremony, Josiah made the people pledge to obey God's laws.

- After renewing God's covenant with the people, Josiah destroyed the pagan altars and idol gods in Jerusalem, including those of Baal and Ashtoreth.

- Josiah traveled throughout Judah and Israel, destroying all signs of idolatry. He got rid of the idol calves set up long ago by King Jeroboam and banished all psychics and mediums from the land.

- Josiah returned to Jerusalem and ordered the priests and Levites to organize a Passover celebration in accordance with the Book of the Law.

- The Egyptian army later marched through Judah on their way to help the Assyrians fight against the Babylonians. King Josiah tried to stop them, but the Egyptians killed him.

- Josiah was king of Judah for thirty-one years and served God throughout his lifetime. Josiah's son Jehoahaz succeeded him as king.

- During Josiah's reign, the prophet Nahum ministered to the Assyrians. The prophet Zephaniah ministered to the people of Judah.

The Prophet Nahum: Nahum, like Jonah, was a prophet sent to the Assyrians in Nineveh to pronounce God's judgment against unrighteousness. About a century earlier, Jonah had delivered God's message to the Assyrians, and they repented of their evil ways. However, with their rise to power, they had become extremely cruel to their enemies and arrogant to God.

Nahum prophesied that Assyria would be destroyed as punishment for their acts of cruelty. Nahum's prophecy was fulfilled in 605 B.C. when the Babylonians destroyed the Assyrian Empire. The message of Nahum is that unrighteousness will be judged. Jesus Christ will execute God's righteous judgment against sin when He returns.

The Prophet Zephaniah: Zephaniah prophesied in Judah during King Josiah's reign. He proclaimed God's judgment against unrighteousness and called the people to repent. Zephaniah's message about the terrible day of the Lord might have encouraged Josiah in his efforts to lead the people of Judah back to the Lord.

Zephaniah also pronounced judgment on Judah's enemies in Philistia, Moab, Ammon, Ethiopia, and Assyria for their acts of cruelty and pride. Zephaniah's message ends with the hope of restoration which will come through Jesus Christ when He will return and live among God's people.

Recommended Bible Reading

2 Kings 18:1–20:21 **Good King Hezekiah**

2 Kings 22:1–23:30 **Good King Josiah**

Romans 13:1–14 **Respect and Love Fulfill God's Commandments**

Meditation & Prayer

A Psalm reminding us not to put our trust in mortal men:

"Praise the LORD.

Praise the LORD, O my soul.

I will praise the LORD all my life;

I will sing praise to my God as long as I live.

Do not put your trust in princes,
     in mortal men, who cannot save.

When their spirit departs, they return to the ground;
     on that very day their plans come to nothing.

Blessed is he whose help is the God of Jacob,
     whose hope is in the LORD his God,

the Maker of heaven and earth,
     the sea, and everything in them—
     the LORD, who remains faithful forever."

(Psalm 146:1–6 NIV)

Dear Lord,

I give You all of the glory, honor, and praise. I will not put my trust in mortal men, for they will only fail me. They cannot save me. All of my help comes from You. You are the source of my blessings and all good things. I will put my trust in You, the God of Jacob, the Maker of heaven and earth, the sea, and everything in them. My hope is in the Lord who remains faithful forever.

Amen

REVIEW QUESTIONS

1. What was Israel and Judah's major sin during the period of the Divided Kingdom? How did it affect their relationship with God?

_____

_____

_____

_____

_____

_____

2. Why did God send prophets to both Israel and Judah? What role did the prophets play during this period?

_____

_____

_____

_____

_____

_____

3. What characteristics of the prophets' ministries were like Jesus' ministry?

_____

_____

_____

_____

_____

_____

4. Why did God pronounce His righteous judgment on Baal worship in Israel during Ahab's reign? How was God's judgment executed?

_____

_____

_____

_____

_____

_____

5. What is a Messianic prophecy? What were some of the Messianic prophecies written by the prophet Isaiah? The prophet Micah?

_____

_____

_____

_____

_____

_____

6. Why was there only one dynasty in Judah?

_____

_____

_____

_____

_____

_____

7. Why were the Samaritans despised by the Jews? What lesson did Jesus teach through the story of the Samaritan woman at the well and the parable of the Good Samaritan? Explain.

_____

_____

_____

_____

_____

_____

8. What did King Hezekiah do that was so foolish? What human character flaw motivated Hezekiah to do this?

_____

_____

_____

_____

_____

_____

9. King Manasseh was the most ungodly of all the kings of Judah. Yet, when he finally humbled himself before the Lord, God forgave him. What does this tell you about God?

_____

_____

_____

_____

_____

_____

PERSONAL REFLECTIONS

10. In what ways do we commit the sin of idolatry today? How has it affected us as a society? Explain.

_____

_____

_____

_____

_____

11. God used a big fish to get Jonah's attention. Has God ever had to get your attention? If so, how did the Lord get your attention and what was your response?

_____

_____

_____

_____

_____

12. What spiritual growth lesson(s) did you learn while reading about the kings who ruled during the period of Israel's Divided Kingdom?

_____

_____

_____

_____

_____

13. What spiritual growth lesson(s) did you learn while reading about the prophets who ministered during the period of Israel's Divided Kingdom?

_____

_____

_____

_____

_____

CLOSING PRAYER

The Apostle Paul encourages God's people to live by faith:

"We have troubles all around us, but we are not defeated. We do not know what to do, but we do not give up the hope of living. We are persecuted, but God does not leave us. We are hurt sometimes, but we are not destroyed. . . . So we do not give up. Our physical body is becoming older and weaker, but our spirit inside us is made new every day. We have small troubles for a while now, but they are helping us gain an eternal glory that is much greater than the troubles. We set our eyes not on what we see but on what we cannot see. What we see will last only a short time, but what we cannot see will last forever."

(2 Corinthians 4:8–9; 16–18 NCV)

Dear Heavenly Father,

Although I cannot see You, I feel Your presence and know You are with me always. You see all my troubles and know my every need. I am hurt sometimes, but not destroyed. Strengthen me physically. Focus me mentally. Renew me spiritually. I will set my eyes on what cannot be seen, for what I see will last only a short time. I will set my eyes on You, O Lord, for You are eternal, and only what I do for Your kingdom will last forever.

Amen

Chapter 8

Captivity, Exile, & Return

Opening Prayer

Dear Heavenly Father,

Reveal Yourself to me in a mighty way as I read about Judah's captivity, exile, and return. Your love and compassion are limitless and unwavering. You continue loving us even when we turn away from You. You show us love and mercy when we no longer love ourselves. Your arms are always outstretched, inviting us to come to You. Thank You Lord for not giving up on Your children. Thank You, Lord, for Your merciful outpouring of love and grace!

Amen

CHAPTER SUMMARY

CAPTIVITY, EXILE, & RETURN

(Ezra, Nehemiah, Esther, Jeremiah, Lamentations, Ezekiel, Daniel, Habakkuk, Haggai, Zechariah, & Malachi)

All the kings of the Northern Kingdom of Israel were ungodly. After many years of evil kings leading the nation further and further into idolatry, Israel became an irreversible abyss of immorality and unrighteousness. God's patience finally ran out. The Lord executed His righteous judgment against the nation. Israel was captured by the Assyrians in 722 B.C. and the people were exiled just as the prophets had predicted.

The Southern Kingdom of Judah had a few good kings and the rest were ungodly. From time to time, Judah's good kings led the people back to the Lord. As a result, God showed mercy to Judah and delayed judgment against the nation.

Finally, Judah became so entrenched in idolatry that God said the people had become more evil than the pagan nations around them. God could no longer tolerate the depths of immorality and sin, so His righteous judgment was executed against Judah. One hundred years after Israel's capture, King Nebuchadnezzar of Babylon invaded Judah. He carried captives (exiles) back to Babylon in 605 B.C. and again in 597 B.C. Judah's kings rebelled against Nebuchadnezzar by refusing to make annual payments. He eventually returned to Judah a third and final time in 586 B.C. King Nebuchadnezzar and the Babylonians were ruthless. They demolished the Temple and totally destroyed the city of Jerusalem. More captives were carried away to Babylon.

Eight hundred years earlier, God told His people through the prophet Moses that failure to keep the covenant agreement would result in Israel being scattered among other nations. Their land would become desolate and their cities would lie in ruins (Leviticus 26:33). This prophecy and others had now come true.

The Persians conquered the Babylonians in 539 B.C. They took control of the territories and the people previously ruled by the Babylonians, including the Jewish exiles. After the fall of the Babylonian Empire, King Cyrus of Persia issued a decree in 538 B.C. This decree allowed the Jewish exiles to return to Jerusalem and rebuild the Temple. Those who returned started the task of rebuilding the Temple, but met with opposition from local residents. As a result, the Temple was not finished until 515 B.C. Jerusalem's city wall was finally restored in 445 B.C.

Not all the Jewish exiles returned to Judah when Cyrus' decree was issued. A young woman named Hadassah, also called Esther, and her family were among those who did not go back. They chose to stay in Persia. Through a series of God-orchestrated events, Esther became queen of Persia. God used Queen Esther to save the Jews from annihilation. The Jewish holiday known as Purim commemorates this event as the time when the Jews' sorrow was turned into joy.

	Approximate Timeline	**Location**	**Biblical Scriptures**	**Author**
Judah's Captivity & Exile	609 B.C.–586 B.C.	Judah & Babylon	2 Kings 23–25 2 Chronicles 36	Unknown Ezra
The Fall of Babylon	539 B.C.–538 B.C.	Babylon & Judah	Daniel 5–6	Daniel
The Decree to Return	536 B.C.–515 B.C.	Babylon & Jerusalem	Ezra 1–6	Ezra
The Story of Queen Esther	479 B.C.–465 B.C.	Susa in Persia	Esther 1–10	Unknown
Restoring & Rebuilding	458 B.C.–430 B.C.	Babylon & Jerusalem	Ezra 7–10 Nehemiah 1–13	Ezra Nehemiah

MAP OF KEY LOCATIONS

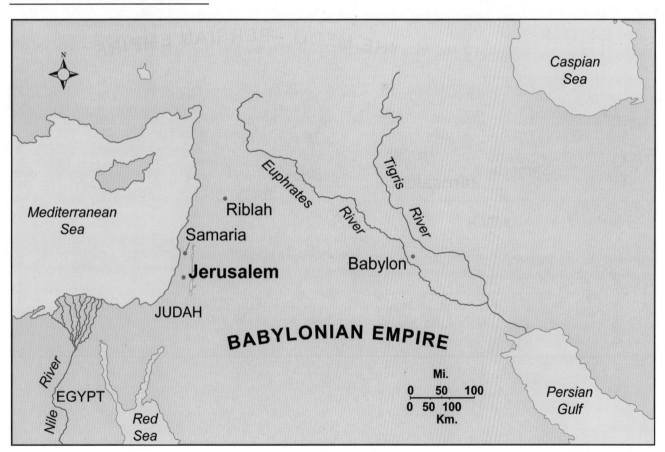

Map of Key Locations

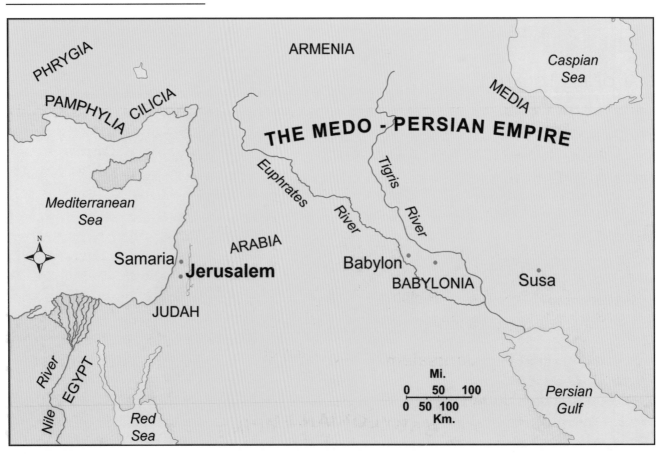

DANIEL

"'O King, live forever!' said Daniel. 'My God sent his angel, who closed the mouths of the lions so that they would not hurt me. I've been found innocent before God and also before you, O king. I've done nothing to harm you.'" (Daniel 6:21–22 MSG)

SECTION 1: JUDAH'S CAPTIVITY & EXILE

Southern Kingdom Kings of Judah	Date B.C.	Prophets	Date B.C.
Jehoahaz (Ungodly)	609	Jeremiah	627–586
Jehoiakim (Ungodly)	609–598	Habakkuk	612–589
Jehoiachin (Ungodly)	597	Obadiah	598–580 (?)
Zedekiah (Ungodly)	597–586		

Jehoahaz, King of Judah: (2 Kings 23:31–34; 2 Chronicles 36:1–4; Jeremiah 3:10; Jeremiah 23)

• King Jehoahaz was not like his father, good King Josiah, but was like the other ungodly kings of Judah.

• Good King Josiah had implemented numerous religious reforms; however, according to the prophet Jeremiah, the people had not sincerely returned to the Lord, but only pretended to be sorry.

• When Josiah died and his son Jehoahaz took over the kingdom, the people again openly practiced idolatry.

• The Lord prophetically announced to Jeremiah, *"Woe to the shepherds who destroy and scatter the sheep of my pasture!"* (Jeremiah 23:1 ESV).

• God said a time would come when He would place a Righteous Branch on King David's throne.

• The Lord told Jeremiah the Righteous Branch's name is *Jehovah-Tsidkenu*, which means "The LORD Is Our Righteousness" (Jeremiah 23:5–6).

Note: *Jehovah-Tsidkenu* is the Hebrew name God revealed to Jeremiah. In this Messianic prophecy, God told Jeremiah He would send a Righteous Branch, One Who is upright, wise, and just. Jesus Christ is the Righteous Branch. He is blameless, guiltless, holy, innocent, and sinless. We are made righteous through Jesus Christ when we accept Him as our Lord and Savior.

• Jehoahaz had reigned as king for only three months when the Egyptian pharaoh seized control of Judah and demanded payment.

• Pharaoh took Jehoahaz to Egypt as a prisoner and left another of Josiah's sons, Jehoiakim, to rule Jerusalem. Jehoiakim collected a special tax to meet Egypt's demand for payment.

Jehoiakim, King of Judah: (2 Kings 23:35–24:7; 2 Chronicles 36:5–8; Jeremiah 36)

• Jehoiakim was another ungodly king. He did not listen to Jeremiah, who repeatedly warned him about the certainty of God's judgment against sin.

• By this time, the Assyrians' power was on the decline. They joined forces with the Egyptians to fight the Babylonians, who were rising in power.

• King Nebuchadnezzar of Babylon conquered both Egypt and Assyria. The Assyrian Empire fell and came to an end.

- In 605 B.C., Nebuchadnezzar invaded Jerusalem, looted the Temple, and demanded annual payments from King Jehoiakim.

- Nebuchadnezzar carried some of Jerusalem's royal family members and noblemen back to Babylon with him. The prophet Daniel was included in this first group of exiles.

Note: Daniel was a young boy when he was carried away into captivity along with other royal family members in 605 B.C. Daniel was very intelligent, and among those chosen by Nebuchadnezzar's palace officials to be taught the language and culture of Babylon. After three years of training, Daniel became an advisor in Nebuchadnezzar's palace.

- King Jehoiakim made payments to the Babylonians for three years and then rebelled. Jehoiakim was king for eleven years and then died. His son Jehoiachin succeeded him as king.

Jehoiachin, King of Judah: (2 Kings 24:8–17; 2 Chronicles 36:9–10; Jeremiah 29)

- Jehoiachin had been king for three months when King Nebuchadnezzar and the Babylonians returned in 597 B.C.

- King Jehoiachin surrendered to Nebuchadnezzar. They took him in chains to Babylon, along with members of the royal family, officials, and prominent citizens of Judah. The prophet Ezekiel was included in this group of exiles.

Note: Ezekiel was being trained for the priesthood in Jerusalem when King Nebuchadnezzar marched into Jerusalem for the second time in 597 B.C. The Babylonians carried Ezekiel away into captivity along with thousands of others when King Jehoiachin surrendered. When Ezekiel reached Babylon, the Lord called him as a prophet to minister to the people. While Daniel was advising in the palace, Ezekiel was ministering to Israel in the streets of Babylon.

- Nebuchadnezzar left another of Josiah's sons, Zedekiah, to rule in Jerusalem.

- After this invasion, the prophet Jeremiah sent a letter to the exiles in Babylon, letting them know they should prepare themselves for a lengthy stay.

- Jeremiah prophesied that Judah's captivity would last for a period of seventy years and then God would allow them to return home to Jerusalem.

Zedekiah, King of Judah: (2 Kings 24:18–25:5; 2 Chronicles 36:11–16; Jeremiah 37–38)

- King Zedekiah was ungodly like his brothers and stubbornly refused to pay tribute to King Nebuchadnezzar. The Babylonians returned and laid siege to Jerusalem, preventing anyone from coming in or going out.

- The Egyptian army mobilized their forces to help Judah. When the Babylonians heard about this, they left their siege in Jerusalem for a while and headed south to battle the Egyptians.

- King Zedekiah called for the prophet Jeremiah and asked him to pray for Judah. Jeremiah told the king he should not put his faith in the Egyptians, for the Babylonians would return and burn Jerusalem to the ground.

- Jeremiah was falsely charged with treason and thrown into a dungeon. Zedekiah secretly met with Jeremiah and asked if he had received a word from the Lord. Jeremiah again told the king he would be defeated.

- Jeremiah then said to Zedekiah, *"What crime have I committed? . . .Where are your prophets now who told you the king of Babylon would not attack you or this land? Listen, my lord the king, I beg you. Don't send me back to the dungeon . . . for I will die there"* (Jeremiah 37:18–21).

- After this, Zedekiah had Jeremiah removed from the dungeon and imprisoned in the courtyard of the palace guards.

- Several men wanted Jeremiah put to death because he was telling the people that they would die if they stayed in Jerusalem but would live if they surrendered to the Babylonians.

- These men took Jeremiah out of prison and lowered him into a cistern (well). Jeremiah was left to die, but a palace official heard about it and pulled him to safety.

- Zedekiah secretly met with Jeremiah again, asking if he had heard from the Lord. Jeremiah advised him to surrender. Jeremiah told the king he would live and Jerusalem would not be destroyed if he turned himself over to Nebuchadnezzar.

- Zedekiah said he was afraid to surrender. The king stubbornly refused to trust God and sent Jeremiah back to the palace prison.

- Nebuchadnezzar's army returned to Jerusalem and laid siege to the city again. Jerusalem was under siege a total of three long years.

- All food supplies totally ran out, and the people were starving to death.

- In 586 B.C., the Babylonian army finally broke through the walls of the city.

- When King Zedekiah and his palace soldiers saw the Babylonians at the city gates, they waited until nightfall and then attempted an escape.

- The Babylonians caught Zedekiah and took him to Nebuchadnezzar, who made the king watch while his sons were killed.

- Nebuchadnezzar then gouged out Zedekiah's eyes and took him in chains to Babylon.

The Prophet Jeremiah: Jeremiah was very young and preparing for the priesthood when the Lord called him to be a prophet. He faithfully ministered in Jerusalem with passion and endurance during the reign of Judah's last five kings. Jeremiah's ministry was filled with prophecies, object lessons, and many tears as he repeatedly warned the people and relentlessly tried to get them to return to God.

Jeremiah prophesied about the captivity and exile. He was ignored, threatened, and eventually put in prison. He also prophesied that Judah's captivity would last for a period of seventy years. Judah's captivity lasted from 605 B.C. to about 538 B.C., when King Cyrus' decree was issued. The foundation of the Temple in Jerusalem was laid in 536 B.C., which was about seventy years after Judah's initial capture and exile.

Jeremiah also offered a message of hope. He prophesized that a time was coming when God would place a Righteous Branch on King David's throne, a King who would rule with wisdom and who would be called "The Lord Our Righteousness." This prophecy was fulfilled through Jesus Christ, our Righteous King.

The Prophet Habakkuk: Habakkuk prophesied in Judah probably during the reign of King Jehoiakim. Habakkuk was deeply distressed by the immorality, violence, and corruption polluting Judah. Habakkuk asked the Lord, *"How long will these injustices go unpunished?"* God's response was that the Babylonians would soon become a powerful force that would sweep across the land and conquer nations in their path, including Judah.

After hearing this, Habakkuk was troubled that God would use such unrighteous people to punish Judah. God told Habakkuk He was aware of the extreme cruelty of the Babylonians and they too would be punished. God does not overlook or tolerate sin. Habakkuk prayed God would have mercy on Judah. He was comforted by the Lord's response and rejoiced in the God of salvation. We too can rejoice in Jesus Christ, the Lord of our salvation.

Jerusalem's Fall: (2 Kings 25:2–26; 2 Chronicles 36:17–21; Jeremiah 39–43)

- The Babylonians marched through the city of Jerusalem, destroying everything in their path and killing people. They burned down the Temple, the royal palace, all the important buildings, and demolished the city's wall.

- They rounded up those who were still alive and took everyone—except a few poor people—to Babylon.

- Nebuchadnezzar ordered his men to find Jeremiah and give him whatever he wanted. They found Jeremiah and asked him if he wanted to stay or go to Babylon. Jeremiah chose to stay.

 The Prophet Jeremiah's Lamentations: Jeremiah is often called the weeping prophet because of the many tears he shed after witnessing the total destruction of his beloved city. He was devastated by Jerusalem's fall and mourned deeply as he wrote Lamentations, a sad funeral song, for generations to remember. Lamentations describes the consequences of Judah's sin, yet offers hope in the midst of suffering.

Jeremiah's ministry was much like that of Jesus. Both were men of sorrow, grief-stricken over the people's sins, rejected and despised.

- The Babylonians appointed a man named Gedaliah to govern the few poor people left behind in Judah. Jeremiah was placed under Gedaliah's care.

- Gedaliah told the poor people that the Babylonians would not harm them if they submitted to their rule.

- A couple months later, a member of Judah's royal family assassinated Gedaliah and his men. The few Babylonian soldiers assigned to oversee those left behind were killed also.

- The assassin took the poor people who had been under Gedaliah's care—along with Jeremiah—as hostages. Johanan, a man loyal to Gedaliah, later killed the assassin.

- Johanan freed the hostages. They fled to Bethlehem, where they discussed their situation and tried to determine what they should do next.

- Johanan and the poor people were afraid of what the Babylonians would do when they discovered Gedaliah and their soldiers had been killed.

- They went to the prophet Jeremiah and asked him to find out from the Lord if they should flee to Egypt or stay in Judah.

- God spoke to Jeremiah ten days later and told him the people should stay and not go to Egypt.

- God revealed that the Babylonians would soon destroy Egypt in the same way they had devastated Jerusalem, but the people would be safe in Judah.

- When Jeremiah delivered God's message to the people, they panicked and did not believe him. They ignored Jeremiah and fled to Egypt.

- The captivity was painful for those exiled in Babylon. Families were separated from their loved ones and marched over 700 miles (1,127 kilometers) to Babylon. Many of the exiles died en route.

 Note: Although the Jews were subject to the Babylonians' idolatrous rule, they maintained their identity while in captivity as the people who served God. The pain of captivity caused the Jews to seek the Lord. God purified His people as they began to see the falsehood of idolatry and the truth of God. The Jews rid themselves of the evil practice of idolatry and introduced pagan societies to the One True God. They no longer had a Temple for worship, but it is believed synagogues were established during this period as a place for teaching and practicing their religion while in a foreign land.

- While in captivity, God gave the prophet Ezekiel numerous visions and prophetic messages. In one of Ezekiel's visions, God described the future city of Jerusalem.

- God said the name of the city (Jerusalem) would be Jehovah-Shammah, which means "The LORD Is There" (Ezekiel 48:35).

 Note: *Jehovah-Shammah* is the Hebrew name for new Jerusalem. *Jehovah-Shammah* is the place where God will always be present.

RECOMMENDED BIBLE READING

2 Kings 25:1–30 **The Fall of Jerusalem**

Jeremiah 39:1–43:13 **Jeremiah's Account of Jerusalem's Fall**

Hebrews 12:1–29 **A Call to Obedience**

SECTION 2: THE FALL OF BABYLON

Kings of Babylon	Date	Prophets	Date
	B.C.		B.C.
Nebuchadnezzar	605–562	Daniel	605–536
Evil-merodach	562–560	Ezekiel	593–571
Neriglissar	560–556		
Labishi-marduk	556		
Nabonidus	556–539		
Belshazzar (co-regent)	553–539		

King Jehoiachin in Exile: (2 Kings 25:27–30)

- After Nebuchadnezzar's death, his son Evil-merodach ascended to the throne of Babylon.

- Evil-merodach was kind to King Jehoiachin and released him from prison. He gave Jehoiachin an allowance to live on and let him dine at the king's table until the day of his death.

- Jehoiachin's grandson was Zerubbabel, who would later lead the first group of exiles back to Jerusalem.

The Prophet Daniel: Daniel was carried away to Babylon during the first exile in 605 B.C. He received training in Babylonian culture and became an advisor in the palace. Although Daniel lived among pagans, he remained fully devoted to the One True God. Daniel was gifted with the power to interpret dreams and was highly respected by officials and King Nebuchadnezzar himself for this ability.

Daniel prophesied the Temple would be rebuilt. Afterwards the Messiah would come and be killed, appearing to have accomplished nothing (Daniel 9:24–26). This prophecy was fulfilled through Jesus Christ.

The Prophet Ezekiel: Ezekiel was carried away to Babylon during the second exile in 597 B.C. Daniel had been in Babylon for eight years when Ezekiel arrived. Ezekiel saw visions of God's presence leaving the Temple. He prophesied about Jerusalem's certain destruction. The Lord told Ezekiel that Judah would not be spared, not even for the sake of righteous men like Noah, Daniel, and Job.

Ezekiel also prophesied about the future restoration of Israel. He passionately proclaimed that a Good Shepherd would come and lead God's people. God would live among His people and sanctify them with His presence. Jesus Christ is the Good Shepherd. He lives in us and sanctifies us.

The Writing on the Wall (Daniel 5)

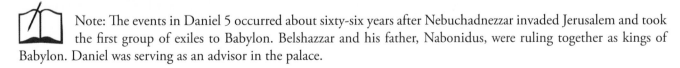

Note: The events in Daniel 5 occurred about sixty-six years after Nebuchadnezzar invaded Jerusalem and took the first group of exiles to Babylon. Belshazzar and his father, Nabonidus, were ruling together as kings of Babylon. Daniel was serving as an advisor in the palace.

- Years after the exile, King Belshazzar of Babylon held a royal banquet one evening for his nobles.

- While everyone was drinking and celebrating, the king ordered his servants to bring in the sacred goblets Nebuchadnezzar had taken from the Temple in Jerusalem so that he and his guests could drink from them.

- The king's servants brought in the sacred goblets and served wine in them to Belshazzar and his guests.

- As King Belshazzar and his guests drank wine from the sacred goblets, they offered toasts to their idol gods honoring them with words of praise.

- Suddenly, a hand appeared and began writing on the palace wall. Belshazzar watched in terror as the hand wrote a message in a foreign language.

- The panic-stricken king immediately summoned Babylon's wisest men to interpret the message.

- The wisest men of the kingdom examined the message, but they were unable to interpret or explain it. This terrified the king even more.

- Overhearing the commotion, the Queen Mother told the king about Daniel. She explained that Daniel was a man of God with great insight who would be able to interpret the message. The king summoned Daniel.

- When Daniel arrived, he chastised the king for failing to humble himself in reverence to God.

- Daniel told Belshazzar that he and his guests had dishonored God when they drank wine from the sacred goblets while praising their idol gods.

- Daniel interpreted the writing saying God had numbered the king's days, the king had been weighed on scales, and he had failed to measure up.

- Daniel then told Belshazzar his kingdom would be divided and given to the Medes and Persians.

- King Belshazzar was killed that very night, and Darius the Mede took over the kingdom.

Note: The Medes and Persians joined forces and conquered the Babylonian Empire in 539 B.C. History tells us that Cyrus was the first king of the Persian Empire. Darius the Mede, who took over the kingdom, is thought to have either been a governor appointed by Cyrus to rule Babylon for a period of time, or was another name for Cyrus, himself.

The Lions' Den (Daniel 6)

- Daniel's knowledge and abilities impressed Darius the Mede. Daniel soon became one of Darius' most trusted advisors.

- When the other palace administrators learned Darius planned to promote Daniel, they looked for a way to destroy Daniel's reputation.

- The administrators could not find anything in Daniel's character to discredit him, so they devised a scheme to have him condemned for religious reasons.

- The administrators convinced Darius to issue a decree stating that anyone caught praying to a god or a human other than the king for the next thirty days would be thrown into the lions' den.

- Daniel heard about the decree but continued to pray three times a day to the Lord God—just as he had always done.

- The administrators caught Daniel praying to the Lord God and reported him to the king. They told Darius that Daniel had ignored his decree and should be condemned to death in the lions' den.

- Darius liked Daniel. When Darius heard Daniel had disobeyed the law, he regretted that he had signed such a decree.

- Darius tried to save Daniel, but he could not because a decree issued by a king could not be rescinded. He reluctantly sentenced Daniel to death. Daniel was arrested and thrown into the lions' den.

- The next morning, Darius rushed to the entrance of the lions' den to see if Daniel's God had miraculously spared his life.

- Darius shouted Daniel's name. Daniel answered, saying God had sent an angel to shut the lions' mouths. Daniel had been in the den with the lions all night long but they never so much as scratched him.

- King Darius had the conniving administrators and their families thrown into the lions' den. He then issued a decree stating that everyone in his kingdom should show reverence and honor to Daniel's God.

- Daniel lived the rest of his life in Babylon as a highly respected advisor of the royal palace.

RECOMMENDED BIBLE READING

Daniel 5:1–30 **Daniel and the Handwriting on the Wall**

Daniel 6:1–28 **Daniel in the Lion's Den**

Hebrews 13:1–25 **Godly Love**

SECTION 3: THE DECREE TO RETURN

Kings of Persia	Date B.C.	Jewish Leaders	Date B.C.	Prophets	Date B.C.
Cyrus	539–530	Zerubbabel	538–516	Daniel	605–536
Cambyses	530–522				
Darius	522–486			Haggai	520–516
				Zechariah	520–516

 Note: Darius, who succeeded Cambyses, was not the same as Darius the Mede mentioned in Daniel.

King Cyrus' Decree (Ezra 1–3)

- After the Medes and Persians conquered the Babylonians, the Jewish exiles found themselves under Persian rule. Cyrus of Persia became king and realigned the region to form the Persian Empire.

- King Cyrus issued a decree during the first year of his reign, allowing the Jewish exiles to return home and rebuild the Temple in Jerusalem.

- According to the prophet Jeremiah, the Jewish exiles would be in captivity for a period of seventy years. King Cyrus' decree freed the exiles and fulfilled Jeremiah's prophecy. (Jeremiah 25:11; 29:10)

 Note: King Cyrus' decree also fulfilled Isaiah's prophecy about a man named Cyrus, who would call for the rebuilding of Jerusalem and the Temple. Amazingly, Isaiah called Cyrus by name in a prophecy written about 100 years before Jerusalem was destroyed and about 150 years before Cyrus became king of the Persian Empire. (Isaiah 44:28)

- After the decree was issued, a few exiles from the tribes of Judah and Benjamin started planning a return trip to Jerusalem. Neighbors and friends of the returning exiles donated supplies and offerings for the journey.

- King Cyrus ordered officials to give the returning exiles thousands of sacred items Nebuchadnezzar had taken from the Temple in Jerusalem.

- About 50,000 Jews made the journey back to Judah under the leadership of Zerubbabel, the grandson of King Jehoiachin and descendant of King David.

- When the exiles arrived in Judah, they settled their families first, and then gathered together in Jerusalem to rebuild the altar at its original site.

- The returned exiles were afraid of the non-Jews who had settled in Jerusalem. Yet, they rebuilt the altar in spite of their fears and offered sacrifices to the Lord.

- Two years after rebuilding the altar, the returned exiles started the task of rebuilding the Temple. When the foundation of the Temple was completed, the returned exiles gathered together to give honor and praise to the Lord.

- The older exiles who remembered the splendor of the first Temple were overcome with sadness and cried when they saw the newly laid foundation.

- The exiles who were too young to remember the first Temple were overjoyed and began shouting praises to the Lord.

Opposition to the Rebuilding of the Temple: (Ezra 4:1–4)

- The local, non-Jewish residents had been hostile to the exiles ever since they returned. When the local non-Jews asked if they could help rebuild the Temple, the returned exiles refused.

- Zerubbabel, who had become the governor of Judah, told the local non-Jews that the returned exiles would rebuild the Temple by themselves without any outside help. When the local non-Jews heard this, they became angry.

- The local non-Jews opposed the rebuilding of the Temple. They plotted against the returned exiles, hiring lawyers and sabotaging the work effort.

Opposition to the Rebuilding of Jerusalem's Wall: (Ezra 4:5–23)

- Much later, after the Temple had been rebuilt, the local non-Jews sent letters to the Persian kings Xerxes and Artaxerxes, opposing efforts to rebuild Jerusalem and its wall.

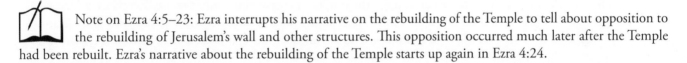 Note on Ezra 4:5–23: Ezra interrupts his narrative on the rebuilding of the Temple to tell about opposition to the rebuilding of Jerusalem's wall and other structures. This opposition occurred much later after the Temple had been rebuilt. Ezra's narrative about the rebuilding of the Temple starts up again in Ezra 4:24.

Rebuilding Stopped: (Ezra 4:24)

- Opposition to the rebuilding of the Temple was so strong the returned exiles became discouraged and stopped. The rebuilding effort remained at a standstill throughout the rest of King Cyrus' reign.

Rebuilding Starts Up Again: (Ezra 5–6; Haggai 1–2; Zechariah 1–8)

- During the second year of King Darius' reign, the prophets Haggai and Zechariah started their ministries. They encouraged the returned exiles to finish the task they had started.

- The Lord spoke through the prophet Haggai saying, *"Why are you living in luxurious houses while my house lies in ruins?"* (Haggai 1:4).

- Zerubbabel and the other returned exiles responded to God's call. The task of rebuilding the Temple started up again in earnest.

- When the local non-Jews discovered that the returned exiles were working on the Temple again, they tried to stop them.

- The local non-Jews went to the construction site, demanding to know who had given permission for work to start up again.

- The returned exiles ignored their demands and refused to let anything hinder their progress.

- The local non-Jews sent a letter to King Darius asking if King Cyrus, his predecessor, had issued a decree allowing the exiles to rebuild the Temple in Jerusalem.

- When King Darius received the letter, he ordered a search of the Babylonian archives. King Cyrus' decree was found.

- King Darius sent a message back to the local non-Jews in Jerusalem, ordering them to stop interfering with efforts to rebuild the Temple. When the local non-Jews received King Darius' response, they complied.

- The prophets Haggai and Zechariah continued to encourage the returned exiles. Haggai prophesied saying, *"The future glory of this Temple will be greater than its past glory, says the Lord of Heaven's Armies"* (Haggai 2:9).

- God spoke through Zechariah saying, *"My Temple will be rebuilt . . . and measurements will be taken for the reconstruction of Jerusalem* (Zechariah 1:16b).

- The Temple was completed in 515 B.C., more than twenty years after the first exiles had returned to Jerusalem.

- The Temple was dedicated with offerings and sacrifices. About one month later, the returned exiles celebrated Passover.

The Prophet Haggai: God called both Haggai and Zechariah to minister to the returned exiles and urge them to finish rebuilding the Temple. Haggai told the returned exiles that they were experiencing difficulties because they had failed to put God first. Haggai assured the returned exiles that God was on their side and would again fill the Temple with His glory.

God sent a message to Zerubbabel through the prophet Haggai telling him that he (Zerubbabel) had been specially chosen (as a descendant of King David) and would be honored with royal status and authority (Haggai 2:20–23). God honored His promise to Zerubbabel through Jesus Christ. Zerubbabel's name appears in the lineages of both Mary and Joseph as an ancestor of Jesus Christ (Matthew 1:12; Luke 3:27).

The Prophet Zechariah: Zechariah was younger than Haggai, but ministered during the same time period. Zechariah reminded the returned exiles that God had been angry with their ancestors because of disobedience. Zechariah encouraged them to return to the Lord and continue the task of rebuilding the Temple. Zechariah's visions about the Temple's future glory and God's promise to restore Jerusalem motivated the returned exiles to finish rebuilding the Temple.

Zechariah's visions and messages provide some of the clearest Messianic prophecies, which were fulfilled by Jesus Christ. Zechariah foretold that Jerusalem's righteous yet humble king would come into the city riding a donkey (Zechariah 9:9). He pictured the Messiah as a Good Shepherd, who would be rejected for thirty pieces of silver and the silver would be thrown to the potter (Zechariah 11:4–13). The Shepherd would be struck down and His sheep would be scattered (Zechariah 13:7). Zechariah prophesied that Jerusalem would mourn for One who had been pierced (Zechariah 12:10) and described a time when the Lord will rule over the earth (Zechariah 14).

RECOMMENDED BIBLE READING

Ezra 1:1–11	**King Cyrus' Decree**
Ezra 3:7–13	**The Foundation of the Temple**
Luke 12:1–12	**Jesus Teaches Against Hypocrisy**
Romans 14:1–23	**Warning Against Judging Others**

SECTION 4: THE STORY OF QUEEN ESTHER

Kings of Persia	Date	Jewish Leaders	Date
	B.C.		B.C.
Xerxes (aka Ahasuerus) Esther's husband	486–465	Queen Esther	479–465

Note: Most Jewish exiles did not return to Jerusalem when Cyrus' decree was issued. Esther's family was among those who did not go back. Esther's story takes place in the Persian city of Susa after the Temple has been rebuilt but before Ezra's return to Jerusalem. Chronologically, the story of Esther happens between Ezra 6 and 7. Xerxes succeeded Darius as king of Persia.

Queen Vashti Is Banished: (Esther 1)

- King Xerxes hosted a large banquet in the capital city of Susa during the third year of his reign for all the nobles and officials of the Persian Empire.

- After celebrating for a full six months, the king held another banquet exclusively for his servants and palace officials.

- There was plenty of wine on hand and everyone was told to drink as much as they wanted.

- King Xerxes was in high spirits from drinking wine when he ordered his attendants to bring Queen Vashti to the banquet hall.

- The king wanted to show off the queen to the other men and dazzle them with her beauty.

- The king's attendants delivered the message, but Queen Vashti refused to come. This made the king very angry.

- After consulting advisors, King Xerxes banished Queen Vashti for disobeying his order. He then issued a proclamation declaring that every man should be ruler of his own home.

Esther Becomes Queen: (Esther 2)

- The king's personal attendants came to him later and suggested that a search be conducted throughout the empire for beautiful young women. The king was told he could then choose a new queen from among them.

- King Xerxes liked this idea. He ordered officials to roundup beautiful young women from all over the empire and bring them to the palace.

- A Jewish man named Mordecai, whose family had been exiled, was living in Susa at the time with his lovely young cousin Hadassah, also called Esther.

- Mordecai adopted Esther after her parents died and was raising her as his own daughter.

- The king's officials found Esther and took her—along with many other beautiful women—to the palace, where they became part of the king's harem.

- Esther and the other women received beauty treatments and special training for an entire year.

- Esther did not tell anyone she was Jewish because Mordecai had instructed her not to reveal her nationality to anyone.

- After a year of beauty treatments, the women were selected one-by-one to spend a night with the king. When it was Esther's turn, she so impressed the king that he fell in love with her and made her his queen.

- After becoming queen of Persia, Esther continued to keep her Jewish identity a secret from everyone, including the king.

- One day Mordecai overheard two palace guards plotting to assassinate the king. He told Esther, and she warned the king. After verifying Mordecai's story, the king had the two guards put to death.

Haman's Plot to Kill the Jews: (Esther 3)

- King Xerxes promoted a man named Haman to the position of second in command of the empire.

- Palace officials were ordered to bow down when Haman passed by to show their respect. Mordecai refused to obey this command.

- When Mordecai was asked why he would not bow down in front of Haman, he answered that it was because of his Jewish ancestry.

 Note: Jewish law prohibited bowing in reverence to anyone or anything other than the Lord God.

- Haman was outraged when he heard about Mordecai and wanted to do more than just kill Mordecai. He wanted to annihilate all of the Jews as well.

- Haman devised a plan to kill the Jews. He then cast lots (also known as purim) to determine when to put his plan into effect. The date chosen was March 7th.

- Haman went to the king and suggested that a decree be issued to kill a certain group of people who were deliberately disobeying the law. In response, the king delegated his authority to Haman and told him to do whatever he wanted.

- Haman used the king's authority to issue letters, decreeing that all Jews must be killed on March 7th, the date chosen by lots (purim).

- When the people heard the decree, they were shocked and confused.

Esther Approaches the King: (Esther 4–7)

- Jews everywhere wept as they fasted and prayed for a miracle. Mordecai tore his clothes and put on sackcloth and ashes, as was the custom when in mourning.

- When Queen Esther heard about Mordecai's distress, she sent a messenger to find out what was troubling him.

- Mordecai sent a message back to Esther, explaining the problem and asking her to beg the king to help the Jews.

- Esther responded saying the king meets only with those he wishes to see and he had not asked for her in over a month. She explained that anyone appearing before the king uninvited would be put to death.

- When Mordecai received Esther's response, he sent another message to her saying, *"And who knows but that you have come to royal position for such a time as this?"* (Esther 4:14b NIV).

- Esther responded differently this time. She told Mordecai to ask the Jews to pray for her because she was going to approach the king even if it meant her death.

- After three days of fasting and praying, Esther walked into the palace hallway near the throne room. The king became concerned when he saw Esther standing there. He asked her what she wanted.

- Esther did not tell the king what she really wanted, but politely invited the king and Haman to a banquet she planned to prepare for the two of them.

- The king accepted Esther's invitation and attended the banquet with Haman later that day. While there, the king asked Esther again what she wanted.

- Esther would not say. She invited the king and Haman to come back again the next day for another banquet. She promised to explain everything then.

- Haman went home that evening and bragged to his family and friends about his prestige and power. However, he was still very upset that Mordecai would not bow down in front of him or show any kind of respect.

- Haman's wife and friends suggested he ask the king to hang Mordecai for failing to obey the law. Haman agreed with their suggestion and had a gallows built for Mordecai's hanging.

- The night before attending Esther's second banquet, the king remembered he had never rewarded Mordecai for reporting the plot against his life.

- The next day, Haman went to the palace with plans of talking to the king about hanging Mordecai. Before Haman could say anything, the king asked what should be done to honor a man for his loyalty.

- Haman could not imagine the king wishing to honor anyone but himself, so he responded that the king should treat such a man like royalty.

- Haman went on to say the king should order one of his nobles to lead the man through the streets shouting to everyone, *"This is what is done for the man the king delights to honor!"* (Esther 6:9b NIV).

- The king liked Haman's suggestion and ordered him to do this for Mordecai. Haman was forced to lead Mordecai through the streets, honoring him in front of everyone in Susa.

- Later that evening, Haman and the king attended Esther's second banquet. When the king asked Esther what she wanted, she explained that Haman had ordered the annihilation of her people.

- The king was furious when he heard this and sentenced Haman to death. The gallows originally built for Mordecai's hanging was used to hang Haman.

Esther Saves The Jews: (Esther 8–10)

- Although Haman had been put to death, the decree against the Jews was still in effect.

- Esther begged the king to spare the Jews, but the king explained that once a decree had been issued with the king's authority, it could not be revoked.

- King Xerxes gave Esther and Mordecai permission to issue another decree in his name stating Jews everywhere could unite and defend themselves on March 7th, the day Haman's plan would go into effect.

- On March 7th, both decrees went into effect. Many of the royal officials, nobles, and governors helped the Jews defeat their enemies.

- Afterwards, Mordecai suggested the event be celebrated annually in remembrance of the time when the Jews' sorrow had been turned into joy.

- The Jews agreed with Mordecai, and the Feast of Purim was established as an annual Jewish holiday.

- King Xerxes promoted Mordecai as his second-in-command, the position once held by Haman. Mordecai became well known and was greatly respected as a man who worked in the people's best interest.

 Note: The Feast of Purim is a Jewish holiday still celebrated to commemorate the time when Queen Esther saved her people from annihilation.

 God used Queen Esther as a savior. She interceded for her people and was willing to die to save them.

RECOMMENDED BIBLE READING

Esther 2:1–20 **Esther Becomes Queen**

Esther 4:1–7:10 **Esther Intercedes for the Jews**

Matthew 5:1–12 **God's Blessings**

Luke 12:13–33 **Jesus Teaches about Worry**

SECTION 5: RESTORING & REBUILDING

Kings of Persia	Date	Jewish Leaders	Date	Prophets	Date
Artaxerxes I	465–424	Ezra	458–430		
		Nehemiah	445–432	Malachi	430–400

 Note: Artaxerxes succeeded Xerxes, Queen Esther's husband, as king of Persia.

Ezra Returns Leading the Second Group of Exiles: (Ezra 7–10)

- During the seventh year of King Artaxerxes' reign, a devout priest named Ezra made arrangements to lead a second group of exiles to Jerusalem.

- King Artaxerxes authorized Ezra's trip and gave him a generous offering for the Temple in Jerusalem.

- Ezra thanked God for the provisions and led the people in fasting and prayer before leaving for Jerusalem.

- Ezra specifically asked the Lord to take care of them as they traveled because they did not have a military escort for protection.

- After giving thanks and praise to God, Ezra and the returning exiles began their journey. God answered their prayers, and the group arrived safely in Jerusalem a few months later.

- Ezra was shocked and greatly disturbed when he discovered many of the Jews in Jerusalem had intermarried with local non-Jews and were practicing pagan religions.

- Ezra was even more upset to learn some of the worst offenders were the priests and leaders of the community.

- Dumbfounded and outraged, Ezra tore his clothes and pulled out his hair, as was the custom when in deep distress. He then fell to his knees, weeping and praying for hours.

- As Ezra called out to God, a large group of people gathered around and began confessing their sins and unfaithfulness to the Lord.

- One of the Jews suggested that those who had intermarried with pagan women should divorce their wives.

- Ezra called a meeting in Jerusalem and told the Jews they must separate themselves from the non-Jewish pagans in accordance with God's laws.

- The repentant Jews divorced their wives and sent them away with their children.

Nehemiah Returns Leading the Third Group of Exiles: (Nehemiah 1–2)

- During the twentieth year of King Artaxerxes' reign, a man named Nehemiah was serving as the king's cupbearer in the capital city of Susa. Nehemiah was responsible for pouring the king's wine.

- Nehemiah learned things were not going well in Jerusalem. The city's wall was still lying in ruins.

- Nehemiah broke down in tears and mourned for several days, fasting and praying to the Lord.

- One day while Nehemiah was serving wine, the king noticed he was sad and asked what was wrong. Nehemiah explained that Jerusalem's wall was lying in ruins.

- The king asked how he could help. Nehemiah prayed first and then requested permission to return to Jerusalem.

- The king gave Nehemiah letters authorizing his trip and equipped him with supplies. The king also provided an armed escort for protection.

- When Nehemiah arrived in Jerusalem, he surveyed the ruined wall of the city and organized the rebuilding effort.

Nehemiah Rebuilds the Wall: (Nehemiah 3–7)

- Nehemiah assigned people to work on rebuilding the section of the wall closest to where they lived.

- When the local non-Jews discovered the wall was being rebuilt, they protested and tried to stop the effort.

- Nehemiah armed the Jews with weapons and assigned half of them to work on the wall while the other half stood guard.

- Nehemiah soon learned the wealthy Jews were prospering from the misfortunes of the poor Jews, causing them more hardship and suffering.

- Nehemiah was outraged and made the wealthy Jews return the land and money—with interest—they had taken from the poor.

- The local non-Jews continued their opposition. In spite of their efforts, the wall was completed in fifty-two days.

Ezra Restores Worship: (Nehemiah 8–12)

- Ezra read the Book of the Law to the people, while the priests helped everyone understand its meaning.

- The people were touched. They cried as they listened to the Word of God. Nehemiah, Ezra, and the priests exhorted the people to stop crying and celebrate, for it was a holy day.

- While reviewing the Book of the Law, Ezra discovered the Feast of Tabernacles (also known as the Festival of Shelters or Booths) was to be celebrated as a reminder of God's protection in the wilderness.

- The people responded to God's Word and built tent-like structures for the festival. They celebrated for seven days. Ezra read from the Book of the Law each day.

- The Israelites later gathered to repent and confess their sins. The Book of the Law was read aloud again and the priests retold the story of the Jews' history.

- The people solemnly promised to obey God's laws and to take care of the Temple with their tithes and offerings.

- Most people had settled in areas of Judah outside of Jerusalem. The city itself was sparsely populated.

- The Jewish leaders, who were among the few people living in Jerusalem, asked a tenth of the people to move inside the city's wall. Those who agreed to resettle in Jerusalem were commended for their obedience.

- Nehemiah organized a ceremony in Jerusalem to dedicate the new wall. Choirs marched through the city, singing and giving thanks to God as the people celebrated and offered sacrifices to God.

Nehemiah's Religious Reforms: (Nehemiah 13; Malachi 1–4)

- Nehemiah stayed in Jerusalem for twelve years and then went back to Babylon for a while. When Nehemiah returned to Jerusalem, he discovered the people were not living in obedience to God.

- Nehemiah was upset when he found out one of the Jews' known enemies had been given a storeroom in the Temple. Nehemiah threw the man's belongings out of the Temple and had the room cleansed.

- Nehemiah also discovered the Levites had stopped performing their religious duties because the people were not tithing and bringing their offerings to the Lord.

- Nehemiah called the people to obedience, and they responded. The Levites re-instituted worship services. The people began supporting the Temple with their tithes and offerings.

- Nehemiah discovered other areas of disobedience as well. Some people were not observing the Sabbath; some were intermarrying with non-Jews.

- Nehemiah addressed the various areas of disobedience and admonished the people to keep God's laws.

- The prophet Malachi ministered to the Jews in Jerusalem after Nehemiah's religious reforms.

The Prophet Malachi: Malachi ministered in about 430 B.C. and was the last of the Old Testament prophets. After Malachi, God did not speak to mankind again until 400 years later, when He sent an angel with a message for Zechariah, John the Baptist's father.

Malachi reminded the people of God's great love. He chastised the priests for offering unworthy sacrifices that dishonored God. The priests were offering defective animals to God and letting the people keep the best ones for themselves. The priests were supposed to lead the people, but they were causing them to stumble. People were marrying pagan women, divorcing their faithful wives, and cheating God of tithes and offerings.

Malachi prophesied that God would send a messenger to prepare the way for the Messiah (see Malachi 3:1–3; 4:4–6). This prophecy was fulfilled through John the Baptist, forerunner of Jesus Christ..

RECOMMENDED BIBLE READING

Ezra 9:1–10:17	**Ezra Leads the People Back to God**
Nehemiah 4:1–6:19	**Nehemiah Rebuilds the Wall**
Romans 15:1–13	**Live to Please God**
Galatians 5:1–26	**Spirit-directed Living**

MEDITATION & PRAYER

Jeremiah reminds us that God's love never runs out

"God's loyal love couldn't have run out,
    his merciful love couldn't have dried up.

They're created new every morning.
    How great your faithfulness!

I'm sticking with God (I say it over and over).
    He's all I've got left.

God proves to be good to the man who passionately waits,
    to the woman who diligently seeks.

It's a good thing to quietly hope,
    quietly hope for help from God.

It's a good thing when you're young
    to stick it out through the hard times."

(Lamentations 3:22–27 MSG)

Dear God,

I thank You for Your love that never runs out and Your mercy that never dries up. Both are created new every morning. Great is Your faithfulness! I will passionately wait on You and diligently seek Your face. I will quietly hope and place my faith in You, for You are more than enough to take care of all my needs.

Amen

Review Questions

1. Nebuchadnezzar and the Babylonians invaded Jerusalem on three separate occasions. What did Nebuchadnezzar demand from Judah's kings? How did Judah's kings respond? Describe the outcome of each invasion and how it affected the Jews.

_____

_____

_____

_____

_____

_____

2. How did God use Jeremiah during Judah's final years? What was Jeremiah's message and how was it received? How was Jeremiah's ministry like Jesus' ministries?

_____

_____

_____

_____

_____

_____

3. How did God use the prophets Daniel and Ezekiel in Babylon?

_____

_____

_____

_____

_____

_____

4. Who conquered the Babylonians? What happened the night before Babylon's fall?

_____

_____

_____

_____

_____

_____

5. What was King Cyrus' decree? What prophecies in Scripture were fulfilled through Cyrus' decree?

_____

_____

_____

_____

_____

_____

6. Who was Zerubbabel? How did God use him to fulfill His promise to King David?

_____

_____

_____

_____

_____

_____

7. How did God use the prophets Haggai and Zechariah after the exiles' return?

_____

_____

_____

_____

_____

_____

8. Who was Esther? How did God use her to save the Jews?

_____

_____

_____

_____

_____

_____

9. Who was Ezra? How did God use him to rebuild and restore Jerusalem?

_____

_____

_____

_____

_____

_____

_____

10. Who was Nehemiah? How did God use him to rebuild and restore Jerusalem?

_____

_____

_____

_____

_____

_____

_____

PERSONAL REFLECTIONS

11. God disciplined Israel and Judah, allowing them to be captured and exiled. What is the purpose of discipline? How did you benefit from your parents' discipline? What were the benefits of Judah's captivity?

_____

_____

_____

_____

_____

_____

12. The returned exiles had to be reminded of their obligation to finish rebuilding the Temple. Why is it so easy to forget about our obligations to God?

_____

_____

_____

_____

_____

_____

13. What did God reveal to you about His character through His Hebrew names, *Jehovah-Tsidkenu and Jehovah-Shammah*?

_____

_____

_____

_____

_____

_____

14. God used a multitude of ordinary men and women to accomplish His work. What are you doing for God's kingdom?

_____

_____

_____

_____

_____

_____

15. What does God want to accomplish through you? Take a moment and write a prayer in which you ask God, "What do You want to accomplish through me?"

_____

_____

_____

_____

_____

_____

CLOSING PRAYER

The Apostle Paul tells us that nothing can separate us from God's love:

"Who shall separate us from the love of Christ? Shall tribulation, or distress, or persecution, or famine, or nakedness, or peril, or sword? As it is written:

'For Your sake we are killed all day long;
We are accounted as sheep for the slaughter.'

Yet in all these things we are more than conquerors through Him who loved us. For I am persuaded that neither death nor life, nor angels nor principalities nor powers, nor things present nor things to come, nor height nor depth, nor any other created thing, shall be able to separate us from the love of God which is in Christ Jesus our Lord."

(Romans 8:35–39 NKJV)

Dear Lord,

Who can ever separate me from Your love? You see all my problems and take care of all my needs. You lead me, guide me, protect me, comfort me, restore me, and so much more. Your love penetrates my inner being, renewing my strength and giving me true life. I am more than a conqueror because of Your love. I am convinced that nothing will ever separate me from Your great love, which is revealed in Christ Jesus.

Amen

ESTHER

"Then Esther sent this answer to Mordecai: 'Go and get all the Jewish people in Susa together. For my sake, fast; do not eat or drink for three days, night and day. I and my servant girls will also fast. Then I will go to the king, even though it is against the law, and if I die, I die.'" (Esther 4:15–16 NCV)

REVIEW ANSWERS

Chapter 1

1. The Trinity is one God in three persons; God, the Father; Jesus, the Son; and the Holy Spirit. All three members of the Trinity were present during creation. (Genesis 1:1; Genesis 1:26; John 1:1–3; John 1:14–15; Colossians 1:15–17)

2. Satan tempted the woman by questioning what God said; distorting God's Word; appealing to man's spirit of pride, physical appetite, and need for power and control. (Genesis 3:1–6)

3. Before the Fall, man enjoyed an intimate, personal relationship with God. After the Fall, man was spiritually separated from God. The relationship was severed and in need of restoration. (Genesis 1–2)

4. God demonstrated justice when he banished Adam and Eve from the Garden. God held them accountable for their actions. There were consequences for their disobedience. God showed mercy when he covered Adam and Eve with animal skins and allowed them to live outside of the Garden. (Genesis 3:8–24)

5. A *Picture of Redemption* or a *Foreshadowing of Jesus Christ* is when Scripture gives a preview of how God would send Jesus Christ to save mankind and restore our relationship with Him. It is also any scripture that illustrates an aspect of Jesus' character or mission, or one that provides a symbolic representation of Jesus as Redeemer and Savior.

6. The ark was a savior. (Genesis 6–8)

7. Noah demonstrated faith by obeying God and building an ark. God shut Noah and his family inside the ark and kept them safe from the floodwaters. (Genesis 6–9)

8. Covenant is a term used to describe the various promises and agreements God entered into with mankind, and man entered into with his fellow man. When God enters into a covenant, He commits Himself and declares to bring promised blessings to pass some time in the future. The covenant with Abram (Abraham) was that through his offspring, all the nations of the earth would be blessed. This covenant was fulfilled through the death and resurrection of Jesus Christ. (Genesis 12:2–3; Galatians 3:8)

Chapter 2

1. Abraham demonstrated faith when he obeyed God, left his father's home in Haran, and moved to Canaan. Abraham's willing submission to God's covenant of circumcision was another demonstration of faith. On another occasion, Abraham was willing to sacrifice his only son in obedience to God. God rewarded Abraham by declaring him righteous because of his faith and making Abraham the father of many nations. All the nations of the world have been blessed through Abraham's offspring. Without faith, it is impossible to please God. We are saved by our faith, not our works. (Genesis 6–9; Genesis 12–25; Hebrews 11:1–22)

2. Abraham, out of fear, said that Sarah was his sister. Abraham agreed with Sarah and slept with Hagar so that he could father a child. Jacob deceived his brother, Esau, out of his birthright and deceived his father, Isaac, out of Esau's blessing. It was inconsiderate and somewhat arrogant of Joseph to share his dreams with his father and brothers. Job's suffering was so great that he made a number of accusations against God. God knows our human frailties and

He knows our heart. God continued to bless Abraham, Jacob, Joseph, and Job because He is forgiving and infinitely merciful. (Genesis 12–50; Job 3–31)

3. Their faith increased with each encounter with God. They each demonstrated spiritual growth as follows: Abraham trusted God and was willing to sacrifice his son in obedience to the Lord; Jacob wrestled with God for a blessing; Joseph recognized his brothers' misdeeds were part of God's plan to save the Israelites; Job had an encounter with God and acknowledged His sovereignty. (Genesis 22–50; Job 42)

4. Through a series of God-orchestrated events, Joseph interpreted Pharaoh's dream, telling him there would be prosperity followed by famine. Pharaoh rewarded Joseph for this interpretation, making him second in command over all of Egypt and placing him in charge of food supplies. When the famine occurred, Joseph was able to save his family by giving them food and arranging for them to live in Egypt. Joseph became a savior for his family. (Genesis 37–50)

5. Judah (Jacob's fourth son) received God's covenant promise. Jesus was a descendant of Judah. Jacob blessed Judah, saying his brothers would praise him and the scepter would never depart from Judah. (Genesis 49:8–10)

6. Joseph was a shepherd and Jesus is the Good Shepherd. Both Joseph and Jesus' lives were endangered and they were taken to Egypt. Joseph and Jesus were sold for silver; falsely accused; forgave those who wronged them; and saved their nation. (Genesis 37–50)

7. Job was a righteous man who served the Lord. God allowed Job to suffer financial, personal, and physical loss as a test of his faith. Although Job did not understand the reason for his suffering, he continued to trust in the Lord. God rewarded Job's faith, restoring his health and wealth. The story of Job is included in this chapter because it occurred around the same time period as that of the Hebrew patriarchs (Abraham, Isaac, and Jacob) and is a story of faith. Job's story shows that some Gentiles (non-Jews) of this period knew God and had personal relationships with Him. (Job 1–42)

Chapter 3

1. When Moses was eighty years old, he experienced an encounter with God through a burning bush. God wanted to use Moses to deliver the Israelites from slavery and lead them out of Egypt to Canaan, the promised land. Initially, Moses was reluctant to do God's work and wanted God to choose someone else. Eventually, Moses yielded and obeyed. Moses grew spiritually to become a great leader and prophet of the nation of Israel. (Exodus 3–4)

2. Both Moses and Jesus were saved at birth from a decree that baby boys were to be killed. Moses was a shepherd and Jesus is the Good Shepherd. Both were deliverers, leaders, law-givers, prophets, mediators, and intercessors. (Exodus 1–35)

3. The Lord sent a series of plagues as a demonstration of His power. There were ten plagues in all: The water of the Nile River was turned to blood; Frogs took over the land; Gnats infested men and animals; Flies invaded Egypt, but not Goshen where the Israelites lived; Egypt's livestock died, but not Israel's; Boils (sores) infected the Egyptians, but not the Israelites; Hail devastated Egypt, but not Goshen; Locusts destroyed everything left after the hail; Darkness covered Egypt for three days, but not Goshen; and Egypt's firstborn sons and firstborn animals were killed, but Israel's were spared. God also parted the Red Sea so that the Israelites could escape from the Egyptians. (Exodus 7–11, 14:15–31)

4. God instructed the Israelites to smear lamb's blood on the doorframes of their houses. At midnight, God's destroyer (angel of death) killed all the firstborn sons and animals in Egypt that did not have blood on the doorframes. The

Israelites' firstborn were spared because the angel of death saw the blood on their doorframes and passed over their houses. The story of Passover foreshadows the significance of the blood. Jesus is our Passover Lamb, the One who delivers us from the slavery of sin. (Exodus 11–12; John 1:29; 1 Corinthians 5:7; 1 Peter 1:19)

5. The Feast of Unleavened Bread is celebrated in remembrance of the Israelites' hurried flight from Egypt. They left in such a hurry that their bread did not have time to rise. The bread was unleavened or without yeast. Leavening (yeast) is used in Scripture to represent sin. Unleavened bread symbolized freedom from slavery and sin. (Exodus 12; Matthew 16:5–12; Mark 8:15; Luke 12:1; Galatians 5:9)

6. God guided the Israelites with a pillar of cloud by day and a pillar of fire by night. God provided manna for food and water for them to drink. God protected them from disease and gave them victory over their enemies. (Exodus 13–17)

7. In the covenant of the Old Testament, God promised that Israel would be His treasured possession and the Israelites vowed to keep the Laws God gave them through Moses. The covenant was sealed with animals' blood. In the New Testament covenant, God promises mankind salvation through faith in Jesus Christ as their Lord and Savior. The New Testament covenant is sealed with the blood of Jesus Christ. Without the shedding of blood, there can be no remission of sin. (Exodus 20–24; Leviticus 17:11; Matthew 26:28; Luke 22:20; Romans 10:5–10; Hebrews 9:15, 22)

Chapter 4

1. The outer courtyard had an altar for offerings and sacrifices and a basin for the priests to cleanse themselves. Christ is our offering and perfect sacrifice. He has cleansed us with His blood. The Ark represented God's presence and now Jesus lives in us and is with us always. The golden lamp stand symbolized Christ as the Light of the World. The bread symbolized Christ as the Bread of Life. The altar of incense symbolized Christ as our Intercessor. (Exodus 35–40)

2. It signified the end of intercession and atonement by priests as a way to God. Jesus is now our High Priest. We can boldly enter into God's presence through faith in Jesus Christ. (Exodus 35–40; Matthew 27:51; Hebrews 10:19–22)

3. Offerings and sacrifices provided foreshadows of Jesus who would atone for our sins, satisfy God's demand for justice, mediate for us, purify us, and pay the price for our sins. Jesus was a perfect offering without defect and was God's very best. We can now stand in God's presence in the Most Holy Place through the blood Jesus shed for us. (Leviticus 1–7; Hebrews 8–9)

4. Priests were responsible for making offerings and sacrifices repeatedly to atone for the peoples' sins. Jesus, our High Priest, atoned for our sins once and for all with His blood on the cross. (Leviticus 8–10; Hebrews 8–9)

5. When the Israelites reached Canaan's southern border, twelve spies were sent to survey the land. Ten spies reported that the Israelites could not take the land because giants were living in Canaan. Joshua and Caleb insisted that the Israelites could take the land with God's help. The people listened to the negative report of the ten spies and were punished for their unbelief. They tried to move forward into Canaan at Kadesh Barnea without God's blessings and suffered a major defeat. (Numbers 13–14)

6. Moses' first speech was a review of the Israelites' forty year journey. Moses' second speech was a review of God's laws and commandments. Moses' third speech was a review of God's covenant. Moses explained they would be blessed if they kept God's laws and cursed if they did not keep God's laws. These speeches were to prepare Israel spiritually and mentally for what lay ahead. (Deuteronomy 1–34)

7. God told the Israelites to go into Canaan fighting and conquer the land. They were to annihilate the people and their altars, and were not to form relationships with the Canaanites, or make deals, or intermarry with them. (Deuteronomy 7)

Chapter 5

1. A major portion of Joshua is about the military battles Israel fought to take possession of the promised land. (Joshua 1–12)

2. Joshua's name means, *The Lord is Salvation*. Joshua is the Hebrew equivalent of Jesus in Aramaic. Joshua was Moses' assistant. He was already a respected warrior and leader. God divinely appointed Joshua leader of Israel. Both Moses and Israel's high priest commissioned Joshua as Moses' successor. God instructed Joshua, telling him obedience to the law would result in success. God told Joshua He would not leave or fail him. (Exodus 17:8–16; 24:13; 32:17; 33:11; Numbers 13–14, 26–27; 34:17; Deuteronomy 1, 3, 31, 34; Joshua 1; Matthew 1:21)

3. The Ark was where the presence of God resided and reminded the people that God was with them. (Exodus 25:10–22; Exodus 40; Numbers 7:89)

4. God fought the battle. God miraculously caused the walls of the city to fall down. (Joshua 6)

5. Rahab was a prostitute who lived at the entrance of the city of Jericho. She helped the two Israelite men who came to spy on the city. Rahab believed in the God of Israel. Jesus Christ was a descendant of Rahab. (Joshua 2, 6; Matthew 1)

6. Those accused of a killing could go to a city of refuge for safety until a trial could be convened. This protected the rights of those involved in an accidental killing and guaranteed them the right to a trial. (Joshua 20–21)

7. A Judge was the name Israel gave to people God empowered to perform His special work. Judges were rulers, deliverers, military leaders, saviors, liberators, administrators of justice, settlers of disputes, counselors, and much more.

8. The Book of Judges tells Israel's history from Joshua's death to the period prior to Israel's first king. It tells of Israel's repeated cycles in which the people would fall into idolatry; Israel's enemies would oppress them; Israel would then cry out to God for help; God would empower or raise up a judge to save them from their enemies; Israel would serve the Lord; and then fall into idolatry again.

Chapter 6

1. The role of the kinsman-redeemer is outlined in Leviticus 25:25, *"If one of your countrymen becomes poor and sells some of his property, his nearest relative is to come and redeem what his countryman has sold."* Jesus is our kinsman-redeemer (Leviticus 25:25; Hebrews 2:17)

2. Ruth was King David's grandmother and an ancestor of Jesus Christ. (Ruth 4; Matthew 1)

3. Samuel was Israel's last judge, prophet, and priest. He led Israel back to God and anointed Saul and David as kings. (1 Samuel 1–10)

4. Saul's downfall was disobedience, envy, and fear. First, Saul offered a sacrifice to God instead of waiting for Samuel, the priest. Second, Saul did not completely destroy the Amalekites and all of their livestock as God had commanded.

Saul became jealous of David and tried to kill him. Finally, he consulted a medium to bring Samuel back from the dead. (1 Samuel 11–31)

5. David was a man after God's own heart. He conquered Jerusalem and made it Israel's capital. David brought the Ark to Jerusalem. He conquered enemies that should have been defeated much earlier. He showed kindness to Jonathan's son, Mephibosheth. He prepared detailed plans for the Temple and donated gold and silver towards its construction. David wrote 73 of the 150 Psalms. (1 Samuel 13:14; Acts 13:22; 2 Samuel; 5–10; 1 Chronicles 11–29)

6. David committed adultery with Bathsheba and arranged to have her husband, Uriah, killed. The consequences of these sins were that David's child with Bathsheba died. David's household was in turmoil and rebelled against him. Later, David took a census that displeased God and the Lord sent a plague that killed thousands of people. (2 Samuel; 11–20; 24)

7. Solomon was one of the wisest men who ever lived. Solomon built the Temple using David's plans. He was responsible for numerous building projects in Israel and established the nation as a center of commerce. He wrote the Book of Proverbs, Ecclesiastes, and the Song of Solomon. His downfall was disobedience. He married pagan women and allowed them to influence his religious life with the practice of idolatry. (1 Kings 2–11; 2 Chronicles 1–9)

Chapter 7

1. Both Israel and Judah turned away from God and fell into idolatry. Idolatry caused the people to abandon God and so God abandoned them, but was never far away. God continued to pursue the people through the prophets. Idolatry caused the nations to become unrighteous and immoral, which separated them from God.

2. Since both Israel and Judah had turned away from God and fallen into idolatry, the prophets were divinely chosen to deliver the Lord's message and remind the people of their covenant relationship with God. Prophets instructed the people to obey God's laws; pointed out sin and unrighteousness; urged the people to come back to God; and warned the people of the consequences of sin.

3. The prophets delivered God's message here on earth to the people; confronted sin; performed miracles; prophesied about future events, many of which have since come to pass; pronounced God's righteous judgment; called people to repent and come back to God; and were rejected by the people.

4. Baal worship promoted immorality. Prostitution, sex orgies, and the sacrificing of children were a routine part of Baal worship all of which were an abomination to God. The Lord used Jehu to rid Israel of Baal worship. Jehu destroyed all traces of Baal worship in Israel. (2 Kings 9–10)

5. A Messianic prophecy is one that foretold of the coming of the Messiah. The word "Messiah" in Hebrew is translated as "Christ" in the Greek, and "Anointed One" in English. Isaiah prophesied that God would send a Messiah to save his people (Isaiah 9:6 - 7); and the Messiah would be born of a virgin (Isaiah 7:14). Isaiah told us the Messiah would come to serve the needy (Isaiah 61:1 - 2); and would be performing miracles (Isaiah 35:5 - 6). Isaiah described Him as One who would suffer, be rejected, and would die as a perfect sacrifice for our sins (Isaiah 53). Isaiah also told us the Messiah would swallow up death forever (Isaiah 25:8). Micah told us the Lord himself would come and lead us (Micah 2:13); and the Messiah would be born in Bethlehem Ephrathah. (Micah 5:2)

6. There was only one dynasty in Judah because God had promised King David that his kingdom would last forever. (2 Samuel 7:12–13)

7. The Samaritans were not racially, culturally, or religiously pure. God loves everyone and is not partial. Jesus taught us that man might look on the outside, but God looks at the heart. (Deuteronomy 10:17–18; John 4:7–26; Acts 15:8–9)

8. Hezekiah showed the Babylonian ambassadors all the treasures and wealth of Israel. This was an act of pride. Hezekiah arrogantly took all the credit for his success instead of giving God the glory. The Babylonians returned and destroyed Jerusalem, taking everything Hezekiah had so proudly shown them. They also took Hezekiah's descendants as captives just as Isaiah had prophesied. (2 Kings 20:12–19; 2 Chronicles 32:24–31; James 4:6)

9. We serve a very loving God who cares deeply about all of us. God will forgive and save those who come to Him with a truly repentant heart no matter how great the sin. God loves everyone and does not want anyone to perish. (Romans 10:8–10; 2 Peter 3:9)

Chapter 8

1. In 605 B.C., Nebuchadnezzar invaded Jerusalem, looted the Temple, and demanded annual payments from King Jehoiakim. Nebuchadnezzar then carried some of Jerusalem's royal family and noblemen to Babylon. Daniel was included in this first group of exiles. Jehoiakim made payments to the Babylonians for three years and then rebelled. Nebuchadnezzar returned to Jerusalem in 597 B.C. He took Jehoiachin in chains along with the royal family, officials, and more prominent citizens, including Ezekiel. Zedekiah, king of Judah, refused to pay tribute to the Babylonians. Nebuchadnezzar invaded Jerusalem a final time in 586 B.C. He gouged out Zedekiah's eyes, totally destroyed the Temple, and burned the city. With the exception of a few poor people, everyone was taken to Babylon. (2 Kings 23–25; 2 Chronicles 36)

2. Jeremiah ministered to the Jews in Jerusalem during Judah's final years. His ministry was filled with prophecies and many tears as he repeatedly warned the people about God's judgment against sin and tried to get them to return to God. When Jeremiah advised the Jews to surrender to the Babylonians, he was called a traitor and was thrown in prison. Both Jeremiah and Jesus were grief-stricken, rejected, and despised. (Jeremiah 1:25, 29, 36–43)

3. Daniel was trained in Babylonian culture and became a well-respected advisor in the palace. Daniel interpreted dreams and had visions about the future. While Daniel was ministering in the palace, Ezekiel was preaching in the streets of Babylon to the people of Israel. Ezekiel had numerous visions and prophesies. (Daniel 1–12; Ezekiel 1–48)

4. The Medes and Persians conquered the Babylonians. King Belshazzar of Babylon hosted a banquet for his nobles. The king and his guests toasted their idol gods and drank wine from the sacred goblets taken from the Temple in Jerusalem. Suddenly, a hand appeared and wrote a message on the wall. Daniel interpreted the message and told the king that his kingdom would be divided and given to the Medes and Persians. King Belshazzar was killed that very night and Darius the Mede took over the kingdom. (Daniel 5)

5. Cyrus' decree allowed the exiles to return to Jerusalem and fulfilled Jeremiah's prophecy, which stated that the exiles would be in captivity for seventy years. Isaiah's prophecy about a man named Cyrus calling for the rebuilding of Jerusalem and the Temple was also fulfilled. (Ezra 1; Jeremiah 25:11; 29:10; Isaiah 44:28)

6. Zerubbabel was King Jehoiachin's grandson and a descendant of King David. Zerubbabel led the first group of exiles back to Jerusalem and became Judah's governor. Zerubbabel was an ancestor of Jesus Christ, fulfilling God's promise to David. (Ezra 1–5; Matthew 1:12; Luke 3:27)

7. God called both Haggai and Zechariah to minister to the returned exiles and encourage them to finish rebuilding the Temple. (Ezra 5:1; 6:14; Haggai 1–2; Zechariah 1–4)

8. Hadassah, also called Esther, was a young Jewish exile who lived in Susa with her cousin Mordecai. King Xerxes fell in love with Esther and made her his queen. Esther approached the king uninvited and asked him to save the Jews. Esther's actions could have meant her death, but the king ordered Haman's death instead. The king gave Esther and Mordecai permission to issue a decree that allowed the Jews to defend themselves. (Esther 1–10)

9. Ezra was a priest who led a second group of exiles to Jerusalem. He was responsible for restoring worship in accordance with the laws of Moses. (Ezra 7–10)

10. Nehemiah was the king's cupbearer and led a third group of exiles to Jerusalem. He led the effort to rebuild Jerusalem's wall. Both he and Ezra were in Jerusalem during the same time period and led religious reforms. (Nehemiah 1–13)

HOW WE GOT THE OLD TESTAMENT

Our Old Testament is the same as the Hebrew Bible (Jewish Bible), which was written in Hebrew and Aramaic as God revealed Himself to men. Some of our Old Testament books are in a different sequence from those in the Hebrew Bible, but the text is the same. God revealed the first five books of the Bible to Moses in about 1445 B.C. Prophets, priests, kings, and other men of God were divinely inspired and continued authoring writings until about 430 B.C.

The original Hebrew text was meticulously copied by scribes, men who were trained in procedures for copying text in a way that would ensure accuracy. These men understood they were preserving the very Word of God and approached their job with reverence. It is said that scribes kept records of the exact number of words and alphabets each writing should contain and used these records to verify the accuracy of copied writings.

Copies of the original text were passed down from generation to generation. These copies are called manuscripts. In Jesus' day, manuscripts of the Hebrew Bible were called "The Holy Scriptures" and were used to teach God's Word. It is widely accepted that the manuscript Jesus taught and quoted from was a Greek translation of the Hebrew Bible called the Septuagint.

As a result of the strict rules and safeguards adhered to by scribes, the Hebrew text has been transmitted with very few copyists' errors. According to Bible scholars, none of these errors or differences among manuscripts has affected the overall meaning or message of any passage of Scripture. Furthermore, ancient manuscripts found near the Dead Sea, dating from second century B.C. to first century A.D., are virtually identical to the text used to translate our present day Old Testament.

Other Old Testament books exist which were never included in the Hebrew Bible. These books are commonly referred to as the Apocryphal books of the Old Testament. Many of these Apocryphal books tell of Jewish history during the few centuries before Jesus' birth and provide a picture of Jewish life in Palestine between the Old and New Testaments. While these books are included in the Catholic Bible and earlier copies of the Protestant Bible, they are not included as canonical books in our modern-day Bible.

 Note: The word *canon* literally means "cane" or "measuring rod" and is the measure used to authenticate a book of the Bible.

There are many reasons why the Apocryphal books were not included in our Bible. However, the major reason is that these books were never included in the Hebrew or Jewish Bible and were never referenced in Scripture by Jesus or His apostles. The tests for canonicity of the Old Testament books as used in our English or Protestant Bible are as follows:

- ✓ Was the book included in the original Hebrew Bible?

- ✓ Was the book quoted by Jesus or the apostles?

- ✓ Was the book accepted by the early church fathers?

- ✓ Does the book have intrinsic qualities of inspiration?

ORGANIZATION OF THE OLD TESTAMENT

Old Testament

The Old Testament provides a record of God's relationship and interactions with mankind before the birth of Jesus Christ. There are thirty-nine Old Testament books in our English or Protestant Bible. These books are arranged in four major divisions as follows:

The Law or Pentateuch (5 books)

The first five books of the Old Testament provide an account of God's relationship with early mankind and the patriarchs (Abraham, Isaac, and Jacob). God promised to give the land of Canaan to these patriarchs, and He established the nation of Israel through their descendants. The nation was later enslaved by the Egyptians and suffered 400 years of bondage. God miraculously delivered Israel from slavery and gave the nation laws and procedures for worship through the prophet Moses. When Moses died, his assistant Joshua took over leadership of Israel.

- ✓ **Genesis**
- ✓ **Exodus**
- ✓ **Leviticus**
- ✓ **Numbers**
- ✓ **Deuteronomy**

History (12 books)

These twelve books provide details of Israel's history after Moses' death, starting with the battles the nation fought for possession of Canaan under Joshua's leadership. Canaan was later called "Israel." The nation of Israel's history continues in these books with the period of the judges; the period of the kings; Israel's fall, captivity, and exile; and finally Israel's return to Jerusalem and the rebuilding of the Temple.

- ✓ **Joshua**
- ✓ **Judges**
- ✓ **Ruth**
- ✓ **1 Samuel**
- ✓ **2 Samuel**
- ✓ **1 Kings**
- ✓ **2 Kings**

✓ **1 Chronicles**

✓ **2 Chronicles**

✓ **Ezra**

✓ **Nehemiah**

✓ **Esther**

Poetry (5 books)

These five books are written in poetic literary style. Here we find divinely inspired expressions, thoughts, and questions on topics such as pain and suffering, life, wisdom, love, and God. The books of poetry highlight the fact that a close personal relationship with God is needed to live a good life, full of purpose and direction.

✓ **Job**

✓ **Psalms**

✓ **Proverbs**

✓ **Ecclesiastes**

✓ **Song of Solomon (Song of Songs)**

Prophecy (17)

Men divinely chosen by God wrote the books of prophecy to remind Israel of their covenant with Him. The Lord communicated with the prophets through visions, dreams, angels, and at times, audibly. The prophets delivered God's message to the people, instructing them to obey God's laws. The prophets pointed out sin, urged the people to return to God, warned about the consequences of sin, and often were inspired by God to reveal future events.

The books of prophecy are categorized as major and minor writings. It is important to keep in mind that the terms "major" and "minor" are a reference to the size of the prophet's book and not the significance of its content. Although the major prophets wrote more Scripture, the minor prophets' writings are as important as those of the major prophets.

Major Prophets (5)

✓ **Isaiah**

✓ **Jeremiah**

✓ **Lamentations**

✓ **Ezekiel**

✓ **Daniel**

Minor Prophets (12)

✓ **Hosea**

✓ **Joel**

- ✓ **Amos**

- ✓ **Obadiah**

- ✓ **Jonah**

- ✓ **Micah**

- ✓ **Nahum**

- ✓ **Habakkuk**

- ✓ **Zephaniah**

- ✓ **Haggai**

- ✓ **Zechariah**

- ✓ **Malachi**

TIMELINE OF OLD TESTAMENT BOOKS

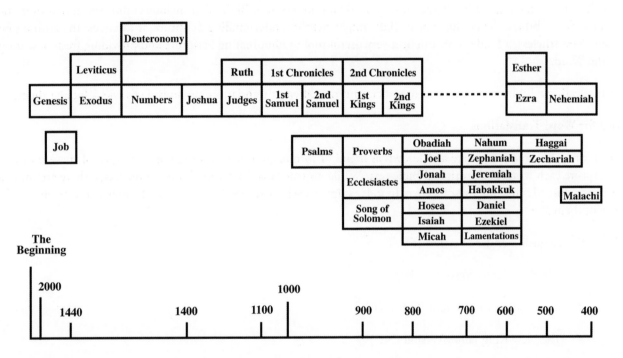

Note: Old Testament books are sequenced according to when events in each book occurred, and not according to when books were written.

SELECTING A BIBLE

The Bible was written in Hebrew, Greek, and some Aramaic. If we were able to read Hebrew, Greek, and Aramaic, there would be no need for the various Bible versions or translations. Since most of us cannot read the Bible in its original languages, Bible scholars have taken it upon themselves to translate it for us. The various Bible versions are actually different translations of our Bible. There is only one Protestant Bible, but it has been translated in various ways.

You will want to find a good Bible that you can read and understand. Bibles that include comments and author's notes are called Study Bibles. While this type of Bible might help in understanding Scripture, it interjects the author's point of view. Nevertheless, a Study Bible can be a very useful tool in illuminating Scripture and providing fresh new insights into the Word.

When selecting a Bible, it is important to understand the different translation methods. Let's take a look at them.

Word for Word Translations

"Word for word" translations are also known as literal or formal equivalent translations. The goal of these translations is to capture each word of the original Bible text. While no true "word for word" translation exists, there are some that come very close to achieving this objective. In today's times, we have several "word for word" translations to choose from. A few of them are:

- ✓ English Standard Version (ESV)
- ✓ The King James Version (KJV)
- ✓ New American Standard Bible (NASB)
- ✓ The New King James Version (NKJV)

Thought for Thought Translations

The second type is the "thought for thought" translation, also called "dynamic equivalent" translation. The objective of these translations is either to capture the thought of the sentence—or—to capture the thought of the paragraph of the original text. In "thought for thought" translations, ensuring that each word of text is represented in the translation becomes less important, while achieving a translation that maintains the overall thought of the original text becomes the primary goal. Examples of these translations are as follows:

- • Capture the Sentence
  - ✓ The Amplified Bible (AMP)
  - ✓ Contemporary English Version (CEV)
  - ✓ New Century Version (NCV)
  - ✓ New International Version (NIV)

- ✓ New Living Translation (NLT)

- Capture the Paragraph

  - ✓ The Message (MSG)

  - ✓ The Living Bible (LB)

COMPARISON OF BIBLE TRANSLATIONS

Hebrew Transliteration	KJV	NKJV	NASB	NIV	NLT	MSG
Proverbs 16:3						
Gol ʾel- Yahweh maʾaseykaa wᵃyikonuw machsh ᵃboteykaa	Commit thy works unto the LORD, and thy thoughts shall be established.	Commit your works to the LORD, and your thoughts will be established.	Commit your works to the LORD and your plans will be established.	Commit to the LORD whatever you do, and your plans will succeed.	Commit your actions to the LORD, and your plans will succeed.	Put God in charge of your work, then what you've planned will take place.
Isaiah 26:3						
Yeetser caamuwk titsor shaalowm shaalowm kiy bᵃkaa baaTuwach	Thou wilt keep him in perfect peace, whose mind is stayed on thee: because he trusteth in thee.	You will keep him in perfect peace, whose mind is stayed on You, Because he trusts in You.	The steadfast of mind You will keep in perfect peace, Because he trusts in You.	You will keep in perfect peace him whose mind is steadfast, because he trusts in you.	You will keep in perfect peace all who trust in you, all whose thoughts are fixed on you!	People with their minds set on you, you keep completely whole, Steady on their feet, because they keep at it and don't quit.
Psalms 36:5–7						
Yahweh bᵃhashaamayim chacdekaa ᵃmuwnaatᵃkaa ʿad- shᵃchaaqiym Tsidqaatᵃkaa kᵃharreey- ʿeel mishpaaTekaa tᵃhowm rabaah ʾAadaam- uwbᵃheemaah towshiyaʿ Yahweh ʾElohiym Uwbneey ʾaadaam bᵃtseel kᵃnaapeykaa yechecaayuwn	Thy mercy, O LORD, is in the heavens; and thy faithfulness reacheth unto the clouds. Thy righteousness is like the great mountains; thy judgments are a great deep: O LORD, thou preservest man and beast. How excellent is thy loving kindness, O God! therefore the children of men put their trust under the shadow of thy wings.	Your mercy, O LORD, is in the heavens; Your faithfulness reaches to the clouds. Your righteousness is like the great mountains; Your judgments are a great deep; O LORD, You preserve man and beast. How precious is Your loving kindness, O God! Therefore the children of men put their trust under the shadow of Your wings.	Your loving-kindness, O LORD, extends to the heavens, Your faithfulness reaches to the skies. Your righteousness is like the mountains of God; Your judgments are like a great deep. O LORD, You preserve man and beast. How precious is Your loving-kindness, O God! And the children of men take refuge in the shadow of Your wings.	Your love, O LORD, reaches to the heavens, your faithfulness to the skies. Your righteousness is like the mighty mountains, your justice like the great deep. O LORD, you preserve both man and beast. How priceless is your unfailing love! Both high and low among men find refuge in the shadow of your wings.	Your unfailing love, O LORD, is as vast as the heavens; your faithfulness reaches beyond the clouds. Your righteousness is like the mighty mountains, your justice like the ocean depths. You care for people and animals alike, O LORD. How precious is your unfailing love, O God! All humanity finds shelter in the shadow of your wings.	God's love is meteoric, his loyalty astronomic, His purpose titanic, his verdicts oceanic. Yet in his largeness nothing gets lost; Not a man, not a mouse, slips through the cracks. How exquisite your love, O God! How eager we are to run under your wings,

271

OLD TESTAMENT SUMMARY OF MAJOR EVENTS

Biblical Event	Approx. Date (B.C.)
Abram's Birth	2166
Abram Arrives in Canaan	2091
Isaac's Birth	2066
Jacob's Birth	2006
Job's Story	Between 2000–1800
Abraham Dies	1991
Joseph's Birth	1915
Isaac Dies	1886
Jacob Dies	1859
Joseph Dies	1805
Moses' Birth	1526
Exodus from Egypt	1446
God Gives the Ten Commandments	1445
Joshua Commissioned / Moses Dies	1406
Israel Arrives in Canaan	1406
Joshua Allocates Land to Tribes	1398
Judges Empowered to Rule	1375–1050
Ruth's Story	Between 1375–1050
Samuel's Birth	1105
Saul Becomes King	1050
David Becomes King	1010
Solomon Becomes King	970
Temple Completed by Solomon	959
The Kingdom Is Divided	930
Israel (Northern Kingdom) Falls	722
Judah (Southern Kingdom) Is Captured	605
1st Exile	605
2nd Exile	597
Jerusalem Falls / 3rd Exile	586
Fall of Babylon	539

Biblical Event	Approx. Date (B.C.)
King Cyrus' Decree	538
Zerubbabel Returns Leading 1st Group	538
Altar Rebuilt	537
Temple's Foundation Laid	536
Temple Rebuilt	515
Xerxes Becomes King of Persia	486
Esther Becomes Queen of Persia	479
Esther Saves Jews	473
Ezra Returns Leading 2nd Group	458
Nehemiah Returns	445
Jerusalem's Wall Rebuilt	445

HEBREW NAMES OF GOD

Hebrew Name	Pronunciation	Translation	Meaning
Elohim	e-lo'-him, el'-o-hem	God	Primary name used in the Old Testament when referring to God as Creator.
El Elyon	el e-li'-on	God Most High	Supreme and Sovereign Ruler of the universe.
Adonai	a-do'-ni	Lord	Master. The One who is in authority and should be obeyed.
El Roi	el roi	The God Who Sees	The One who is omnipresent and sees all.
El Shaddai	el shad'-i	God Almighty	The All-Powerful and All-Sufficient One.
Jehovah-Jireh	je-ho'-va ji'-re	The LORD Will Provide	The Provider. The One who takes care of our every need.
Yahweh (Jehovah)	yah-weh, (je-ho'-va)	The Self-Existent One	The personal name of the One True God.
Jehovah-Rapha	je-ho'-va ra'-fa	The LORD Who Heals	The Great Physician and Healer.
Jehovah-Nissi	je-ho'-va nis'-i	The LORD Is My Banner	The Conqueror. The One who gives victory over the enemy.
Jehovah-Mekoddish-kem	je-ho'-va me-kad-dish-kim	The LORD Makes You Holy	The One who sanctifies.
Jehovah-Shalom	je-ho'-va sha'-lom	The LORD Is Peace	The One who gives peace.
Jehovah-Sabaoth	je-ho'-va sa-ba'-oth	The LORD of Hosts	The One who has multitudes in his service.
Jehovah-Raah	je-ho'-va ra'-ah	The LORD Is My Shepherd	The Shepherd. The One who takes care of His flock.
Jehovah-Tsidkenu	je-ho'-va tsid-ke'-nu	The LORD Is Our Righteousness	The One who makes us righteous.
Jehovah-Shammah	je-ho'-va sham'-a	The LORD Is There	New Jerusalem, where God will reside forever.

OLD TESTAMENT SACRIFICIAL OFFERINGS

Name of Sacrifice	Purpose of Sacrifice
Burnt Offering	An animal without defect was sacrificed to atone for individual sin and express devotion to God.
Grain Offering	The very best of one's flour or grain was offered and burned in reverence to God, acknowledging that all is given to us by God.
Fellowship or Peace Offering	An animal without defect was sacrificed and its fat burned as an expression of one's desire for peace and fellowship with God.
Sin Offering	An animal without defect was sacrificed and its fat burned as an offering to purify and cleanse one's unintentional sins.
Guilt Offering	An animal without defect was sacrificed to make restitution for injuries against others and sins against God.

JEWISH HOLY DAYS, FEASTS AND FESTIVALS

Name of Event	When Observed	Purpose of Observance
Sabbath	Every 7 Days	To honor God's sacred day of rest. No work was performed.
Sabbath Year	Every 7 Years	To allow the land to rest. No crops were planted.
Year of Jubilee	Every 50 Years	To celebrate restoration. All property was returned to its original owner.
	Annually	
Purim	Feb/March	To remember Israel's deliverance during the time period of Esther's reign as Queen of Persia.
Passover	March/April	To remember Israel's deliverance from slavery in Egypt.
Unleavened Bread	March/April	To celebrate the exodus from slavery.
First Fruits	March/April	To celebrate the first grains of the barley harvest.
Pentecost, (Weeks or Harvest)	May/June	To celebrate the end of the barley harvest and beginning of the wheat harvest.
Trumpets, (Rosh Hashanah)	Sept/Oct	To present offerings in celebration of the Jewish New Year.
Day of Atonement, (Yom Kippur)	Sept/Oct	To atone for the nation's sins. Sacrifices were made to cleanse the priests, people, tabernacle, and altar.
Tabernacles, (Shelters or Booths)	Sept/Oct	To commemorate God's protection and provisions while Israel was in the desert.
Lights, (Dedication or Hanukkah)	Nov/Dec	To celebrate the rededication of the Temple after Israel's revolt in 165 B.C.

THE PROPHETS

Prophet	Time Period	Ministered To	Main Message
Elijah	875–848	Israel	Confronted Israel and Baal worship. Proved that there is only One True God.
Elisha	848–797	Israel	Succeeded Elijah in Israel. Performed mighty miracles for the needy.
Obadiah	855–840 (?) or 598–580 (?)	Edom	Pronounced judgment against Edom for their pride and harassment of the Jews.
Joel	835–796 (?)	Judah	Warned about the impending Day of the Lord's Judgment.
Jonah	793–753	Nineveh	Admonished the people of Nineveh in Assyria to repent of their sins.
Amos	760–750	Israel	Warned that Israel and Judah would be exiled if they did not repent and turn to God.
Hosea	753–715	Israel	Denounced immorality and ungodliness.
Micah	740–687	Judah	Prophesied about both Israel and Judah's captivity.
Isaiah	740–681	Judah	Warned about God's impending judgment and prophesied about future salvation and restoration.
Nahum	663–654	Nineveh	Prophesied that the Assyrian Empire would be destroyed for acts of cruelty.
Zephaniah	640–621	Judah	Proclaimed God's judgment against sin and called the people to repentance.
Jeremiah	627–586	Judah	Declared God's certain judgment. Was rejected. Expressed deep sorrow and mourned the Fall of Jerusalem.
Habakkuk	612–589	Judah	Prayed about the people's immorality. God answered with a message of hope.
Daniel	605–536	Babylon	Advised and interpreted dreams for kings in Babylon. Prophesied about future events.
Ezekiel	593–571	Babylon	Prophesied about Jerusalem's certain destruction and urged the people to repent.
Haggai	520–516	Judah	Encouraged the rebuilding of the Temple. Foretold of God's glory filling the Temple.
Zechariah	520–516	Judah	Urged the people to return to God and finish rebuilding the Temple.
Malachi	430–400	Judah	Reminded the people of God's great love and chastised the priests for dishonoring God.

GLOSSARY

Abomination–A term used to describe an utterly abhorrent and loathsome situation.

Altar–A raised mound of earth or stone or other type of platform used for sacrifices and praising God.

Anoint–To rub with oil in a ceremony of consecration. The practice of anointing with perfumed oil was common among the Hebrews.

Armor-bearer–An attendant who carried a soldier's equipment. Usually an officer selected by kings and generals because of his bravery.

Armor of God–God is the faithful protector of His people and is often referred to as a shield for those that put their trust in Him. In other words, putting on the armor of God is having faith that He will protect you.

Ark of the Covenant–The chest containing the two stone tablets inscribed with the Ten Commandments, kept in the holiest part of the ancient Jewish Tabernacle. It was the central symbol of God's presence with the people of Israel.

Ashtoreth–An idol goddess frequently referred to as the wife of Baal, the sun god.

Apostle–A New Testament word, meaning one who is sent on a mission. Jesus commissioned His twelve disciples as apostles and made an appearance after His death to commission Paul as an apostle.

Atone–To reconcile or make amends for sin.

Baal–A male idol sun-god that was a Canaanite fertility god. Baal worship was a demoralizing form of idolatry.

Bible–A compilation of writings, written by men inspired by God. It is the written Word of God and God's message to mankind.

Bible Translations–The various renderings of Biblical manuscripts from their original language (Hebrew, Aramaic, or Greek) to English or some other language. Some manuscripts have been translated "word for word," while others use a "thought for thought" translation method. (See the Introduction section titled, "Using this Study", for a list of Bible versions and translations used in this study.)

Birthright–In ancient times, an honor given to the oldest son, which included the privilege of becoming the family's leader as well as inheriting a double portion of the family's wealth upon his father's death.

Blessed–Holy; sacred; consecrated. Enjoying great happiness.

Blessings–Good wishes or approval. The gift of divine favor or blessings because of God's special favor.

Book of the Law–The laws God gave to Moses.

Cast lots–A number of small stones or pebbles were placed in a container and then drawn or cast out at random one by one. The Israelites frequently cast lots as a method of ascertaining God's divine will.

Canaanites–A general term used to reference all the various peoples that lived in Canaan.

Circumcision–Removal of the male's genital foreskin. God initiated this rite as a sign of His covenant with Abraham. Circumcision has been performed from generation to generation among Abraham's (Jewish) descendants, identifying them as part of God's covenant with Abraham.

Concubine–A mistress; a woman living in a socially recognized state of cohabitation without being legally married.

Conjured–In primitive or superstitious rites, to summon (a demon or spirit) as by a magic spell.

Consecrate–To make sacred or holy.

Covenant (Testament)–Used to describe the various promises and agreements God entered into with mankind, and man entered into with his fellowman. When God enters into a covenant, He commits Himself and declares to bring promised blessings to pass some time in the future.

Crucifixion–To put to death by nailing or binding to a cross and leaving to die of exposure.

Crucifixion, The–Refers to the crucifying of Jesus Christ.

Cup bearer–A person who fills and serves the wine cups in a king's palace. Often a trusted and high ranking official in the courts of Ancient Near Eastern kings who was responsible for serving wine at the king's table and protecting the king from poisoning.

Devil (See Satan)

Divination–The act or practice of trying to foretell the future and determine answers to questions hidden to humans by occult means.

Dynasty–A succession of rulers from the same line of descent.

Fall–To yield to temptation; to do wrong; to sin

Fall, The (The Fall of Man)–Refers to the first man and woman's (Adam and Eve's) rejection of God's rules, which marked the beginning of sin and unrighteousness in the world.

Fleece–The wool covering of a sheep or similar animal.

Foreshadow–To be a sign of (something to come); to indicate or suggest beforehand.

Foreshadowing of Jesus Christ (Picture of Redemption)–A scriptural preview of how God would send Jesus Christ to save mankind and restore our relationship with Him. It is also any scripture that illustrates an aspect of Jesus' character or mission, or one that provides a symbolic representation of Jesus as Redeemer and Savior.

Gentiles (non-Jews)–Any person who is not a Jew. Historically among Jews, heathens (people regarded as uncivilized) and pagans (people with little or no religion) were considered to be Gentiles.

Glean–To pick up grain left behind by harvesters.

God–The Creator of the universe and everything in it. He is not limited by time or space and has no beginning and no end. God is all-knowing, all-powerful, and in all places at all times.

Grace–Unmerited or undeserved favor.

Handmaiden–A woman or girl servant or attendant.

Hebrew–Any member of a group of Semitic peoples tracing their descent from Noah's son Shem, Abraham, Isaac, and Jacob; an Israelite or Jew. The word also refers to the ancient Semitic language of the Israelites, in which most of the Old Testament was written.

Hebrew Names of God–(See Appendix 7)

Holy–Dedicated to religious use; belonging to or coming from God; sacred. Being spiritually perfect or pure; untainted by evil or sin.

Holy Spirit–The Spirit of God. The third being in the Trinity with God the Father and Jesus the Son. After Jesus' resurrection, the Holy Spirit came to live within the minds and hearts of Christians as a Comforter and Guide to all who have accepted Christ.

Host–Those in God's heavenly army (angels).

Intercessory Prayer–A petitioning of God's special favor for someone other than oneself.

Israel–A people and a nation. Jacob's descendants are the people and nation. Israel is the name given to Jacob after his struggle with God. The name was later given to Jacob's descendants, the twelve tribes of Israel, called Israelites. It is also used in reference to the land God gave to Jacob's (Israel's) descendants.

Jesus Christ–God made human. The second being in the Trinity with God the Father and the Holy Spirit. God became a man, in the person of Jesus, and lived among us to show us how to live a life that is righteous and pleasing to God.

Jews, Jewish–A person descended from the ancient Hebrews of Biblical times. A person whose religion is Judaism.

Judge–The name Israel gave the people God empowered to perform His special work. At a time when Israel had no elected leader and there was no standing army, God used Judges to accomplish His will and rescue Israel from their enemies.

Kinsman-redeemer–A close relative who recovers his kinsman's property. According to Jewish law, if an Israelite became poor and had to sell his property, his close relative should pay the price to redeem or recover it.

Lamp stand–In ancient times, there were no candles and therefore no candlesticks. Lamps were oil-fed and had a wick. In the Tabernacle and the Temple, lamps were on stands and burned olive oil.

Leprosy–A generic term applied to a variety of skin disorders. Its symptoms range from white patches on the skin, to running sores, to the loss of digits on the fingers and toes. For the Hebrews, it was a dreaded malady which rendered its victims ceremonially unclean—that is, unfit to worship God.

Leavening–Yeast used to make bread rise.

Levite–A member of the tribe of Levi, Jacob's third son. The name often applies only to those descendants of Levi who assisted the priests and handled more routine duties in support of the Tabernacle.

Lord's Supper, The–Also called "The Last Supper," "Communion," and "Eucharist." The central Christian rite in which bread and wine are consecrated and distributed as the body and blood of Jesus or as symbols of them. It is a memorial service celebrated by the church to signify Jesus' sacrificial death for humankind's sin. This observance was established by the Lord Himself at the Last Supper when He symbolically offered Himself as the paschal Lamb of atonement and commanded all Christ-followers to remember His death.

Lots–(See Casting Lots)

Manna–A Hebrew word, which means "What is it?" The food substance provided by God to the Jews during their exodus from Egypt.

Mediate–To settle or bring about reconciliation.

Mediator–one who intervenes between two parties who are in conflict, with a view to reconcile them. Christ is the one and only mediator between God and man. He makes reconciliation between God and man by his all-perfect atoning sacrifice.

Medium–A person through whom communications are thought to be sent, to the living, from spirits of the dead.

Messiah–An expected savior or liberator of a people or country; a Hebrew word which is translated as "Christ" in Greek, and "Anointed One" in English.

Nazarite–One who had taken a vow to dedicate his life to God's service for either a specific period of time or for a lifetime. Among the ancient Hebrews, he was a person who vowed to abstain from wine, leave his hair uncut, and avoid touching a corpse.

New Testament–The second of two main divisions of the Bible, containing 27 books of God-inspired messages and history covering the period just prior to Jesus' birth to about 100 years after Jesus' death.

Old Testament–The first of two main divisions of the Bible, containing 39 books of God-inspired messages and history covering the period of time from the beginning of the universe to about 400 years before Jesus' birth.

Passover–The most important Jewish holiday, commemorating the Jews' deliverance from Egyptian bondage. It is kept in remembrance of the Lord's angel of death *passing over* the houses of the Israelites when the first born of all the Egyptians died. The Israelites' children were spared because of the blood smeared on their doorposts.

Patriarch–One of the scriptural fathers of the human race or of the Hebrew people (Abraham, Isaac, Jacob and the twelve sons of Jacob (Israel)). A patriarch is a ruling ancestor who may have been the founding father of a family, tribe, clan, or nation.

Pharaoh–The title of the kings of ancient Egypt: often used as a proper name in the Bible.

Picture of Redemption (See Foreshadowing of Jesus Christ)

Pilgrimage–A journey to a shrine or holy place.

Plunder–To take by force (as in war). As a noun, it is loot or goods seized in war.

Praise–An expression of approval, esteem, or commendation. For Christians it is thanking God for what He has done. Thus, to praise God is to proclaim His merit or worth.

Priest–Mankind's representative before God, authorized to perform sacred rites and intercession. According to the Laws of Moses, only Aaron's descendants could serve as priests.

Purim–A Jewish holiday, also called the Feast of Lots, commemorating the deliverance of the Jews by Queen Esther from a genocidal massacre of the Jews plotted by Haman.

Righteous–Acting in a just, upright manner; doing what is right; virtuous.

Righteous Branch–A reference to the Righteous One (Jesus Christ), whom God told Jeremiah that He would place on King David's throne (See Jeremiah 23:5–6).

Righteousness–The actions and positive results of a sound relationship within a local community, or between God and a person or between God and His people. In the Bible, righteousness is the fulfillment of the terms of a covenant between God and humanity.

Redeem–To buy back. To save from captivity by paying a ransom. Biblically, to deliver from sin and its penalties, as by a sacrifice made for the sinner.

Redeemer–A person who redeems or sets free. This title is especially applied to Christ. He redeemed us from all evil by the payment of a ransom with His life.

Redemption–Deliverance by payment of a price. The purchase back of something that has been lost, by the payment of a ransom. Christ's blood or life, which he surrendered for us, is the "ransom" by which the deliverance of his people from the servitude of sin and from its consequences is secured.

Sacrifice–The act of offering the life of a person or animal, or some object; a selling or giving up of something at less than its supposed value. Christ was the sacrificial lamb that redeemed us.

Salvation–Being saved or rescued from danger, evil, difficulty, or destruction. Biblically, freedom from the power and penalties of sin.

Satan (Devil)–A supernatural adversary and rival of God. Satan is an accuser and opposes God's people tempting them to do evil. He is the enemy of all humankind and righteousness. Satan is usually identified as *Lucifer*, the leader of the fallen angels from heaven.

Savior or savior–A person who saves: When written with a small letter "s" (savior), it means one who saves from danger or destruction. When the letter "s" is capitalized (Savior), the reference is to God (Old Testament) or Jesus Christ (New Testament). Jesus is the One who offers the free gift of salvation. He will save anyone who believes in Him.

Scepter–A wand or baton used by kings as a symbol of authority.

Sin–Rebellion against God and rejection of God's Word which leads to misdeeds or actions that we know are wrong. Sin causes us to miss God's purpose for our life, and to surrender to the power of evil rather than to God.

Spirit-directed–Led by the Holy Spirit.

Spiritual separation–The barrier created between mankind and God after the first man and first woman (Adam and Eve) sinned. Their unrighteousness created a rift in the relationship man had once enjoyed with God because our righteous and holy God could not coexist with sin and unrighteousness.

Staff–A stick, rod, or pole. In the Bible, rods and staffs were used as walking sticks, for defense, for punishment, and for measurement. Staffs were also used as symbols of authority.

Tabernacle (Tent of Meetings)–A mobile tent-like structure used as a place of worship. The Israelites carried it with them through the desert as they traveled on their way to Canaan.

Testament–(See Covenant)

Threshing floor–A place used to beat grain out of its husk.

Tithe–One tenth of one's earnings set aside as a gift to God.

Trinity–Our one God is three distinct beings: God the Father; Jesus the Son; and the Holy Spirit. All three are fully God, and yet these three beings are one God, and not three Gods.

Unleavened bread–Bread baked without yeast so that it does not rise. Unleavened bread is a symbol of freedom from slavery.

Unrighteous, Unrighteousness–Wicked; sinful.

Worship–To have intense love or admiration for; to show religious devotion or reverence for; For Christians, to worship is to glorify God for who He is.

BIBLIOGRAPHY

Arthur, Kay, *LORD, I Want To Know You*, Colorado Springs, Colorado, Waterbrook Press, 1992, 2000

Benware, Paul N., *Survey of the Old Testament*, Chicago, Illinois, Moody Publishers, 1988, 1993

Bromiley, Geoffrey W. (EDT), *International Standard Bible Encyclopedia*, Eerdmans Publishing Company, 1979

Halley, Henry Hampton, *Halley's Bible Handbook with the New International Version*, Grand Rapids, Michigan, Zondervan Publishing House, 2000

Henry, Matthew, *Matthew Henry's Concise Commentary on the Whole Bible*, Nashville, Tennessee, Thomas Nelson Publishers, 1997

Lightfoot, Neil R., *How We Got the Bible*, Grand Rapids, Michigan, Baker Books, 1963, 1988, 2003

Nave, Orville J., *The New Nave's Topical Bible*, Grand Rapids, Michigan, Zondervan Publishing House, 1969

Strong, James, LL.D, S.T.D., *The Strongest Strong's Exhaustive Concordance of the Bible*, Grand Rapids, Michigan, Zondervan, 2001

Sumrall, Lester, *The Names of God*, New Kensington, Pennsylvania, Whitaker House, 1993

Unger, Merrill F., *Unger's Concise Bible Dictionary*, Grand Rapids, Michigan, Baker Book House, 2001

Study Bibles

Life Application Study Bible, New Living Translation, 1988, 1989, 1990, 1991, 1993, 1996 by Tyndale House Publishers, Inc., Wheaton, IL

The Open Bible, New King James Version, 1997, 1990, 1985, 1983 by Thomas Nelson, Inc., Nashville, Tennessee.

ABOUT BIG PICTURE MINISTRIES

John and Lorna Nichols are the co-founders of Big Picture Ministries, LLC, an organization devoted to encouraging spiritual growth through the study of God's Word. John and Lorna currently live in Chesterfield, Missouri, and are members of Grace Church-Saint Louis, a non-denominational church, where both are facilitators, leaders, and mentors for Jesus Christ.

Big Picture Ministries provides resources and services designed to help people better understand the message of the Bible. The goal of Big Picture Ministries is to encourage Bible reading and Bible study, and to promote spiritual growth. Our vision is to glorify God by providing tools designed to help people develop a deeper, more meaningful relationship with the Lord.

If you are interested in leading a Big Picture Ministries group study, please visit our Web site or call for information about bulk order discounts.

Big Picture Ministries, LLC
P.O. Box 67
Chesterfield, MO 63006-0067

Web site: www.bigpictureofthebible.com
Phone: (636) 536-0197   Fax: (636) 536-0138

Please feel free to contact us with your comments or questions. Our e-mail address is:
info@bigpictureofthebible.com

Big Picture of the Bible—New Testament
Coming in 2008!